About This Book

Why is this topic impo. ......

At any given moment, every day, people come together as groups—to share experiences, opinions, skills, and resources, and to work toward accomplishing goals. The process sounds simple and fairly straightforward but, in reality, the road to accomplishment can be obstructed by meanderings, bypasses, roadblocks, and detours at almost every turn. Helping to create a group experience that is productive and deeply satisfying to its members can make the difference between success and failure. Hands-on activities and learning games provide experiences for group members to focus the energy that exists as a part of the group process. This synergy can result in increased productivity, good feelings, and a real sense of success and accomplishment for the group as well as the organization.

What can you achieve with this book?

The New Encyclopedia of Group Activities is designed for anyone who works with groups and who wishes to help them become more effective. Using an experiential approach, these hands-on structured exercises give group members the opportunity to analyze the experience and apply these insights to work and life situations. Because it is an extensive collection, the activities and learning games can be used in many different settings and for a wide variety of purposes. Some topics that are covered include change, collaboration, communication, conflict, feedback, negotiation, planning, problem solving, trust, and values clarification, among many others. These activities provide a practical resource for increasing the awareness and skills of group members in both content and process areas.

How is this book organized?

The Introduction to the book provides background on its purpose and intended audience, a product description, an explanation of the Experiential Learning Model, and a glossary of key concepts. The Facilitator's Guidelines section includes information on how to use the activities, the role of the facilitator, and guiding principles on debriefing an activity. For ease of use, the activities contained in the book are divided into five sections, each one preceded by a brief introduction: Group Process, Task-Oriented Process, Relationship-Oriented Process, Communication, and Personal Awareness. Each exercise contains complete facilitation instructions that cover the goals, group size, time required, materials, physical setting, process notes, variations, and all necessary handouts. Activity selection guidelines and a topic matrix table are included to help in selecting the most appropriate activity for your specific learning needs.

About Pfeiffer

Pfeiffer serves the professional development and hands-on resource needs of training and human resource practitioners and gives them products to do their jobs better. We deliver proven ideas and solutions from experts in HR development and HR management, and we offer effective and customizable tools to improve workplace performance. From novice to seasoned professional, Pfeiffer is the source you can trust to make yourself and your organization more successful.

ⓟ Essential Knowledge Pfeiffer produces insightful, practical, and comprehensive materials on topics that matter the most to training and HR professionals. Our Essential Knowledge resources translate the expertise of seasoned professionals into practical, how-to guidance on critical workplace issues and problems. These resources are supported by case studies, worksheets, and job aids and are frequently supplemented with CD-ROMs, Web sites, and other means of making the content easier to read, understand, and use.

ⓟ Essential Tools Pfeiffer's Essential Tools resources save time and expense by offering proven, ready-to-use materials—including exercises, activities, games, instruments, and assessments—for use during a training or team-learning event. These resources are frequently offered in looseleaf or CD-ROM format to facilitate copying and customization of the material.

Pfeiffer also recognizes the remarkable power of new technologies in expanding the reach and effectiveness of training. While e-hype has often created whizbang solutions in search of a problem, we are dedicated to bringing convenience and enhancements to proven training solutions. All our e-tools comply with rigorous functionality standards. The most appropriate technology wrapped around essential content yields the perfect solution for today's on-the-go trainers and human resource professionals.

Pfeiffer
www.pfeiffer.com   *Essential resources for training and HR professionals*

Lorraine L. Ukens

The NEW
Encyclopedia
of
GROUP ACTIVITIES

Pfeiffer
A Wiley Imprint
www.pfeiffer.com

ISBN 0-7879-6854-4 (loose-leaf); ISBN 978-1-11815-7558 (pbk)

Acquiring Editor: *Martin Delahoussaye*	Interior Design: *Gene Crofts*
Director of Development: *Kathleen Dolan Davies*	Cover Design: *Chris Wallace*
Developmental Editor: *Susan Rachmeler*	Illustrations: *ICC*
Production Editor: *Nina Kreiden*	
Editor: *Rebecca Taff*	Printed in the United States of America
Editorial Assistant: *Laura Reizman*	HB Printing 10 9 8 7 6 5 4 3
Manufacturing Supervisor: *Bill Matherly*	PB Printing 10 9 8 7 6 5 4 3 2

➤ Contents

Section 2: Task-Oriented Process   139

Section 4: Communication   295

Section 5: Personal Awareness 375

This book is dedicated to my parents, Helen and Jerry Maas, who provided me with my first real group experiences by way of Gerri, Rich, Jerry, and Jan.

➤ Introduction: Getting the Most from This Resource

Purpose

Groups are everywhere. They are the fundamental building blocks of our society. They take such diverse forms as departmental work groups, planning committees, boards of trustees, social clubs, play groups, sports teams, and self-help groups, to name a few. As such, they provide the means for task accomplishment, growth and development, socialization, and social support.

Basically, a group is a collection of two or more individuals who are to some degree in dynamic interrelations with one another. Each group has its own uniqueness, and it is this uniqueness that complicates the search for ways to help groups be successful. Because of this complexity, some people have never experienced being a part of a successful group. Even more difficult is knowing how to create one. How do you create a group experience that is both productive and deeply satisfying to its members?

When people come together to meet and work in groups, a certain energy is produced. If focused with skill, this energy can result in increased productivity, good feelings, and a real sense of success and accomplishment. To begin this journey, you need to understand the group with which you are working. You should consider such factors as how much the members interact with one another, how each person is related to other members, the size of the group, the group goals, the group's unity (cohesiveness), and the way the group has changed over time. It is the combination of these crucial characteristics that guide the flow of behavior in groups; that is, the group dynamics. The information gleaned from examining a group's existing dynamics will allow you to take the first steps in designing an effective training program for creating a more successful group.

The activities and learning games in this collection were developed for use in a variety of programs and courses to increase skills in areas related to the effective functioning of groups. Covering a wide spectrum, these exercises can be used to examine process as well as content dimensions of group structures, task and relationship processes, communication, and personal awareness. Whether searching for a serious foundational process activity or for a light transitional learning game, group facilitators will find something to meet their needs.

Audience

The New Encyclopedia of Group Activities is designed for anyone who works with groups and who wishes to help them become more effective. It can be used by trainers, facilitators, teachers, and consultants as well as by group or team leaders, managers, and supervisors. These persons may have a variety of titles or positions, but the essential aspect is that the person is charged with the responsibility to conduct a structured learning experience within a group environment. Because of the wide range of activity types and topics, there are exercises that can be used by less experienced facilitators and those that require a higher level of facilitation experience. However, the majority of the activities can be conducted successfully by anyone with basic facilitation skills.

How This Resource Is Organized

The New Encyclopedia of Group Activities provides facilitators with a large assortment of reproducible activities and learning games that can be used in many different group settings and for a wide variety of purposes. The activities range from very simple designs that consume little training time and require little, if any, advance preparation on the part of the facilitator to more complex designs that consume several hours and do require some advance preparation. The classification of the activities in this book is somewhat arbitrary since they can be adapted for different training purposes. Although any given activity could belong to a number of classifications, each is categorized in alphabetical order within five categories according to its most probable use.

The categories used for classifying the activities are Group Process, Task-Oriented Process, Relationship-Oriented Process, Communication, and Personal Awareness. The contents of these categories are described briefly in the following paragraphs and are presented in greater detail in the introductory pages of the designated category divisions.

Group Process

This category includes a wide variety of activities that address issues concerned with the dynamics of the group: icebreakers, getting acquainted, group norms, member roles, leadership, dimensions of group effectiveness, diversity, change management, organizational culture, and closure.

Task-Oriented Process

This category of activities examines those functions that contribute to accomplishing a job, including planning, goal setting, problem solving, creativity, risk taking, decision making, and the use of resources.

Relationship-Oriented Process

This category of activities explores maintaining good working relationships within the group, including group cohesiveness, trust, collaboration, conflict management, and negotiation.

Communication

The activities in this category deal with various aspects of communication, including communication styles, nonverbal communication, listening, feedback, and coaching skills.

Personal Awareness

This category includes activities that focus on the individual as a key component in the group process. The exercises emphasize self-disclosure, values clarification, ethics, sensory and feelings awareness, perceptual set, motivation, and personal growth and development issues.

Explanation of the Experiential Learning Model

Experience is a rich resource for adult learning. People retain knowledge more easily when they experience things in an unforgettable way, and hands-on activities help induce this result in learning situations. Experiential learning involves active participation in a planned event, an analysis of what is experienced, and the application of the experience to work and life situations.

Structured activities and games put people in situations that do not always look like work, but that actually contain analogies to situations they encounter on the job. This allows participants opportunities to take a close look at themselves and how they do things. They can think back to what made them act or react in a certain way on the job or in personal relationships and walk away with a new way to respond to an actual situation when it occurs. The ability to transfer the learning back to the workplace is critical; training is effective only if the information can be applied. A training "experience" turns the event into an interactive form of learning, as the individual makes the actual cognitive link, not the facilitator or "trainer."

The facilitator should remember that adult learners share certain characteristics. They share strong feelings about learning situations in general. Because they have a good deal of first-hand experience, they bring a wealth of ideas to contribute. Adult learners also have established values, attitudes, and tendencies. This means that they have set habits and strong tastes that affect their learning. Most importantly, adults generally have more to lose when it comes to pride, respect, and reputation. Experiential activities and games, when used properly and sensitively, can help alleviate many of the fears that adults associate with the learning process and allow for a comfortable environment of discovery. Participants can be given opportunities to explore new views and practice new skills in a safe environment.

Experiential learning can be viewed as a dynamic sequence of events. The Experiential Learning Cycle (see Figure I.1) begins with the event itself, as experienced by the participant. This provides the basis for the discussion that comes afterward. Because all the participants have been provided with the same experience, they are able to focus on a common base. The next four phases of the cycle constitute the

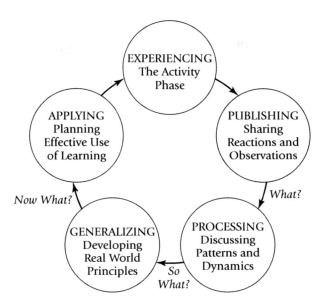

Figure I.1.   The Experiential Learning Cycle

Source: J. W. Pfeiffer & J. E. Jones, *The Reference Guide to Handbooks and Annuals*. San Francisco: Pfeiffer, 1972–1999.

debriefing or feedback segment, which helps the group to make the connection between the exercise and what is to be learned from it. Debriefing generally should begin by having individuals share feelings, reactions, and observations about the experience. Next, there should be a discussion of what happened in general. The group as a whole examines the interactions, patterns, and group dynamics that may have occurred. This is a pivotal step in the process and it is critical for the connection between the event and real-life situations to be discussed.

Participants begin to generalize about what has been learned from the experience. By identifying patterns, participants can abstract inferences, generalizations, learnings, and principles that apply to their own situations. This is the time to introduce the actual concepts being taught. The final stage involves application of what was learned, at which time the group can identify actions for more effective behavior in the future. This is where the transfer of skills from the classroom to the workplace occurs. Some of the more common methods utilized to accomplish this objective include the addition of structured goal-setting and action-planning procedures after the activity.

Glossary of Key Concepts

Change management   The ability to accept and make changes in a planned and managed or systematic fashion; to plan, initiate, realize, control, and stabilize change.

Coaching   A discussion and feedback process aimed at exerting a positive influence on the motivation, performance, and development of others.

Cohesiveness (cohesion)   The strength of the relationships linking the members of a group to one another and to the group as a whole; the internal bonding of a group.

Collaboration   The ability to work together to produce an integrated joint effort, such as found in the concept of teamwork.

Communication   The transmission of information and understanding between individuals, including how people, talk, listen, and put forth their ideas.

Conflict management   The process of managing differences among ideas, perceptions, beliefs, and goals of individuals.

Creativity   The ability to be inventive, imaginative, or original.

Decision making   The process of identifying and evaluating potential courses of action and then choosing from the various options.

Diversity   The quality of having difference or variety.

Feedback   The delivery of reassurance, praise, and corrective information to group members.

Goal setting   The establishment of a direction for action or a specific quantity of work to be accomplished.

Group   A collection of two or more individuals who are to some degree in dynamic interrelations with one another.

Group process (dynamics)   The flow of behaviors in a group; how things are happening rather than what is happening.

Icebreaker   The means for individuals to mix together or become better acquainted with one another at the beginning of a session.

Leadership   The ability to influence and direct the behaviors of others.

Negotiation   The reciprocal bargaining process that is a basis of agreement between opposing parties.

Organizational culture   The expectations and practices of the organization, including shared philosophy, attitudes, rituals and ceremonies, and belief about the direction of the organization.

Perception   The view individuals have of things in the world around them and its effect on concept formation and behavior.

Planning   The use of strategies, objectives, and specification that precede an action.

Problem solving   The use of skills to solve something capable of solution, such as a puzzle, as well as coping with difficulties that present problems in real life.

Relationship-oriented process   The functions that help maintain good working relationships within the group.

Resource use   The interpretation of data and information, as well as the use of available supplies.

Risk taking   The degree to which one is willing to perform an action that is deemed to result in negative consequences.

Self-disclosure   The process of sharing personal information with others that they would not normally know or discover.

Stereotypes   Cognitive generalizations about the qualities and characteristics of the members of a particular group.

Task-oriented process   The functions within a group that contribute to accomplishing a job.

Team   An interdependent group of people who rely on the close coordination of collaborative effort and mutual support to accomplish a common goal.

Trust   Confidence in the integrity, ability, character, and truth of an individual or process.

Values clarification   The definition and prioritization of beliefs and things in life that are important to the individual.

Facilitator's Guidelines

The facilitator's main emphasis in experiential learning is to assist in a process of inquiry, analysis, and decision making with the learners, rather than merely to transmit content knowledge. He or she must be able to help the participants make the connection between the experience and the intent of the learning. Therefore, it is important that the activity itself be set up, run, and processed properly with a tie back to the real world. For the activities and games to have learning value, there must be a good match between the metaphors and analogies of the event to real-life issues. The joy of full discovery generally comes after the exercise or even after the participants leave the session.

How to Use the Activities

Certain questions need to be asked by the facilitator who is contemplating using an activity as an intervention in a training event. The following set of considerations is intended to help the facilitator select and develop designs that are both relevant and effective.

1. *What are the goals of the group and why was it formed?* Structured activities are designed for a variety of purposes, but their most effective use is within programs that are aimed at specific learning goals.

2. *At what stage is the group in its development?* Different issues surface at various stages of group development, and some activities are particularly useful at some points in group life.

3. *How ready are the participants to take risks and to experiment?* Some activities may be threatening to a few participants and may evoke a degree of anxiety and defensiveness. It is useful, therefore, to establish an experimentation norm in training in that participants should be expected to "stretch" their boundaries somewhat. However, a participant should never be forced to volunteer or participate in an activity. Such a participant can become a part of the group experience by being assigned to the role of observer.

4. *What content modifications can I make for an effective, appealing design?* Local issues and concerns can be incorporated into the activity materials and processes in order to heighten the possibility of learning transfer. The inclusion of company goals, policies, roles, issues, cases, and so on can result in developing actual work norms and avoiding the impression of simply "game playing."

5. *What advanced preparations need to be made?* Appropriate rooms (with the right kinds of furniture and equipment) should be selected, and the furniture prearranged so that the participants are seated in preparation for the first phase of the process. If any materials are required, they must be duplicated and/or assembled. It is helpful to become familiar with the process instructions beforehand in order to be comfortable with running the activity and to anticipate any potential problems.

6. *How rigid are the time constraints for the session?* It is important not to generate more data than can be adequately processed within the session. It is better not to use an activity than to leave too much data "hanging" at the end. One consideration is to anticipate which elements of the design can be speeded up or expanded, if necessary.

Being able to design an effective and creative training program depends on having as vast a repertoire of experiences as possible that draw on the following modes of learning: games, simulations, role playing, creative physical activity and exercise, fun intergroup competition, real-life micro-activities (such as interviewing, problem solving, or counseling), structured debates, and the use of straight lecture and theory.

The facilitator needs to weave together a series of activities that help to move a group through its various stages of development, that reflect the pace at which the group can learn, and that provide a balance of structure, process, cognitive information, challenge, risk taking, intensity, and humor. Like a master puzzle, sequencing the activities into a comprehensive design places each piece in relation to the others. The beginnings are essential because they set the stage and lay the groundwork for the success or failure of the entire design and for the credibility and acceptance of the facilitator. The main portion of the learning experience can come from a single extended activity or it can result from a series of shorter activities that transition smoothly from one to the other. The ending should assimilate the activity through an interactive debriefing period integrating the cognitive information with practical application to the real world.

The Role of the Facilitator

The process of interactive learning does not happen on its own. Rather, it happens through the guidance of a group facilitator, and how this leader performs that role influences learning outcomes. During a session, the facilitator's role is to carry out the activity so that there is movement in the direction of learning.

Unless an activity calls for the facilitator to take an active role, participants should be allowed to experience the event on their own. They should be allowed the freedom to make mistakes because this in itself is an excellent way to examine the situation and learn from its outcomes. Unless otherwise noted in the process instructions, the facilitator should intervene only on questions of procedure and only to give as much detail as possible to answer the inquiries without influencing the results.

The facilitator's behavior models what is to be expected from the group. A primary objective is active involvement, and that should be evident to all participants from the outset. Some ground rules (norms) that the facilitator should establish are that:

- *People should be listened to and recognized.* The facilitator acknowledges questions and comments. Diverse opinions should be encouraged so that participants gain other insights that lead toward growth and development. This establishes a sense of respect and inclusion in the group.

- *The training environment is a safe place to be.* The facilitator reassures participants that what happens in the group remains in the group. Participants should be encouraged to express themselves without fear of ridicule or reprimand, and members who are uncomfortable with certain topics should be supported in their efforts and encouraged to take a chance. This encourages participants to try new behaviors in a safe climate.

- *Objectivity is encouraged.* The facilitator remains objective to participant comments and expressions in all activities. This helps a group look at what is happening and learn from it.

- *Feelings are important.* The facilitator encourages expressions of feelings. Feelings influence how much change will be considered, how much effort is expended, and whether energy goes toward action or toward defensiveness. Expression of feelings is vital if the group is to use its energy toward resolving problems and understanding the processes occurring.

- *We learn from doing things and analyzing them.* The facilitator links the learning experience to real-life application by providing a conceptual framework to help in analyzing a particular outcome.

This aids in the process of learning what has occurred: what was felt, how that can be dealt with differently in a similar situation, what new behavior might be attempted, and what insights were gained. This sets the stage for participants to analyze what is happening to them as individuals, in their relationships with others, and in the group as a whole.

Listed below are some general guidelines for the facilitator to follow during the activity that can help provide group members with a meaningful experience.

- Prepare the group so that members know why they are there and what will be accomplished.

- Encourage everyone to participate fully.

- Give clear directions.

- Never allow only one "right" experience.

- Be alert to body language in response to group exchange and interaction.

- Use process/content observation during the activities. (*Process observation* examines what is happening as far as group dynamics are concerned, and *content observation* involves what the participants are talking about.)

- Show enthusiasm and interest; you must believe in what you are doing.

- Stay in control; don't let the group get off track or stuck in one place.

- Do not assume an authoritarian position.

- Be flexible; go with the flow if the discussion provides feedback on areas that were not planned.

- Make the experience fun as well as challenging.

Debriefing the Activity

Having the group reflect on its experiences is a critical aspect of experiential learning. It is the point at which the experience is connected to real-world application. When using games and entertaining activities to teach a lesson, it is especially important to underscore the instructional message behind the fun so that participants take the training seriously.

Although the facilitator may have a specific objective for introducing the activity, participants may get something else out of the experience that goes beyond this. Therefore, participant feedback will help determine the direction and composition of the debriefing period. The facilitator should lead the participants to insights by discussing, reflecting, and questioning what was experienced. Rather than telling the learning points of the exercise, an effective leader guides participants into awareness. You know you have had a successful learning event if the participants come away with at least one insight. And remember, failed attempts can yield just as rewarding an experience as successful ones!

Activity Selection Guidelines

Activities and games are meant to be the vehicle through which learning occurs. Facilitators must remember that they are using tools for instruction and keep focusing on the results they want to achieve. The activities presented here can succeed with any subject matter, any segment of the workforce, and any length training program. An activity may be used as the main learning event, or several exercises may be used throughout a training session to reinforce or introduce any number of topics. Because they are so flexible, they offer the additional opportunity to vary conditions in accordance with the needs of a specific group. However, the activity that is chosen must fit within the context of the whole instructional process. To assist in the selection of activities by content, a matrix table has been included at the end of this section.

For any given learning objective, there are many possible activities, differing in complexity and in the demands made of the participants.

The facilitator should select activities that are most suitable for the intended audience. The activities cover a wide variety of endeavors, involving such things as solving problems and puzzles, making self-disclosure statements, using role plays, creating objects, playing games, and so forth. In addition, the activities may incorporate work as individuals, in pairs, triads, small groups, or large groups. The actual number of participants often limits the kind of activity that can be used, and environmental factors (such as time, materials, and physical setting) also may impose restrictions.

Activity Format

Each activity follows a basic format, as explained below. If there is no pertinent information for a particular section (if, for example, an activity requires no materials), the heading for that section has been omitted.

Goals   In this section, the primary goals of the activity are stated. They are specific in that they state what should occur; they are less specific in terms of the result of that occurrence, in order to permit inductive learning (learning through discovery). For example, if a goal is "to examine" or "to explore" the effects of a particular procedure, the activity will involve the dynamics of examining or exploring. What is learned, however, may differ from participant to participant or from group to group, depending on the participants' backgrounds and their unique experiences during the activity.

Group Size   This section identifies information connected with suggested group size and composition in terms of minimum or maximum number of participants, the number and size of the subgroups, or a restriction that the activity should be conducted with an intact or ongoing work group.

Time Required   The time listed for an activity allows for conducting the exercise, group or individual reports, and a debriefing discussion. It is only an estimation since the length of the activity depends on several variables: the number of participants, the extent and style of the debriefing, and so on. A good guide to follow is that the larger the number of participants, the longer the activity will take. This is not a hard-and-fast rule, but it is a rather good indicator of what happens in larger groups because the group reports and debriefing generally take longer.

Materials   This section specifies any handouts required and the quantities of each. Audiovisual items such as newsprint flip charts, felt-tipped markers, paper and pencils, and any other special materials also are listed if the activity design requires them. Please note that some Variations may require additional or different materials than those listed in this section.

Physical Setting   This section deals with participants' needs in connection with an activity. For example, the design may call for a room that is large enough for subgroups to work on a task assignment without disturbing one another; a room that allows the participants to move around in an unrestricted fashion; a room with tables for each subgroup; and so on. When an activity requires writing surfaces, the facilitator may distribute clipboards or use tables or desks, whichever is preferable.

Process   In this section, the step-by-step procedure is presented in terms of what the facilitator does and says and what the participants do in the appropriate sequence. For most activities, a list of questions is provided for the concluding discussion (debriefing) that tie back to the goals of the activity. However, the facilitator should feel free to include any additional questions that meet the outcome needs of the group.

Variations   This section presents adaptations that may vary the activity's content, sequence, time, materials, size or group composition, complexity of process, and so on. It is not possible to list all adaptations for any activity; and, if no variations are specified, the facilitator should not assume that none should be tried. Structured activities like the ones in this book invite experimentation, and facilitators are encouraged to alter the designs for their own unique purposes.

Notes to the Facilitator   The notes in this section present information that guides the facilitator in conducting the activity. The information may consist of answers to puzzles, specific content background, or cautionary notes about higher-risk conditions pertaining to the processing of an activity.

Handouts   All handouts required to conduct the activities are printed on separate pages included at the end of the activity format for ease of duplication and distribution to the participants. Copies of handouts are also included on the accompanying CD-ROM.

Activity Topic Matrix

A matrix of the activities and their topics is provided in Table I.1.

Resources

The following books are recommended as companion pieces because they provide additional activity sources and further information on group facilitation.

McLaughlin, M., & Peyser, S. (2004). *The new encyclopedia of icebreakers*. San Francisco: Pfeiffer.

Pfeiffer, J. W. (Ed.). (1989). *The encyclopedia of group activities: 150 practical designs for successful facilitating*. San Francisco: Pfeiffer.

Reddy, W. B. (1994). *Intervention skills: Process consultation for small groups and teams*. San Francisco: Pfeiffer.

Schwarz, R. M. (2002). *The skilled facilitator: A comprehensive resource for consultants, facilitators, managers, trainers, and coaches, new and revised*. San Francisco: Jossey-Bass.

Ukens, L. L. (1997). *Working together: 55 team games*. San Francisco: Pfeiffer.

Ukens, L. L. (1999). *All together now: A seriously fun collection of interactive training games and activities*. San Francisco: Pfeiffer.

Zander, A. (1994). *Making groups effective* (2nd ed.). San Francisco: Jossey-Bass.

Table I.1. Activity Topic Matrix

	Change Mgt.	Closing	Cohesion	Collaboration	Communication	Conflict Mgt.	Creativity	Decision Making	Diversity	Feedback/Coach	Goal Setting	Icebreaker	Leadership	Listening	Negotiation	Norms/Roles	Org. Culture	Perception	Planning	Problem Solving	Resource Use	Risk Taking	Self-Disclosure	Trust	Values
All Tied Up			X	X								X													
Alternative Solutions				X				X												X					X
Anecdotal Appreciation				X			X														X				
Animal Appeal							X		X											X		X			
Appearances Can Be . . .				X																					
At Issue						X		X									X	X							
At the Movies		X						X								X									
At Wit's End				X			X									X		X		X					
Back to the Future			X		X		X									X									
Beam Bounce			X	X								X	X				X								
Big Pushover			X			X																			
Blind Faith			X		X																			X	
Body Basics					X													X							

(Continued)

Table I.1. Activity Topic Matrix (Continued)

	Change Mgt.	Closing	Cohesion	Collaboration	Communication	Conflict Mgt.	Creativity	Decision Making	Diversity	Feedback/Coach	Goal Setting	Icebreaker	Leadership	Listening	Negotiation	Norms/Roles	Org. Culture	Perception	Planning	Problem Solving	Resource Use	Risk Taking	Self-Disclosure	Trust	Values
Bouncers			X	X								X													
Bumper-Idiom			X	X														X							
Button Up				X		X																			
Change of Position	X				X							X	X			X									
Chip In												X						X							
Cite Unseen								X												X					
Clash Action						X										X				X					
Close Calls					X									X											
Close Resemblance				X																X					
Coming Together			X						X			X						X					X		
Communal Cave			X				X				X					X									
Connectable																		X		X					
Converse Proceedings					X									X											

	1	2	3	4	5	6	7	8	9	10	11	12	13	14	15	16	17	18	19
Count Down											X								
Counter Attack						X	X				X	X							
Cross-Circulation							X									X			
Culture Connection										X	X								
Dingbats			X	X									X	X					
Do or Taboo?							X			X			X	X					
Don't Label Me				X									X						
Down to Basics		X	X																
Drawing on the Group		X											X						
Dumlelop			X										X		X				
Early Dismissal	X							X			X		X	X					
Eye of the Beholder								X		X	X		X	X					
Fab Five						X			X									X	
Favorable Outlook							X		X										
Feedback Forum			X					X			X								X
Final Debriefing	X									X									
Fishing for Feedback			X					X		X			X	X					
Fit Figure										X									

(Continued)

Table I.1. Activity Topic Matrix (Continued)

Activity	Change Mgt.	Closing	Cohesion	Collaboration	Communication	Conflict Mgt.	Creativity	Decision Making	Diversity	Feedback/Coach	Goal Setting	Icebreaker	Leadership	Listening	Negotiation	Norms/Roles	Org. Culture	Perception	Planning	Problem Solving	Resource Use	Risk Taking	Self-Disclosure	Trust	Values
For Shore	X			X			X	X											X	X					
Full Circle												X				X		X					X		
Gender Bender					X				X							X	X	X							
Getting the Message Across				X	X			X		X				X	X										
Give and Take				X			X												X	X					
Give Me Shelter	X		X																		X				
Goal Mining			X					X			X														
Going Around in Circles	X			X	X													X							
Group Assembly			X	X	X	X										X									
Having a Ball	X											X	X												
High Impact																X		X					X		
"Hip" Hop	X				X		X																		
How Sweet It Is				X				X			X										X				

Idea Shuffle										X										
In the Company of . . .							X							X		X		X	X	
In the Middle								X													
In the Spirit of Things								X	X	X											
Infomercial									X	X				X							
Inner Circle												X									
Inside and Out						X					X					X		X			
It Figures								X	X								X				
It's in the Mail								X								X	X				
Keep on Role-ing												X					X		X		
Lead On						X				X						X					
Let Me Show the Way									X												
Listen to Me					X			X	X							X					
Lofty Goal				X	X						X					X					
Mad Hatter's "Team" Party						X		X										X			
Making a Commitment								X										X	X	X	
Making Contact							X					X				X					
Material Evidence												X	X	X							

(Continued)

Table I.1. Activity Topic Matrix (Continued)

	Change Mgt.	Closing	Cohesion	Collaboration	Communication	Conflict Mgt.	Creativity	Decision Making	Diversity	Feedback/Coach	Goal Setting	Icebreaker	Leadership	Listening	Negotiation	Norms/Roles	Org. Culture	Perception	Planning	Problem Solving	Resource Use	Risk Taking	Self-Disclosure	Trust	Values
Me, Myself, and I																X		X					X		
Mentoring Memoirs				X						X			X			X									
Mind Benders					X		X											X		X					
Mind Mingle		X						X																	
Mirror Image																		X							
Model Behavior				X		X												X		X					
Music Box												X				X									
Name Game																X				X					
New Twist on Things				X												X		X							
Not Me!					X							X						X					X		
Oh, Domino	X			X												X									
On the Move				X				X												X					
On Top of Things				X							X									X					

	1	2	3	4	5	6	7	8	9	10	11	12	13	14	15	16	17	18
Oobleck	X										X							
Opposites Attract									X	X	X	X		X			X	
Organizational Pulse												X	X					
Otherwise									X		X							
Our Song	X							X							X			
Patent Pending		X						X				X			X			
Paying Your Dues	X					X	X				X							X
Perceptual Dimensions	X				X						X							
Personal Links	X	X																
Picture That!	X																	
Picture This!	X										X							
Piecing It All Together	X	X						X				X						
Pipe Dreams	X	X						X								X		
Point of View	X				X							X				X	X	
Positive Charge	X			X														
Powers of Observation											X	X						
Pride and Prejudice	X				X													
Prospect-Us	X						X				X							X

(Continued)

Table I.1. Activity Topic Matrix (Continued)

	Change Mgt.	Closing	Cohesion	Collaboration	Communication	Conflict Mgt.	Creativity	Decision Making	Diversity	Feedback/Coach	Goal Setting	Icebreaker	Leadership	Listening	Negotiation	Norms/Roles	Org. Culture	Perception	Planning	Problem Solving	Resource Use	Risk Taking	Self-Disclosure	Trust	Values
Proverbially Speaking																	X	X							
Question Mark					X					X				X						X					
Rapid Fire		X										X											X		
Reading Between Lines				X	X																				
Rhyme Time							X											X		X					
Risky Business								X														X			
Role Out							X									X									
Roman Candles							X					X								X					
Rules												X				X									
Rummage Sale			X	X			X																		
Scrambler			X		X															X					
Search for Tomorrow				X												X							X		
Secret Service				X	X											X									

	1	2	3	4	5	6	7	8	9	10	11	12	13	14	15	16	17	18
Seeing Things My Way	X								X				X					
Shake It Up			X				X	X			X				X			
Sounding Board				X		X						X					X	
Spin Off			X			X					X						X	
Splits	X												X	X				
Style							X		X									
Sum–Thing											X	X			X			
Take Flight								X										X
Taking the Lead					X					X								
Tale of the Tape			X	X						X				X				
Taste of Success									X			X						
Team Report Card			X	X								X						
Team Time			X				X								X	X		
Team Totem		X	X		X							X						
Tear It Up				X			X								X		X	
Think About It			X	X											X		X	
Three Blind Mice				X							X			X				
To a "T"							X				X				X		X	

(Continued)

Table I.1. Activity Topic Matrix (Continued)

	Change Mgt.	Closing	Cohesion	Collaboration	Communication	Conflict Mgt.	Creativity	Decision Making	Diversity	Feedback/Coach	Goal Setting	Icebreaker	Leadership	Listening	Negotiation	Norms/Roles	Org. Culture	Perception	Planning	Problem Solving	Resource Use	Risk Taking	Self-Disclosure	Trust	Values
Top Ten																							×		×
Toss Away		×																				×			
Trust Bust																								×	
Turning 21				×		×																			×
Unspoken Meanings					×			×		×															
Value Judgment								×										×							×
Value of Work																									×
Valuing Yourself							×																		×
Weekend Getaway															×		×			×		×			
What You Herd	×										×								×		×		×	×	
Where Are You?																		×					×		
Why's Guise		×																							
Wishing Well								×			×												×		×

⊁ Section 1

Group Process

Introduction to Group Process

Group process refers to the flow of behaviors in a group where the emphasis is on how things happen rather than on what is happening. The Group Process category encompasses the majority of the activities presented in this collection. There are a wide variety of activities that meet a number of purposes: icebreakers, getting acquainted, group norms, member roles, leadership, dimensions of group effectiveness, diversity, change management, organizational culture, and closure.

The use of these activities is dependent on the facilitator's assessment of the group's stage of development, its current structure, and the environment in which it functions. Wise choices of group process activities can help to facilitate group growth, to ease a group through a difficult period or process, and to lead to development of the individuals within the group. In addition, by participating in these kinds of activities, participants can learn what to expect in the ongoing development of their own groups and how to handle various situations that arise within those groups.

Icebreakers and *getting acquainted* activities help to "break the ice" at the beginning of a session or early in the stages of a newly formed group. Session beginnings are important because they set the stage and lay the groundwork for active participation in the experience that will follow. These activities also can be utilized to get participants to mix together and/or to form subgroups. *Closing* activities provide techniques to debrief a session or group experience through a structured exercise.

1

Activities addressing *group norms, member roles,* and *leadership* examine a group's fundamental structure, which is the underlying pattern of stable relationships among the group members. Group norms are social standards or guidelines that describe what behaviors should and should not be performed. If written down, they can become the formal rules of the group. Member roles are sets of behaviors that are characteristic of persons within a particular group context; that is, group members tend to perform certain actions and interact with other group members in a particular way concerning both task and relationship dimensions. Group structure is influenced by *organizational culture*— the expectations and practices of the organization, including shared philosophy, attitudes, rituals and ceremonies, and belief about the direction of the organization. Activities that assess such conditions can help a group define its own structure more clearly.

Since groups are inherently dynamic in nature, it is critical that effective change management become an integral part of a group's function. Activities dealing with *change management* examine the ability for group members to accept and make changes in a planned and managed or systematic fashion; that is, to plan, initiate, realize, control, and stabilize change.

The ability for group members to expand their thinking in new and innovative ways can take a group to a more competitive level of performance. *Diversity* activities encourage participants to accept and celebrate differences and to recognize the contribution of diverse thoughts and ideas to the group effort.

➤ Alternative Solutions

Goals
1. To examine how individual values affect decision making.
2. To practice searching for alternative solutions to problems.
3. To examine the process by which a group makes decisions and discusses problems.

Group Size   Several groups of five or six persons each, preferably from the same organization.

Time Required   Approximately 1 hour.

Materials
1. Paper and a pencil for each participant.
2. A newsprint sheet and a felt-tipped marker for each group.
3. Masking tape.
4. A newsprint flip chart sheet showing a specific values issue or general problem statement for discussion. Some suggestions are listed below:
   • Ways to save time
   • Ways to make work more fun
   • Creative ways to reward employees
   • Ways to give your boss some negative feedback
   • Ways to settle arguments
   • Ways to be more assertive

Physical Setting   A room large enough for groups to work without disturbing one another. Writing surfaces should be provided.

Process
1. Introduce the activity by stating the following:
   "For many people, personal behaviors are often a result of accu-mulated habits (for example, arriving late, reading while eating, or even wearing blue on Mondays). More importantly, behaviors

and ideas are influenced by personal value systems and these values can differ from person to person. Because a group is comprised of separate individuals who can become entrenched in old habits and ideas, a group often makes decisions and does things the same way time after time without looking at all the possible options available."

2. Distribute paper and a pencil to each participant.

3. Present the participants with the specific values issue or general problem statement listed on the prepared flip chart sheet. Ask participants to individually list as many alternatives as possible to address the issue or problem. Encourage them to be specific in stating the alternatives. Allow approximately 5 minutes, and then tell participants to stop.

4. Direct participants to form groups of five or six persons each, preferably from the same work team. Acting as a team (preferably their normal work group), they will have 15 minutes to develop a list of alternative solutions by combining their individual lists and by adding any solutions generated in the group setting.

5. After approximately 15 minutes, stop the discussion. Distribute a newsprint sheet and a felt-tipped marker to each group.

6. Instruct the groups to choose the three alternatives that are best suited to addressing the issue or problem and rank order them. The results are to be listed on the sheet provided. Allow approximately 8 minutes, and then tell participants to stop. Provide masking tape and ask each group to post its newsprint sheet.

7. Ask each group in turn to make a report on its solutions list to the class as a whole. If anyone wants to hear more about a given alternative, he or she may ask for further information.

8. Using a flip chart sheet, lead a concluding discussion based on the following questions:
   - How well did group members work together during the activity? Did all members participate? Why or why not? Did any one person take the lead? If so, how did that happen? How did other members react to this?

- What approach did your group take to identify all possible alternatives to the problem? Did synergy (that is, the group as a whole performing better than the sum of all individuals acting alone) occur during the process? Why or why not? How did this influence the quality of the possible solutions offered?
- How likely would it be to successfully implement these ideas in your workplace? Why or why not?
- How do our personal values impact the decisions we make as individuals? What impact do individual values have on group problem solving and decision making?
- How can a group improve its problem-solving and decision-making processes?

Variations

1. If working with an intact work group, actual problems facing the group or organization may be discussed.
2. Rather than have all groups discuss the same topic, each one may be assigned a different issue or problem.
3. Two or more values issues or problem statements may be assigned to the groups. If this is done, additional time will be required for individual work, group work, and reports.

Note to the Facilitator   When participants are presenting alternatives, do not criticize their contributions but be sure that specific and complete information is provided for each. For example, on a list of ways to reward workers, rather than "give out gifts for extra work," a stronger statement would be "give a $10 gift certificate every time an employee works two hours of unpaid overtime."

➤ Anecdotal Appreciation

Goals

1. To utilize individual group member input for a collective product.
2. To enhance creativity through storytelling.
3. To make the best use of available resources.

Group Size   Several groups of four or five persons each.

Time Required   20 to 30 minutes.

Materials

1. Anecdotal Appreciation cards.
2. Paper and a pencil for each participant.
3. A container (for example, a paper bag or box).

Physical Setting   A room large enough for groups to work without disturbing one another. Writing surfaces should be provided.

Process

1. Prior to the session, prepare the Anecdotal Appreciation cards by writing each of the words provided (or others of your choosing) on a slip of paper or card stock. You should have at least twice as many cards as participants. Place the cards in a container that allows participants to select them easily.
2. At the session, direct the participants to form groups of four or five persons each.
3. Distribute paper and a pencil to each participant. Present the container of cards to the participants and instruct each one to select two cards.
4. Explain that each group will have 10 minutes to combine its words in writing a cohesive, collective story. Each individual is responsible for using the words he or she selected to add to the story.

5. Signal for the task to begin, and then stop the groups after approximately 10 minutes. Ask a representative from each group to read aloud the story that was created.

6. Lead a concluding discussion based on the following questions:
   - How did you feel as an individual member of the group during the activity? Why?
   - What factors hindered the group's ability to accomplish the task? What factors helped the process?
   - How did the group decide the best way to use the resources available (words and individual group members)? Was this an effective plan? Why or why not?
   - Did the group need to make adjustments as the task progressed? Why or why not? Was the final product complete?
   - Why was creativity a factor in this task? Which group had the most creative story? What made it the most creative?
   - What role did individual input have in the collective group effort? How does this relate to teamwork in general?

Variation   Provide each group with a newsprint sheet and felt-tipped markers and have members draw a composite picture representing all the words. The picture must be complete and logical, not eight to ten separate pictures or drawings.

Anecdotal Appreciation Cards

bean	rose	thirsty	tornado
tree	disappear	mad	tide
beaver	volcano	heat	desert
plane	run	hurricane	sugar
love	tattle	beach	empty
brother	shadow	light	sing
spring	tale	cry	ocean
winner	surprise	odor	monster
mistake	friend	mother	fear
eagle	home	laughter	quick
gone	sister	moon	apron
star	baby	dinosaur	sorry
building	error		

➤ At the Movies

Goals
  1. To identify the individual traits and contributions of group members.
  2. To review group performance at the end of a session.
  3. To reach a consensus decision.

Group Size   Several groups of six to eight persons each; works best with groups of seven.

Time Required   40 minutes.

Materials
  1. A copy of the At the Movies Worksheet for each group.
  2. A copy of the At the Movies Resource Sheet for each participant.
  3. Pencils for all participants.

Physical Setting   A room large enough for groups to work without disturbing one another. Writing surfaces should be provided.

Process
  1. Direct the participants to form groups of six to eight persons each. Ask the groups to select one member to act as recorder.
  2. Distribute a copy of the At the Movies Worksheet and a pencil to each group recorder. Provide a copy of the At the Movies Resource Sheet to each participant.
  3. Explain that the groups are to select one of the three movies listed on the worksheet whose theme best represents them as a team. Based on their selection, the groups will then cast each member as one of the seven characters from that movie. If the group has only six members, one character will be left uncast; if there are eight members, one character will have an understudy. Groups will have approximately 20 minutes before they will be

asked to report back on the movie title, cast members, and reasons why the choices were made.

4. Allow approximately 20 minutes, giving a 2-minute warning before time expires, and then stop the discussion.

5. Ask each group in turn to present its report, having each person stand as his or her role is announced. Be sure that the reasons for the choices are explained.

6. Lead a concluding discussion based on the following questions:
   • What impressions and insights did you gain from this activity?
   • How did your group select the representative movie? What approach did your group take to cast the various roles?
   • How difficult was it to obtain a group consensus on these decisions? Why?
   • How was the role of the "dark character" (Wicked Witch, Darth Vader, Gollum) treated? Why was that?
   • What was the outcome of the activity in objective terms?

Variations

1. Distribute a copy of the worksheet and a pencil to each participant and have individual group members decide on the casting of roles. Group members then discuss the choices and reasons, with the group report eliminated.

2. Offer each group the opportunity to select its own movie and cast group members as characters from the chosen movie.

3. Rather than a movie, ask groups to select a book or play from which to cast group members as characters.

At the Movies Worksheet

Instructions: Select one of the movies from the At the Movies Resource Sheet whose theme best represents your group. Cast each group member as one of the story's characters. Explain the reasons for your choices. Fill in the roles and reasons below.

Movie Title and Reason		
Role	Cast Member	Reason

At the Movies Resource Sheet

Wizard of Oz

Dorothy
Scarecrow
Tin Man
Lion
The Wizard
Wicked Witch of the West
Good Witch of the East

Star Wars

Luke Skywalker
Han Solo
Princess Leia
Obi-wan Kenobi
Yoda
Darth Vader
C3PO

Lord of the Rings

Bilbo Baggins
Frodo
Gandalf
Gollum
Aragorn (Strider)
Legolas the Elf
Gimli the Dwarf

➤ At Wit's End

Goals

1. To communicate thoughts and feelings about a group through humor.
2. To envision a group's future state.

Group Size   An intact work group divided into several groups of three or four persons each.

Time Required   1½ to 2 hours.

Materials

1. A set of the five At Wit's End Cartoon pages for each group.
2. Two newsprint sheets and several felt-tipped markers for each group.
3. Masking tape.
4. A newsprint flip chart and felt-tipped markers for recording.

Physical Setting   A room large enough for groups to work without disturbing one another. Writing surfaces should be provided. Wall space is needed for posting newsprint sheets.

Process

1. Begin the session by discussing how laughter can improve group relationships. A humorous approach may help relieve tension and stress as well as improve problem solving and creativity. The use of cartoons to express the thoughts and feelings of group members can help reveal group strengths as well as limitations. Explain that the work group will explore its strengths as well as limitations through a light-hearted approach by becoming cartoonists for the day.
2. Direct the participants to form groups of three or four persons each. Distribute a set of the five At Wit's End Cartoon pages and several felt-tipped markers to each group. Instruct group

members to write a humorous caption for each cartoon provided. Participants should select a humorous phrase that pertains to the work group *as a whole.* Allow approximately 20 minutes.

3. Have the subgroups use masking tape to post their pictures around the room and then allow sufficient time for the participants to walk around and view them.

4. Facilitate a discussion on the general themes of the comments. Discuss ways that the work group can reinforce the positive feelings or change the negative feelings expressed in the thought balloons and captions.

5. Distribute two newsprint sheets to each group. Instruct them to draw two original cartoons—one with a caption or thought balloon that reflects a *positive* aspect of the group 6 months from now and another one for 1 year from now. Allow 30 minutes for the task.

6. Have the subgroups post the sheets and then take turns presenting their cartoons.

7. Convene the total group and discuss ways in which the group can support actions to fulfill these "visions." Record the ideas on the flip chart as they are presented.

At Wit's End Cartoon 1

At Wit's End Cartoon 2

At Wit's End Cartoon 3

At Wit's End Cartoon 4

At Wit's End Cartoon 5

➤ Back to the Future

Goals

1. To promote creativity through imaginative writing.
2. To encourage a sense of group belonging.
3. To explore group issues that may be hidden beneath the surface.

Group Size   Several groups of three to five persons each, from an intact work group or participants who have worked together for some time.

Time Required   30 to 40 minutes.

Materials   Several sheets of paper and a pencil for each group.

Physical Setting   A room large enough for groups to work without disturbing one another. Writing surfaces should be provided.

Process

1. Direct the participants to form groups of three to five persons each. Ask the groups to select one person to act in the role of recorder.
2. Distribute several sheets of paper and a pencil to each group.
3. Explain that the groups will have 15 minutes to write about an imaginary get-together of this whole work group at some future date, in some other location. The story may be in outline form, but the story will be related to the larger group, so notes should be clear enough for that to occur. Tell the participants:
   "Let your imaginations run free as to when and where the group will meet, what group members will look like, and what the group will do. You should write the story without attributing any specific conversations taking place, but include lots of action and activity. The stories should have a definite ending or conclusion."

4. Time the activity for approximately 15 minutes, providing a 2-minute warning before asking the groups to stop.

5. Ask each group in turn to recount its story.

6. Lead a concluding discussion based on the following questions:
   - How were the locations for the future get-together chosen? Did the various locations have anything in common?
   - Did the members of the group stay the same? If not, how did they change?
   - Did relationships among members change? In what ways?
   - What conditions about the group changed the most? What changed the least?

Variation Have each participant write an individual account of the future get-together and ask for volunteers to share stories with the group.

Note to the Facilitator *It is best not to over-structure the discussion following the activity to allow for the sharing of deeper issues that may be at work within the larger group. Do not drive the group toward explorations of particular elements in which you are interested if the group discussion goes in a different but more insightful direction.*

➤ Beam Bounce*

Goals

1. To examine the role of the leader in the group process.
2. To observe how the collaboration of individual efforts contribute to the team effort.
3. To build cohesion within a group.
4. To discuss the vision of an organization.
5. To use as an icebreaker activity at the beginning of a session.

Group Size   Several groups of six to ten persons each.

Time Required   20 to 30 minutes.

Materials

1. A laser pointer for each group.
2. A small pocket mirror for each participant.

Physical Setting   A large open space.

Process

1. Direct the participants to form groups of six to ten persons each. Select one person from each group to act as the group leader.
2. Distribute a laser pointer to each group leader and a mirror to all remaining participants.
3. Explain that the goal of the activity is for the group members to use the mirrors to transmit the laser beam from person to person until all the mirrors are reflecting the beam, which will be started by the leader shining the laser pointer onto the mirror of the first person.

   Note to the Facilitator   Stress the importance of safety in directing the laser beam so that it does not shine into anyone's eyes. To prevent this from occurring, the mirrors should be held at waist level.

*Adapted from Ukens, L. (1997). Reflections. In *Working together: 55 team games.* San Francisco: Pfeiffer.

4. Signal for the activity to begin and allow approximately 10 minutes for the groups to work on the task. Make note of which groups are able to accomplish the task and the various methods used.

5. Lead a concluding discussion based on the following questions:
   - What approach did your group take to accomplish the task? Was it successful? Why or why not?
   - What factors influenced a group's ability to succeed? How did the achievement of each individual contribute to the overall success of the group?
   - How important was the role of the leader? Why? What happens when the leader shifts position?
   - How can we relate what occurred in this activity to the overall concept of leadership within the group process? How does it relate to group member collaboration? To teamwork in general?
   - How is a laser beam like a company vision? Is the vision of your organization clear and straightforward or does it waver, dim, or extinguish? In what ways and why?
   - Does the organizational culture support the vision? In what ways? Why is that?

Variation   Direct the members of each group to form a circle and relay the beam from person to person until it makes a complete circuit around the group.

Notes to the Facilitator   1. *Be aware of the safety issues of using laser pointers in this activity. There is very little danger as long as the beam is not pointed directly at someone's eyes. The majority of the laser pointers used in the U.S. use Class 2 or 3a diode lasers in the 630–680 nm wavelength (red), with a maximum power output of between 1 and 5 mW. The length of exposure to visible lasers is usually limited by the eye's blink reflex, which normally occurs within a quarter of a second. DO NOT use laser pointers that emit a green beam.*

2. The most efficient way to accomplish the task is to have group members form two lines facing one another and spaced very close together, and then relay the beam back and forth from one person to the other.

➤ Change of Position

Goals

1. To examine the discussion behavior of a group as it is affected by changes in physical positioning.
2. To evaluate the effects of change on the individual as well as on the group as a whole.
3. To review the impact of leader control on a group.
4. To set group process guidelines for new teams.

Group Size   Five to fifteen participants.

Time Required   45 minutes to 1 hour.

Materials   A prepared newsprint flip chart with a discussion topic relating to a relevant issue, problem, or previous subject content pertinent to the group. (A discussion in which frequent reference must be made to books, slides or posted material would not be suitable.)

Physical Setting   A large open space with enough movable chairs to accommodate all the participants and the facilitator. The chairs should be placed in a circular pattern.

Process

1. Direct the participants to be seated and take a seat among the participants.
2. Referring to the prepared flip chart, facilitate a general discussion based on the chosen topic.
3. After approximately 5 minutes of discussion, recommend a change in position, moving into the new situation and instructing the participants to follow as quickly and easily as possible. Some possibilities to try:
   - Pull chairs closely together so that knees are touching.
   - Move chairs in a configuration of rows.
   - Stand, rather than sit, in the same locations.

- Stand facing outward, in a tight circle with backs touching.
- Kneel, facing each other.
- Sit on the floor, either in the same locations, farther apart, or closer together.
- Hold hands while seated or standing.
- During any of the position changes, have several people trade their relative positions.

4. Continue the discussion for approximately 5 minutes more, and then recommend a second change in position, moving into the new situation and instructing the participants to follow as quickly and easily as possible. Facilitate the discussion for another 5 minutes, and then recommend a third change in position for the final 5 minutes of discussion. Stop the activity and ask the participants to take comfortable seats.

5. Lead a concluding discussion based on the following questions:
   - How did you feel during this exercise? When did you feel most comfortable? Least comfortable? Why?
   - Which position seemed to create the most disruption for the group? Why?
   - Did the patterns of communication change as the group changed positions? In what way?
   - Which position seemed to provide the "best" discussion? Why do you think that was? Did the quality or content of the discussion change in any way? If so, how did it change?
   - How did you feel about the leader having so much control of the group? What effect did this have on the discussion?
   - How are other group situations affected by seating arrangements, physical arrangement of the group, or physical positioning of the leader in relation to the group?

Variations

1. Instruct a group leader to perform the changes in position rather than you as the facilitator.
2. At the end of each 5-minute discussion period, select a different group member to take the center chair and select a new position

for others to follow. Explore issues of shared leadership during the concluding discussion.

3. In larger groups, one or two members may be asked to serve as observers, remaining outside the group during the content discussions. Prior to the concluding discussion, the observers should be asked to make general observations about the group and what happened, without referring to people by name.

Note to the Facilitator *This exercise may be introduced early in a group's life and may be used as one of the first experiences in creating group process guidelines.*

⊵ Chip In

Goals

1. To become acquainted with members of the group.
2. To discuss the influence of initial assumptions on behaviors.
3. To use as an icebreaker activity at the beginning of a session.
4. To support full participation of members during a session.

Group Size   Eight to twenty participants.

Time Required   15 to 30 minutes.

Materials

1. A prepared newsprint flip chart with the following:
   White = Hobbies and interests
   Blue = Professional experience
   Red = Memorable life event
2. Approximately three to five poker chips (in white, red, and blue) for each participant.
3. An open container such as a basket or coffee can.

Physical Setting   Any room in which the group regularly meets.

Process

1. Prior to the session, conceal the prepared flip chart. Place the poker chips in an open container and situate the container at the entrance to the workshop room (for example, near the sign-in sheets).
2. At the session, as the participants arrive, invite individuals to select as many poker chips as desired.
3. After all the participants have been seated, tell them that each color represents a category. Reveal the information on the prepared flip chart.
4. In a round-robin fashion, ask each participant to share one fact for each poker chip selected, according to the color categories

listed on the chart. For example, someone with two white chips and one red chip would share two details about his or her hobbies and interests and one detail of a memorable life event.

5. Lead a concluding discussion based on the following questions:
   - Why is it important to get to know other members of a group? Does background knowledge of an individual influence initial acceptance or rejection within a group? Why is that?
   - What initial assumptions influenced how many poker chips you took? Were these assumptions supported when you were told the meaning of the chips?
   - How do initial assumptions influence our behaviors in the real world?

Variation   After individuals share their information, provide masking tape or stickers to the participants to place their names on the poker chips. Collect all the chips and use these to select participants to answer questions or perform tasks during the workshop.

◥ Coming Together

Goals
1. To become better acquainted with other members of the group.
2. To compare and contrast the benefits of similarity and diversity within a group.
3. To provide an icebreaker activity at the beginning of a session.

Group Size   Twelve to twenty participants.

Time Required   10 to 20 minutes.

Physical Setting   A room large enough for all participants to form a large circle.

Process
1. Direct the participants to form a large circle, at least one arm's length apart.
2. Explain that each person, going in turn around the circle, must tell one thing about a personal characteristic or experience that is unique. If no one else in the group shares the same characteristic or experience, the speaker takes one step forward. If someone else DOES share the characteristic or experience, the speaker remains in place. Clarify that everyone understands the rules.
3. Select someone to begin and continue around the circle several times or until most people have moved closer to the center of the circle.
4. Lead a concluding discussion based on the following questions:
   • How difficult was it for you to come up with unique personal characteristics and experiences to share? Why?
   • Were you surprised to find others who shared characteristics or experiences that you considered "unique"? Why? Were there more similarities or more differences?
   • How did you feel about moving away from the rest of the group when you revealed something about yourself that no

one else shared? What impact does diversity have on group member relationships?

- How does sharing common characteristics and experiences among group members help a group function more effectively? How can perceived similarity cause stereotyping of people and groups?
- How does the combination of diverse group member characteristics and experiences help a group function more effectively?
- What specific things can group members do to "come together" to build a more cohesive group?

Note to the Facilitator   *In this activity, many people often come up with what they think—and that others might think—are unique experiences, only to find that someone else has that in common with them. This exercise shows not only how different we all are, and how our differences can enrich a group, but also that we have many things in common that we might not expect.*

❖ Communal Cave

Goals
1. To examine the material and nonmaterial needs of the group.
2. To explore the various elements of group dynamics.
3. To build cohesion within a group.

Group Size   Several groups of five to eight persons each, from an intact work group.

Time Required   45 minutes.

Materials
1. A medium-sized cardboard box for each group.
2. One dozen 3-inch by 5-inch index cards and several felt-tipped pens for each group.
3. Masking tape for each group.

Physical Setting   A room with separate tables for each group.

Process
1. Direct the participants to form groups of five to eight persons each.
2. Talk briefly about how primitive man lived communally in caves that provided comfort and safety through both material and nonmaterial means. Say that a work group does a similar kind of thing in its own work environment. Participants will now have the opportunity to furnish communal caves for their current groups.
3. Distribute a cardboard box, one dozen 3-inch by 5-inch index cards, several felt-tipped pens, and masking tape to each group.
4. Explain that the members of each group are to decide on what "furnishings" (material or nonmaterial) they want to include in their cave, represented by the box. They are to print one item per

card and affix the card to the box with masking tape. Groups will have 20 minutes to complete the task.

5. Time the activity, giving the groups a 2-minute warning. End the group work when time has expired.

6. Ask each group in turn to share the "furnishings" of its cave with all the participants.

7. Lead a concluding discussion based on the following questions:
   - What personal impressions and insights did you gain as a result of this activity?
   - What underlying values came into play during the activity?
   - On what basis did your group select its furnishings for the cave? What factors of the group were considered? Did you include more material or nonmaterial items? Why?
   - Did all members of your group agree on the included items? If not, how were conflicts resolved?
   - Were future considerations of the group taken into account? Why or why not? If there were any changes to the current group composition, would you need to make any changes to the things included in your communal cave? If not, why? If so, what things might be different?
   - How can your cave "furnishings" guide the work group in setting its goals?

Variation   Instead of boxes, provide each group with a newsprint sheet to represent the communal cave. Participants can attach the index cards to the sheet, or they can write their answers directly onto the sheet.

➤ Culture Connection

Goals
1. To define culture and identify its various components.
2. To list rules or norms of organizational and team cultures.
3. To compare organizational and team cultures.

Group Size   Several groups of six persons each, from an intact work group.

Time Required   1 to 1½ hours.

Materials
1. A prepared newsprint flip chart with the following two definitions:

    "Culture is the arts, beliefs, customs, institutions, and all other products of human work and thought created by people or a group at a particular time."

    "Culture is the rules for living created by a group of people based on who they are, where they are, and the perceived resources available."
2. Paper and a pencil for each participant.
3. Two newsprint sheets and felt-tipped markers for each group.
4. Masking tape.

Physical Setting   A room large enough for groups to work without disturbing one another. Writing surfaces should be provided. Wall space is required for posting newsprint sheets.

Process
1. Prior to the session, prepare a newsprint flip chart with the two definitions of culture. Conceal the contents of the flip chart.
2. At the session, distribute paper and a pencil to each participant.
3. Ask the individuals to write a personal definition of "culture." Allow a few minutes, and then ask each person to share the

definition with two other people. Using feedback from their partners, instruct the groups to discuss and rewrite their definition of culture to reflect all three of their views.

4. Allow approximately 5 minutes and then ask each triad to share their revised definition with the large group. After all the groups have reported, lead a discussion on the similarities and differences of the various definitions.

5. Ask the groups to take another look at their definitions of culture and decide whether or not they want to make any changes in the way they are worded. Allow a few minutes for discussion.

6. Reveal the definitions written on the prepared flip chart. Refer to the first one and explain that this is a dictionary definition, and then read it aloud. Refer to the second example and explain that this is an alternative definition, and then read it aloud. Ask:
   • Looking at these definitions of culture, how can we apply the definitions to the organization(s) in which we work?
   • How can we apply the definitions to the group(s) in which we work?

7. Direct the participants to form groups of six persons each by combining two triads. Distribute a sheet of newsprint and a felt-tipped marker to each group. Ask the groups to list the characteristics of the organizational culture that exists within their company.

8. After approximately 15 minutes, distribute another sheet of newsprint to each group. Ask the group members to list the characteristics of the group culture in which they work.

9. After approximately 15 minutes, provide masking tape and instruct the groups to post their two lists side by side. Lead a discussion on how closely the group culture meshes with the organizational culture.

10. Lead a concluding discussion based on the following questions:
   • What happens when the group culture does not mesh with the organizational culture?
   • What happens when individuals move from one group to another?

- How do established rules or norms for operation help group members work together more effectively?

Variation Provide the groups with a final newsprint sheet and ask them to generate a list of rules or norms for "living" within the group culture.

➤ Dingbats

Goals
1. To discuss the concepts of collaboration and competition.
2. To explore ways in which we express and perceive communication.
3. To apply creative thinking skills in solving problems.

Group Size   Several groups of three to five persons each.

Time Required   45 minutes to 1 hour.

Materials
1. A set of twelve Dingbats Puzzle transparency units.
2. A newsprint flip chart and a felt-tipped pen for recording.
3. An overhead projector.
4. A clock or timer.
5. A prize for the winning team (optional).

Physical Setting   A room large enough for groups to work without disturbing one another.

Process
1. Prior to the session, duplicate the Dingbats Puzzle Sheets 1 and 2 on transparency film and then cut into individual units.
2. At the session, direct the participants to form groups of three to five persons each. Assign a designation to each group (for example, letter, number, color, and so forth). Write the group designations in columnar format on the flip chart.
3. Explain that the groups will have 3 minutes in which to determine a commonly known word or phrase by viewing a visual riddle. The participants may ask any questions they wish that can be answered by "yes" or "no," and the groups may make as many guesses as they wish. The first group to solve the riddle

will earn one point. Announce that the group earning the most points will be the winner (a prize may be awarded, if desired).

4. Display a Dingbats Puzzle transparency on the overhead projector, responding to any question with a "yes" or "no" answer, and record one point on the flip chart sheet for the group that guesses the puzzle correctly. After 3 minutes, announce the answer if it has not been guessed (*see Note to the Facilitator*). Repeat the process for as many of the remaining puzzles as desired, and then tally the scores.

5. Lead a concluding discussion based on the following questions:
   - What factors influenced behaviors and outcomes in the activity?
   - How did individual perception and past experience play a role in solving these puzzles? How do they relate to our ability to communicate clearly? The puzzles represented one way of communicating ideas. What are some others? Which ways are most efficient and why?
   - How does creative "out of the box" thinking stimulate problem solving? How does time pressure impact creative thinking?
   - How can a group use creativity to improve its problem-solving process?
   - What were your reactions to being placed in competition with the other groups? How did this impact your group's willingness to share its ideas by asking questions or making guesses? Why was that true?
   - Is it possible to compete, yet still collaborate, with others? Why or why not? How does this relate to conditions in the work environment? What are some examples of situations that rely on both competition and collaboration?
   - How can we use the insights gained here to improve a group's ability to perform effectively?

Variation   Duplicate the Dingbats Puzzle Sheet(s) on paper and allow approximately 20 minutes for the members of each group to collaborate in solving the puzzles. Give a prize to the group that solves the most puzzles correctly.

Note to the Facilitator Solutions: (1) *backward glance;* (2) *in the thick of things;* (3) *bend over backwards;* (4) *someone to turn to;* (5) *mixed-up kid;* (6) *positive thinking (thin "king");* (7) *fruit in season;* (8) *easy on the eyes;* (9) *foul ("fowl") language;* (10) *it's up to you;* (11) *down on your luck;* (12) *put two and two together.*

Dingbats Puzzle Sheet 1

ecnalg 1	**SUM12S** 4
THINGS 2	**DKI** 5
BEND DRAW DRAW 3	**+ king** 6

Dingbats Puzzle Sheet 2

SfErAuSiOtN

7

U
S
T
I

10

ee e
——————
iiiiii

8

feathers
horoscope

11

Quack Quack
Cluck Cluck

9

totoo

12

➤ Do or Taboo?

Goals

1. To describe behaviors viewed as unacceptable or expected within the participants' own and other cultures.
2. To examine the impact of forbidden and expected behaviors within groups or organizations.
3. To establish rules for group or organizational behavior.

Group Size   This activity works best with a group of up to twelve participants, preferably an intact work group. If there are more than twelve participants, form groups of four to six persons each, preferably mixing people of different cultures, if possible.

Time Required   1 to 1½ hours.

Materials

1. Four newsprint sheets and a felt-tipped marker for each group.
2. Masking tape.

Physical Setting   Any room in which the group regularly meets. A writing surface should be provided. Wall space is needed for posting newsprint sheets.

Process

1. Introduce the session with the following:
   "Every culture draws limits on what is acceptable behavior. At the same time, there are often some ritual behaviors that are expected to be followed. These 'social rules' can include both verbal and nonverbal behaviors. This session will examine some common (and maybe some not-so-common) cultural taboos and rituals as a means of provoking awareness of the influence of culture on behavior."

2. Give a few examples of some cultural taboos, such as:
   Touching someone's head (Thailand)
   Whistling in public places (Russia, Egypt)
   Showing the sole of your shoe (Southeast Asia)
3. Give a few examples of some cultural rituals, such as:
   Presenting gifts to business partners (Japan)
   Giving flowers to a host (Eastern Europe)
   Bowing to greet someone (Southeast Asia)
4. Distribute two sheets of newsprint and a felt-tipped marker. Instruct the group to title one sheet "DO" and the other one "TABOO."
5. Ask group members to make a list of cultural taboos and expected rituals, either from their own culture or organization (for example, closed doors, separate lunchrooms, formal or casual dress, and so forth) on the appropriate newsprint sheet. Allow approximately 10 minutes for completion of the task. Provide masking tape and instruct the group to post both sheets. Ask the group to share the information on the lists.
6. Distribute two additional sheets of newsprint. Instruct the group to title one sheet "GROUP DO" and the other one "GROUP TABOO."
7. Ask group members to make a list of prohibited and expected behaviors that they would like to establish for their own group. Allow approximately 10 minutes for completion of the task. Instruct the group to post both sheets. Ask the group to share the information on the lists.
8. Lead a concluding discussion with the following questions:
   • What did you learn from this activity?
   • How do we learn what is taboo and what is expected behavior in our own culture? In other cultures?
   • How do we learn what is taboo and what is expected behavior in a work group? In our organization? How effective is this?
   • How will the insights from this exercise help you in the workplace?

Variations

1. Have the group role play or dramatize a group setting using the GROUP DO and GROUP TABOO sheets that were prepared in step 6 above. Allow approximately 10 minutes for preparation, and then ask the group to present the role plays.
2. Have the group discuss the possible consequences of acting in a prohibited or undesirable manner or of ignoring an expected ritual, in terms of teamwork.
3. Ask the group to make a list of American taboos and rituals that would be useful for other cultures to know.
4. Direct participants to form groups of four to six persons each. Instruct the groups to define the terms "taboo," "culture," and "values." Compare the definitions and lead a discussion based on the following questions: "How do these concepts interrelate?" and "What role does perception play in understanding cultural differences?"

Note to the Facilitator   *It is suggested that you gather some research information on various cultural taboos, customs, and rituals before conducting the activity.*

➤ Early Dismissal

Goals
1. To simulate group-member acceptance or rejection.
2. To examine how physical characteristics lead to stereotyping.
3. To identify ways in which groups can become more inclusive.

Group Size   A minimum of sixteen participants.

Time Required   20 to 30 minutes.

Physical Setting   A room with plenty of space so that the participants can move about in an unrestricted fashion to form groups in four separate corners of the room.

Process
1. Select four participants to act as leaders. In private, assign each leader a different physical characteristic that will allow someone to join his or her group. The characteristic should be something very specific, quite obvious, and not too common; for example, glasses, hair color, tennis shoes, blue shirt, and so forth. After the information has been provided, send each leader to a separate corner of the room.
2. Tell the group:
   "The remaining participants are to walk IN SILENCE and approach each of the leaders, extending a hand as if to shake with the leader. The leaders will shake their heads YES or NO to indicate whether or not the person will be able to join that particular group. When someone does join a group, he or she should stand behind the leader so that the next approaching individual can be seen by the leader."
3. Allow all the participants to pass by the leaders at least once. With some luck, a few of the people will not be chosen. Instruct these individuals to pass by each of the leaders at least once, so

that they are rejected by one or two of the leaders again. Then call an end to the game.

4. Ask the leaders only:
   • As a leader, how did you feel about having to reject people?
   • How did people react to being rejected? To being accepted?

5. Ask the other participants:
   • How did you feel when you were accepted into a group? Why?
   • For those rejected by all the groups, how did you feel about not being chosen? Why?
   • Why do you think you were accepted into your particular group? *(Reveal the physical characteristic for each group if the participants do not guess it.)*

6. Lead a concluding discussion based on the following questions:
   • What underlying personal values came into play during the activity?
   • To what extent do physical characteristics contribute to group functioning? How can the physical characteristics of an individual lead to stereotyping? What impact does stereotyping have on personal interactions?
   • How does your experience during this exercise relate to what happens in a real-world setting?
   • What are some ways in which groups can become more inclusive rather than exclusive?

➤ Final Debriefing

Goals
1. To provide a final debriefing session following one or more group activities.
2. To identify skills needed to cooperate as a group.

Group Size   Groups of participants from previous activities.

Time Required   20 to 30 minutes.

Materials
1. A copy of the Final Debriefing Worksheet and a pencil for each participant.
2. A newsprint flip chart and felt-tipped markers for recording.

Physical Setting   A room large enough for groups to work without disturbing one another. Writing surfaces should be provided.

Process
1. Once the activity or series of activities have been completed for the session, distribute a copy of the Final Debriefing Worksheet and a pencil to each participant.
2. Instruct group members to individually reflect on the questions and record a brief response to each. Allow approximately 5 minutes.
3. Instruct participants to discuss their responses to the questions within their groups. Allow approximately 10 to 15 minutes.
4. Ask for volunteers from the groups to provide responses to each of the questions.
5. Lead a concluding discussion based on the following questions, recording relevant issues on a flip chart:
   - Would you recommend group work for any task? Why? What are some examples of tasks that are best supported by group work?

- What is the value of group work? What are the problems with group work?
- What makes someone a good group member?
- How can groups apply these insights to the workplace environment?

Final Debriefing Worksheet

Instructions: Based on your experiences during the previous group activity(ies), discuss the following questions within your group:

1. What kinds of thoughts did you have about other members of your group as you participated in today's activity(ies)?

2. What kinds of thoughts did you have about yourself as you participated in the activity(ies)?

3. What skills were needed to accomplish the activity(ies)? What are some other times in your life when you would need these skills?

4. Did any conflicts arise as the group members worked together? If so, how were the conflicts resolved?

5. What general insights did you gain in regard to working in groups?

➤ Fit Figure

Goals
1. To identify things that help and those that prevent individuals from working together effectively in a group setting.
2. To develop guidelines to help individuals work together more effectively.

Group Size   Several groups of five or six persons each.

Time Required   30 to 45 minutes.

Materials
1. A newsprint sheet and felt-tipped markers for each group.
2. Masking tape.
3. A newsprint flip chart and felt-tipped markers for recording.

Physical Setting   A room with separate tables for each group. Wall space is required for posting newsprint sheets.

Process
1. Direct the participants to form groups of five or six persons each.
2. Explain that, as the basic unit of a group, each individual has a deep impact on how effectively the group performs as a whole. This activity will provide an opportunity to take a look at those things that individuals do that can either help or hinder the group effort.
3. Distribute a newsprint sheet and felt-tipped markers to each group. Ask the groups to draw a large outline of a human figure on the sheet.
4. Tell the groups:

   "Group members are to brainstorm all the things necessary for individuals to do to work well together. Write these inside the outline of the figure. Then discuss all the things that keep individuals from working as a group. Write these on the sheet outside the outline of the figure. You will have 20 minutes to complete the task."

5. Time the activity, giving the groups a 5-minute and a 2-minute warning. End the group work when time has expired.

6. Provide masking tape and instruct the groups to post their sheets. Ask a representative from each group to make a report on their discussion.

7. Lead a concluding discussion by asking the following questions:
   - What general impressions and insights about group work did you gain from this activity?
   - What common issues were identified by the groups?
   - What basic guidelines can a group develop to help individuals work together more effectively? (Record responses on the flip chart.)
   - What things can a group do to help reinforce these guidelines in the workplace?

➤ Full Circle

Goals

1. To share personal information with other members of the group.
2. To become acquainted with other members of the group.
3. To examine the impact of stereotyping on an organization and on the group process.
4. To use as an icebreaker activity at the beginning of a session.

Group Size   Eight to twenty participants.

Time Required   15 to 20 minutes.

Materials   A list of directions to be read by the facilitator. For example:

- Anyone with one sister, move one seat clockwise. If two or more, move two seats.
- Anyone with red hair, move two seats clockwise.
- Anyone who is 40 years or older, move one seat counterclockwise.
- Anyone born in another country, move one seat in any direction.

Physical Setting   A large open space, with one chair for each participant. The chairs should be arranged in a circle.

Process

1. Prior to the session, compile a list of directions for the participants to follow. Make sure that there are lots of categories so that everyone has lots of chances to move. Note that the larger the group, the more directions you will need to include.
2. At the session, instruct the participants to each take a seat. Say: "The goal of this exercise is for you to move around the circle so that you end up back in the same seat as you started. How you move will be determined by a series of directions. As each item is read and it applies to you, move the appropriate

number of seats. If the seat is occupied, stand in front of the
seat until it becomes available, or you move on."

3. Announce each direction on your list, allowing enough time
   between the announcements for the participants to make their
   moves. Continue until at least one member of the group returns
   to his or her original seat.

4. Lead a concluding discussion by asking the following questions:
   - How did you feel about participating in this activity? Why did
     you feel that way?
   - What kinds of things did you learn about other members of
     the group? Why might it be important to know these things?
   - Were you ever reluctant to respond to a direction because of
     what it would reveal about you (for example, age)? Why? How
     does this reflect situations in the work environment?
   - Did everyone in the group have an equal opportunity to
     accomplish the task? Why? How did this make you feel? How
     does this exercise relate to issues of group acceptance? How
     can we relate this to the workplace?
   - How does the use of certain categories of features or
     characteristics contribute to stereotyping? What implications
     does stereotyping have for an organization?
   - How does stereotyping have an effect on the group process?
     What are the implications within a group? How can we avoid
     negative labeling?

➤ Gender Bender

Goals
1. To identify gender-related stereotypes.
2. To discuss the influence of gender-related stereotyping in the workplace.

Group Size
Several same-gender groups of five to seven persons each.

Time Required
40 to 50 minutes.

Materials
1. A copy of the Gender Bender Worksheet and a pencil for each participant.
2. A newsprint flip chart and felt-tipped markers for recording.
3. Masking tape.

Physical Setting
A room large enough for groups to work without disturbing one another. Writing surfaces should be provided. Wall space is needed for posting newsprint sheets.

Process
1. Explain that culture is defined as "the shared way of life of a group of people," and this collectiveness can lead to the stereotyping of people within that culture. In the same way, men and women may hold stereotypical views of one another's expected attitudes and behaviors. Say that this exercise will explore that tendency.
2. Direct the participants to form same-gender groups of five to seven persons each. Distribute a copy of the Gender Bender Worksheet and a pencil to each participant. Read the instructions at the top of the sheet. Allow approximately 15 minutes for groups to complete the task.
3. Tabulate the attributes of all groups using separate newsprint flip chart sheets headed "WOMEN" and "MEN." Post the sheets

using masking tape. Compare and contrast the traits listed for both genders.

4. Lead a concluding discussion based on the following questions:
   - How does popular advertising treat gender-related stereotypes? Have these views evolved over the years? If so, in what way?
   - How do stereotypes lead to erroneous conclusions about groups of people? How can this influence our first impressions of individuals?
   - What impact can gender-related stereotyping have on task assignments in the workplace? How does it impact group member relationships? How does gender-related stereotyping relate to career development issues? What influence does organizational culture have on these issues?
   - What are some specific things that a group can do to alleviate stereotypical thinking in terms of group norms and roles?

Variation   Run the activity using mixed-gender groups rather than gender-specific groups. As an alternative, use mixed-gender groups to complete a second worksheet before collecting data from both groupings.

Gender Bender Worksheet

Instructions: For each list below, select the top six attributes your group believes are most characteristic of that specific gender.

WOMEN are

_____ analytical

_____ assertive

_____ competitive

_____ dominant

_____ empathetic

_____ impulsive

_____ independent

_____ influential

_____ inquisitive

_____ moral

_____ reactive

_____ supportive

MEN are

_____ analytical

_____ assertive

_____ competitive

_____ dominant

_____ empathetic

_____ impulsive

_____ independent

_____ influential

_____ inquisitive

_____ moral

_____ reactive

_____ supportive

➤ Give Me Shelter

Goals

1. To collaborate as a team in accomplishing a task.
2. To build cohesion in a group.
3. To apply creative problem-solving skills.
4. To develop a plan for use of available resources.

Group Size   Several groups of four or five persons each.

Time Required   40 minutes.

Materials

1. Several sections of newspaper and a roll of masking tape for each group.
2. A clock or timer.

Physical Setting   A room with plenty of space for the groups to construct tent structures.

Process

1. Direct the participants to form groups of four or five persons each.
2. Explain that each group will be using newspapers and masking tape to construct a tent that is large enough to shelter all the members of the group from an imaginary rainstorm. Only the materials provided may be a part of the structure; that is, it cannot be connected to or use any other item in its construction. Groups will have 20 minutes to complete the task.
3. Distribute several sections of newspaper and a roll of masking tape to each group.
4. Time the activity for 20 minutes, giving a 2-minute warning before time expires. Determine whether the structures meet the specifications by asking each group in turn to have its members enter their shelter.

5. Lead a concluding discussion based on the following questions:
   - What were your personal reactions to this activity? How did other group members react to it?
   - How well did group members work together during the activity? Why? Could you have interacted with greater harmony during the activity? If so, in what ways?
   - How did your group decide on a structural plan for the shelter? Were you able to build your shelter according to the original plan? Why or why not?
   - If you changed your plan, how well did group members make the adjustment?
   - What factors influenced the behaviors and outcomes in this activity? How are these factors logically related to one another?
   - How can we relate the group shelter to the concept of teamwork?

Variations

1. Ask the groups to judge the structures on the basis of creativity and usefulness.
2. Appoint observers to report back to the total group on task and relationship behaviors within each team.

   Note to the Facilitator   The tent structures are most easily made by using support "poles" made from rolled-up newspapers.

➤ Having a Ball

Goals

1. To demonstrate the need to coordinate individual efforts within a team.
2. To examine the contribution of each individual to the team effort.
3. To explore new ways to adjust to change.
4. To build cohesion within a group.

Group Size   Eight to fifteen participants.

Time Required   15 minutes.

Materials   Four to six small objects in a variety of shapes and sizes that can be easily thrown and caught, for example, rubber balls, Koosh™ balls, sponge balls, crushed paper balls, bean bags, hacky sacks, and so forth.

Physical Setting   A room large enough to allow the participants to form a large circle.

Process

1. Direct the participants to form a circle in which persons stand approximately one arm's length apart.
2. Explain that they are to establish a pattern by throwing an object from member to member in any order so that it makes it way to everyone once, returning to the original person. Players are to remember to whom they throw the object. Once the pattern is set, it is never broken throughout the game.
3. Provide a player (leader) with one of the objects and signal for the task to begin. After the initial pattern has been established, instruct the group to continue passing the object for a few more rounds, and then stop the activity.
4. Explain that as the game continues in future rounds, new objects will be introduced until there are several being thrown at the

same time. Tell the participants to continue passing objects without interruption once the game begins. Remind the participants that they are to use the same throwing pattern set previously.

5. Start the game again with the original object, and after one or two rounds, provide the leader with another object to begin passing. As the rhythm of the pattern becomes smoother, add a third object, then a fourth one. Depending on the size of the group, it should be possible to have as many as six objects being thrown at once.

6. Allow the task to continue for several minutes, but stop the activity as the actions of the group begin to become too chaotic or overly frustrating.

7. Lead a concluding discussion with the following questions:
   • How did you feel during this activity? Why did you feel that way?
   • How does this activity relate to teamwork in general? How does it relate to our ability to deal with change?
   • How difficult was it to adjust your actions when a new object was introduced? Why?
   • What are some examples of specific contributions that individual members might make toward the group effort?
   • What are some suggestions to help a group "juggle" multiple responsibilities more effectively? Suggestions to help integrate additional responsibilities? Suggestions to help adjust to changes in procedures?

Variation   Introduce only two or three objects during the game and instruct the participants to initiate a different pattern with each new object.

➤ "Hip" Hop

Goals

1. To use creative thinking skills to produce a variation on a traditional process.
2. To generate clear and concise instructions for performing a task.
3. To examine the role of behavior modeling and leadership.
4. To discuss the process of introducing and managing change.
5. To provide an icebreaker activity at the beginning of a session.

Group Size   Several groups of five to seven persons each.

Time Required   30 to 40 minutes.

Materials   Paper and a pencil for each group.

Physical Setting   A room large enough for groups to work without disturbing one another.

Process

1. Direct the participants to form one line, one person behind the other, and to perform the "line dance" known as the "Bunny Hop," according to the following instructions:
   Right Foot: Heel, toe, heel, toe
   Left Foot: Heel, toe, heel, toe
   Hop forward, Hop backward
   Hop forward three counts (hop, hop, hop)
   Repeat once or twice
2. Direct the participants to form teams of five to seven persons each. Distribute paper and pencil to each group.
3. Explain that groups will now brainstorm other ways of doing the Bunny Hop by addressing the following questions:
   • What else could be hopping in this dance?
   • What other movements could be made besides hopping?
   • What other formation could this dance take besides a line?

4. Allow approximately 10 minutes for participants to design the movements and steps for a new dance. Encourage the groups to come up with a new and different approach. Stress that the groups are to provide clear and concise instructions for performing their new dances.

5. Ask each group to model its new version of the dance by reading the instructions aloud and then leading the other participants in trying the new dance creation.

6. Lead a concluding discussion based on the following questions:
   • Which was more helpful—the oral instructions or physically modeling the dance steps? Why? How could the instructions have been made clearer?
   • How would your group introduce the new dance to others who now do the traditional Bunny Hop? How do you think they would react to the change? Why?
   • Did you follow the lead of the person in front of you? Why or why not? How does role modeling influence our behavior? How does it aid in managing change? What role does the leader have in the change management process?
   • Why is it important to revisit traditional work processes? How does creativity impact the way in which we do things?

Variation   Ask the participants to create a variation of the traditional "Hokey Pokey" dance.

⊿ Inner Circle

Goals

1. To demonstrate acceptance and rejection to group membership.
2. To investigate the impact of individual characteristics in gaining group membership.
3. To examine how individual acceptance affects participation levels in various groups.

Group Size   Six to twelve participants.

Time Required   15 to 30 minutes.

Physical Setting   A room with sufficient space to allow the participants to form a large circle.

Process

1. Direct the participants to form a circle. Sequentially assign a number to each participant.
2. Instruct participants that, as each person's number is called, the person will step outside the circle and then try to get back in to become a part of the group again. Members in the group are to form a tight circle and try to keep the person from "joining." Slight force may be used, but definitely not excessive force or violence.
3. Randomly announce a number, allow approximately 1 minute or less for the appropriate person to try to reenter the group, and then instruct the person to return to the group if he or she has been unsuccessful. Announce a new number and repeat the process several times. Call most of the numbers, but not all, and then stop the activity.
4. Lead a concluding discussion based on the following questions:
   - How did you feel about this activity in general? How did you feel if you were chosen to leave and then try to force your way

back into the group? How did you feel if you did not have to leave the group?

- What did this exercise tell us about acceptance? What did it tell us about rejection?
- What were the differences among the approaches people took to regain entrance to the group? What were the similarities?
- Did members of the group allow others back in without causing them to use much force? Why or why not? Did anyone use threats or trickery? If so, how did you feel about that approach?
- What characteristics of the individual may have impacted the reentry approach? How does individuality impact one's ability to gain acceptance to some groups?
- How did this activity relate to the amount of participation by individuals that occurs in various kinds of group? Are some groups easier to get into than others? Why is this?

Variation   Rather than assign numbers to participants, ask for volunteers to leave and then try to reenter the group. Encourage people to volunteer, but do not insist that everyone take a turn at "breaking in."

Note to the Facilitator   *Monitor the interactions of the participants during the exercise to assure that there is no undue force employed. You may need to alter the amount of time allowed for "breaking in" depending on individual participant ability.*

➤ Inside and Out

Goals
1. To become better acquainted with other members of the group.
2. To discover similarities and differences among group members.
3. To compare and contrast the benefits of similarity and diversity.
4. To provide an icebreaker at the beginning of a session.

Group Size   Several groups of four persons each.

Time Required   20 to 30 minutes.

Materials   A copy of the Inside and Out Worksheet and a pencil for each group.

Physical Setting   A room large enough for groups to work without disturbing one another. Writing surfaces should be provided.

Process
1. Direct the participants to form groups of four persons each. Ask each group to select one person to act as its recorder/presenter.
2. Distribute a copy of the Inside and Out Worksheet and a pencil to each group. Ask the recorder to write the group members' names on the worksheet, one in each of the four outer segments of the square.
3. Explain that group members are to get to know one another by discussing their various backgrounds, experiences, and interests. The group recorder is to place any items that are shared by *all* group members in the center circle. Items that are true of *one* member only should be placed in the appropriate outside segment.
4. Allow approximately 10 to 15 minutes for completing the task, and then ask the recorder from each group to present some of the documented items.

5. Lead a concluding discussion based on the following questions:
   - What did you personally learn from this activity?
   - Did you find that others in your group had *more* or *less* in common with you than you expected? Give some examples.
   - What are some examples of things that were shared by MOST group members, but not all? When an item was found to be the same for everyone in the group with the exception of one or two members, how did those individuals feel?
   - What are the advantages of having things in common with other members of a group? What are the benefits of having different backgrounds, experiences, and interests?
   - How can a work group use this information to improve its functioning?

Variations

1. Use this activity to compare and contrast elements of two concepts (for example, creativity and diversity).
2. This activity can be used in a problem-solving session to compare and contrast a list of possible solutions.

Note to the Facilitator   The main purpose of this activity is to get the group members to share information about themselves to become better acquainted. By recording only those items that ALL members share or those that belong to only ONE individual, there is an emphasis on the issues surrounding similarity and diversity.

Inside and Out Worksheet

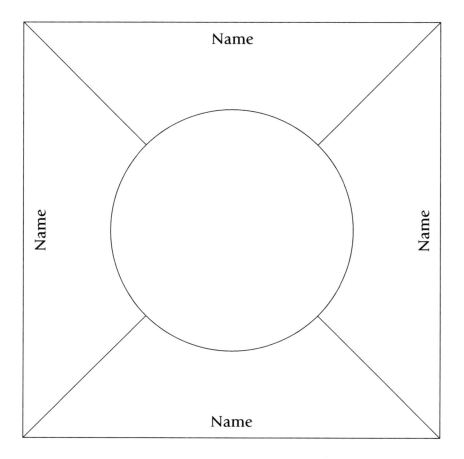

➤ Lead On

Goals

1. To gain insight into leadership skills and actions.
2. To apply problem-solving and sequencing skills.

Group Size   Three groups of four to seven persons each.

Time Required   45 to 50 minutes.

Materials

1. A copy of the Lead On Puzzle and a pencil for each participant.
2. A copy of the Lead On Answer Sheet for each participant.
3. A newsprint sheet and a felt-tipped marker for each group.
4. Masking tape.

Physical Setting   A room large enough for groups to work without disturbing one another. Writing surfaces should be provided. Wall space is needed for posting newsprint sheets.

Process

1. Direct the participants to form three groups of four to seven persons each.
2. Explain that the groups will be working together to complete a word search puzzle that will reveal fourteen words. These words, when combined appropriately, will form three well-known proverbs or wise sayings. Groups will have approximately 10 minutes to solve the puzzle.
3. Distribute a copy of the Lead On Puzzle sheet and a pencil to each participant. Signal for the groups to begin and then call time after approximately 10 minutes or sooner if all the groups have completed the task.

4. Distribute a copy of the Lead On Answer Sheet to each participant. Allow several minutes for the group members to compare their answers. Ask:
   - How well did your group do in completing the puzzle? Why did you do well, if you did? Why did you do poorly, if you did?
   - How did your group approach the task? Was it an effective approach? Why or why not?
   - Did any one person in the group take a leadership role? If so, how did this occur? What specific role did the person play?
5. Explain that the three sayings can be viewed in terms of leadership. To that end, each group will discuss one of the sayings in relation to how a leader could apply the proverb.
6. Assign one saying to each of the three groups and ask that they spend approximately 10 to 15 minutes discussing how the proverb relates to the role of a leader, describing specific examples whenever possible. Distribute a newsprint sheet and a felt-tipped marker to each group for the purpose of recording key points of their discussions.
7. Ask a representative from each group to use masking tape to post the newsprint sheet and share the information from the group's discussion.
8. Lead a concluding discussion by asking:
   - What were some similarities among the three proverbs? Any differences?
   - What impressions and insights did you gain about leadership?

Lead On Puzzle

E	R	M	T	Y	F	T	H	A	N
A	C	S	P	L	E	Y	U	C	T
R	E	N	R	K	N	I	H	T	B
B	R	X	E	C	A	V	K	I	W
D	R	L	H	I	Z	E	X	O	O
J	E	V	C	U	R	G	P	N	R
C	D	I	A	Q	X	E	K	S	D
E	U	R	E	C	U	F	P	H	S
H	O	X	T	K	T	D	I	X	T
T	L	S	L	O	W	L	Y	S	E

WORDS:

SAYINGS:

1)

2)

3)

Lead On Answer Sheet

1. Experience is the best teacher.
2. Actions speak louder than words.
3. Act quickly, think slowly.

E	R	M	T	Y	F	T	H	A	N
A	C	S	P	L	E	Y	U	C	T
R	E	N	R	K	N	I	H	T	B
B	R	X	E	C	A	V	K	I	W
D	R	L	H	I	Z	E	X	O	O
J	E	V	C	U	R	G	P	N	R
C	D	I	A	Q	X	E	K	S	D
E	U	R	E	C	U	F	P	H	S
H	O	X	T	K	T	D	I	X	T
T	L	S	L	O	W	L	Y	S	E

➤ Lofty Goal

Goals
1. To examine the role of the individual in a group effort.
2. To build cohesion within a group.
3. To provide an icebreaker activity at the beginning of a session.

Group Size   Several groups of five to eight persons each.

Time Required   10 to 15 minutes.

Materials
1. A balloon for each participant (use a variety of shapes but only one color per group).
2. Five to ten extra balloons and a marble for each balloon.

Physical Setting   A room large enough so that the participants can move about in an unrestricted fashion.

Process
1. Prior to the session, prepare the extra balloons by inserting a marble into each, inflating them, and tying off the ends. These balloons will be used later in the activity.
2. At the session, direct the participants to form groups of five to eight persons each. Distribute a balloon to each participant, providing each group with a different color. Ask the participants to fully inflate the balloons and to tie them off securely.
3. Explain that each color set of balloons represents a team within an organization and that each balloon shape designates a particular role within each team. The goal of the activity is for all the teams to do their "jobs" by keeping their balloons in the air at all times.
4. Signal for the participants to bounce their balloons into the air and, after a minute, begin to add the extra weighted balloons into the larger group at various locations. Allow the activity to

continue for several minutes, and then call for the participants to stop.

5. Lead a concluding discussion based on the following questions:
   - What were your personal reactions to this activity? How did others seem to react to it?
   - How difficult was it to keep all the balloons in the air? Why? What happened when the extra balloons were introduced?
   - Did an individual maintain responsibility for the original balloon (team role) throughout the activity? Why did this happen?
   - How willing were others on your team to help you keep your balloon in the air?
   - Did members from other teams help you do your job? Who took responsibility for the additional balloons?
   - How does this activity relate to teamwork in general?

Variations

1. Use weighted balloons throughout the entire activity.
2. Assign a separate yet adjacent area of the room for each team to perform the activity. Include the following question in the discussion: How often did you need to move into another team's area to perform your job?
3. As you introduce the weighted balloons, name each one with a cultural or organizational challenge as you enter it into the group. During the concluding discussion, explore the impact of these challenges on the group and ways in which to handle the challenges.

Note to the Facilitator   Placing a marble in the balloon makes it bounce in all different directions and creates an interesting challenge to keep it afloat.

➤ Mad Hatter's "Team" Party

Goals
1. To become acquainted with group members.
2. To provide an icebreaker activity at the beginning of a session.
3. To examine active listening skills.

Group Size
Several groups of five or seven persons each (an odd number of people in each group is required).

Time Required
15 minutes.

Materials
1. A set of Mad Hatter's Question Cards for each group.
2. A timer or stopwatch (optional).

Physical Setting
A large room equipped with a chair for each person. The chairs for each group should be arranged in two equal lines facing one another with one chair at the top or "head" of this arrangement.

Process
1. Instruct the participants to be seated in the prearranged chairs.
2. Explain that the participants are going to take part in a Mad Hatter's "team" party. The person occupying the seat at the "head" of each group is designated as the Mad Hatter. The Mad Hatter will start by reading a question card out loud to the group. Making eye contact with the person across from him or her, each person in the group will respond in turn, starting with the person to the right of the Mad Hatter and continuing down the line on the right and up the line on the left until everyone has answered. Then, everyone moves one chair clockwise, which puts a new Mad Hatter at the head of the group who will read the question on his or her card. This process will continue until all of the questions have been read and answered. Clarify these instructions to be sure that everyone understands the procedure.

3. Distribute a set of Mad Hatter's Question Cards to each group
   and instruct each person to take a card, setting aside any extras.
4. Signal for the task to begin. Stop the groups when everyone has
   had the opportunity to answer all the questions.
5. Lead a concluding discussion based on the following questions:
   - What kinds of things did you learn about other members of
     your group?
   - Was it difficult to answer some of the questions? Which ones?
     Why?
   - How difficult was it to actively listen to the answers made by
     your group members? Why was it difficult?
   - How does this activity relate to the communication process in
     general?

Variations

1. Time each question to be answered by all the group members
   within 30 seconds, then announce "Switch" for everyone to
   move one chair clockwise and a new Mad Hatter to ask his or
   her question.
2. Use the activity as a review of content presented during the
   session. To do so, make a set of question cards that requires each
   group member to list one applicable answer. For example, to the
   question "What factors contribute to effective communication?"
   possible answers might be "active listening," "no jargon," and so
   forth.

   Note to the Facilitator   *Be aware that this activity can become very
   noisy.*

Mad Hatter's Question Cards

I really hate it when	I really like it when . . . .
The best thing that happened to me this week was	The worst thing that happened to me this week was . . . .
My favorite thing to do is	My least favorite thing to do is . . . .
When I feel bad, I	When I feel good, I . . . .

➤ Material Evidence

Goals

1. To communicate views of "group leader" and "group member" through representative items.
2. To compare and contrast perceptions of group leader and group member roles.
3. To examine how the leadership role is perceived.

Group Size   Several groups of four or five persons each.

Time Required   45 minutes to 1 hour.

Materials

1. One prepared paper bag of ten items for each group.
2. A stapler and felt-tipped marker for preparing the bags.
3. A newsprint sheet and a felt-tipped marker for each group.
4. Masking tape.

Physical Setting

A room with a separate table for each group. Wall space is required for posting newsprint sheets.

Process

1. Prior to the session, collect several units (same as number of participating groups) each of ten objects that include such items as feathers, balls, coffee filters, corks, candles, matchbooks, paper cups, string, marbles, glue sticks, compact discs, erasers, bottles of Wite®Out fluid, and so forth. Using the felt-tipped marker, identify half of the bags as "Group Leader" and the other half as "Group Member." Place an identical set of ten items in each bag and staple the bags closed.
2. At the session, direct the participants to form groups of four or five persons each.
3. Distribute a prepared paper bag of items, a newsprint sheet, and a felt-tipped marker to each group.
4. Explain that each group has a bag containing items that represent certain characteristics of the specific role to which it

belongs, either "Group Leader" or "Group Member." Like archeologists, each group will construct a composite profile of the role identified on the bag by examining the material evidence inside and assigning detailed traits or characteristics that are representative of each object. For example, a rubber band might represent "flexibility" for some particular aspect of the role. Groups are to write the assigned role at the top of the newsprint sheet and list the assigned characteristic for each item. Groups will have 15 minutes to complete the task.

5. Signal for the activity to begin. After approximately 15 minutes, announce that the groups are to stop.

6. Provide masking tape and instruct the groups to post their newsprint sheets. Ask each group in turn to report the characteristics of its composite profile.

7. Lead a concluding discussion based on the following questions:
   - How did you feel about assigning traits to your designated role? Why did you feel that way?
   - How did perception play a part in this activity? Did all members of the group have similar ideas for what the items represented? If not, why?
   - Although each bag had the same contents, in what ways did the profiles differ? What were some of the same characteristics for both roles?
   - Comparing your lists for the two roles, what fundamental differences, if any, were perceived to exist between being a Group Leader and being a Group Member? Does this reflect our views on leadership in general? How do these views impact a group and its work?
   - How do the characteristics you identified for each role match the traits of the members of your current work group?
   - How might a role "profile" help clarify group expectations in the workplace?

Variation   Provide each group with a *different* set of ten items, but do not designate roles on the bags. Have each group assemble a composite profile and indicate which role, Group Leader or Group Member, it feels the items would represent.

➤ Mind Mingle

Goals

1. To provide a closing activity to review content or discussion ideas.
2. To look for common relationships among ideas.
3. To discuss the influence of perception on the interpretation of content information.

Group Size   Unlimited participants.

Time Required   10 to 20 minutes.

Materials   A 3-inch by 5-inch index card and a pencil for each participant.

Physical Setting   A room large enough that the participants can move around freely in an unrestricted fashion. Writing surfaces should be provided.

Process

1. Distribute an index card and a pencil to each participant.
2. Ask each participant to write down one content item learned from the session (or alternatively, one idea from the group's previous discussion).
3. Explain that the participants are to walk around the room, mingling with others. On your signal, they are to form triads and discuss each person's item. They are to find a common relationship among all the ideas.
4. Signal for participants to mingle and, after a few seconds, signal for them to form the discussion triads. Allow approximately 3 to 5 minutes for discussion. Repeat the process as many times as

desired, then lead a concluding discussion based on the following questions:

- What were some of the main ideas presented on the cards? Did any individuals have different interpretations of the ideas presented? If so, why might this occur?
- How does individual perception influence the interpretation of content information? What are some examples of this occurring in the workplace?
- How difficult was it to find a common relationship among a variety of ideas? Why was this?
- How can groups use this type of process to make more effective decisions? How can this process help individuals gain a stronger commitment to group decisions?
- How can you use the information gained from this exercise to improve your own group's performance?

Variations

1. During an extended session, provide several index cards for each participant and have them form groups at intermediate times throughout the session and at the end.
2. Using the ideas written on their index cards, have participants mingle and find three or four others who share the same content item or idea. Then have small groups discuss the idea for expanded insights.

➤ New Twist on Things

Goals

1. To discuss the dimensions of task and relationship behaviors within the group process.
2. To list characteristics of task and relationship behaviors.
3. To discuss ways to facilitate effective group process behaviors.

Group Size   Five to twenty participants.

Time Required 40 to 50 minutes.

Materials

1. A strip of 8½-inch × 14-inch paper and a pencil for each participant.
2. Tape and a pair of scissors for every five participants.
3. A newsprint flip chart and felt-tipped markers for recording.
4. Masking tape for posting.

Physical Setting   Any room in which the group regularly meets. Writing surfaces should be provided. Wall space is required for posting newsprint sheets.

Process

1. Prior to the session, cut 8½ by 14-inch paper into strips 14 inches long and approximately 1½ inches wide. On each strip, write "A" on one end and then turn the paper over and write "B" at the opposite end, as shown below:

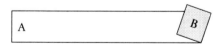

2. At the session, distribute a paper strip and a pencil to each participant. Provide tape to be shared by several participants.
3. Explain that participants are to hold the strips in their hands, give one end a double twist, and tape the ends of the strip

together so that the ends marked "A" and "B" are touching. View the strips to ensure that the results appear to be a figure 8, as illustrated below:

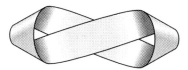

4. Direct the participants to use their pencils to draw a line lengthwise down the middle of the paper strip until the circle is complete. Ask:
   • What occurred? *(The line can be drawn without lifting the pencil from the paper.)*
   • Were your initial perceptions about the loop accurate? Why did this happen?
   • What do you predict will happen if the paper strip is cut along the line that has been drawn?
5. Distribute several pairs of scissors to be shared by groups of participants. Instruct each participant to carefully insert the tip of the scissors into the paper and cut the strip along the pencil line. The result is two connected loops, as illustrated below:

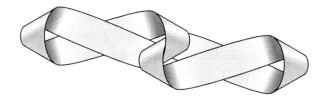

6. Ask the participants:
   • Did the result support your prediction? What was your prediction based on?
   • How do past experiences influence our expectations? How might this cause us to make false assumptions?
   • How might certain assumptions affect how work is accomplished within a group? How can these assumptions affect how group members interact with one another?

7. Explain that the two loops can represent the two basic dimensions of behaviors that exist within every group: *task behaviors* that involve doing the job and *relationship behaviors* that affect how members interact. These two aspects of the group process are equally important and one cannot be separated from the other in supporting the collaborative efforts of teamwork.

8. Ask the participants to identify various behaviors under the Task dimension *(goal setting, problem solving, decision making, strategic planning, resource use, time management)* and then behaviors for the Relationship dimension *(collaboration, conflict resolution, negotiation, leadership)*. Use the flip chart to record feedback and then post the sheet.

9. Ask the participants to brainstorm guidelines that a group can use to help facilitate effective task and relationship behaviors. Use the flip chart to record feedback.

Variation   Rather than have individual participants do their own bands, you can use just one strip to demonstrate the loop, pencil marking, and cutting steps.

Note to the Facilitator   The twisted strip that was created is called a double Mobius band. What is initially perceived as a band with an inner and outer surface is really a continuous one-sided loop. When it is formed, it takes on the shape of a figure 8, the symbol for infinity. Both of these concepts can be related to teamwork, which requires an ongoing effort to provide a link that connects group members. When the band is cut in half, it generates two separate, yet interconnected links. These constitute a systems view of task and relationship behaviors: both are equally important and together they comprise effective teamwork.

➤ Oh, Domino

Goals
1. To provide an icebreaker activity at the beginning of a session.
2. To discover rules that can be applied to solving a problem.
3. To equate making connections to a variety of concepts (teamwork, change, problem solving, and interpersonal relationships).

Group Size   Fifteen to twenty-eight participants.

Time Required   20 to 40 minutes.

Materials
1. A set of double six dominoes (twenty-eight tiles).
2. A clock or stop watch.

Physical Setting   A room large enough that the participants can move about in an unrestricted fashion.

Process
1. Distribute a domino tile to each participant. Place any extra tiles aside.
2. Explain that the participants are to match the dots on the dominoes, connecting them from end to end. The goal of the activity is to make the longest series of connected domino tiles as possible in the shortest amount of time.
3. Allow the activity to run until it comes to a natural conclusion. Note the total number of connected dominoes and the time elapsed.
4. Lead a concluding discussion based on the following questions:
   • How successful were you in making the connections? What factors contributed to your success or lack thereof?
   • Were players willing to rearrange a sequence to accommodate additional tiles? Why or why not? How does this relate to the acceptance of change?

- What observations did you make about the way in which the dominoes connected to one another (that is, rules that might be applied)? If you were to go through the same activity again, would these "rules" help improve the group's performance? Can certain "rules" help solve problems in the workplace? Give an example.
- How can we use this activity as an analogy for working together in groups in terms of teamwork? In terms of problem solving? In terms of introducing change? In terms of interpersonal connections?

Variations

1. An extended discussion can occur on how individuals make interpersonal connections in a variety of situations: between members, across teams, with customers, and so forth.
2. You can use this activity to form smaller groups. Ask the participants to connect the dots on their dominoes with those of other players to form the appropriate number of groups.

   Note to the Facilitator   Some of the observations that might be made during the concluding discussion include such things as: a single occurrence of a particular number will not connect; a "double" acts as a main connector and should be used to start; you may need to change a sequence in order to accommodate a better fit; you are more likely to make all possible connections when you have an even amount of like numbers occurring within the set; only the complete set of twenty-eight pieces assures a perfect connection.

➤ Oobleck

Goals

1. To investigate the effects of fast versus slow change.
2. To explore personal reactions to change.
3. To compare the impact of change on groups versus individual members.
4. To recommend ways for groups to handle change effectively.

Group Size   Several groups of four persons each.

Time Required   30 minutes.

Materials

1. A large mixing bowl, 16 ounces cornstarch, and ½ cup water to make the mixture.
2. A 6-ounce bathroom-size paper cup and sheet of waxed paper for each participant.
3. *Bartholomew and the Oobleck* book by Dr. Seuss (optional).
4. A wet hand towel for each participant.
5. A newsprint sheet and a felt-tipped marker for each group.
6. Masking tape.

Physical Setting   A room with tables where four people can gather together in a group. Wall space is needed for posting newsprint sheets. Trash receptacles are necessary for proper clean-up.

Process

1. Prior to the session, you will need to make the Oobleck. Combine the cornstarch and water in a large mixing bowl about 45 minutes before the session starts. To mix, "lift" the mixture from the bottom of the bowl to the top by slipping your fingers under it, until an even consistency is reached. Just before the session, stir the mixture again, adjusting the amounts of water and cornstarch until the Oobleck flows when you tip the bowl and feels solid when you hit it. Fill the cups with only about half

an inch of the mixture. (Oobleck comes from a Dr. Seuss book titled *Bartholomew and the Oobleck*. In that book, the Oobleck is green. You could make your Oobleck green by adding green food coloring, but this may become a little too messy.)

2. Begin the session by asking if anyone has heard of the Dr. Seuss book *Bartholomew and the Oobleck*. If you have a copy of the book, hold it up. If not, ask the group if anyone knows what Oobleck might be. Inform the group that they will be investigating some Oobleck (without it being green as in the Dr. Seuss book).

3. Direct the participants to form groups of four persons each. Distribute a small cup of Oobleck and a small sheet of waxed paper to each participant.

4. Tell the participants that they will have approximately 5 minutes to investigate the Oobleck by using their fingers and by pouring it onto the waxed paper. Have them make a mental note of the properties of Oobleck as they do their investigation.

5. Observe the group investigations. If no one notices, suggest poking a finger into the Oobleck quickly versus poking a finger into the mixture slowly.

6. After several minutes, stop the group activity. Instruct the participants to do a quick clean-up by wrapping the Oobleck mixture in the waxed paper and discarding it, along with the cups, in the trash receptacles provided. Be sure that a wet hand towel is available for each participant if wash facilities are not available.

7. Distribute a newsprint sheet and a felt-tipped marker to each group. Explain that group members are to record all their observations about the Oobleck. Allow approximately 7 minutes for the task, and then instruct groups to post their sheets with the masking tape.

8. Referring to the sheets, have the groups share their observations on the various properties of the Oobleck mixture.

Note to the Facilitator   *What you eventually are looking for is that someone discovers that the mixture behaves differently if you do something to it fast (like jabbing it with your finger) versus doing*

*something to it slowly (like slowly pushing into it with your finger).
This should lead to a discussion of fast changes versus slow changes to
Oobleck, and finally to fast changes versus slow changes in your
organization.*

9. Lead a concluding discussion by asking the following questions:
   • How are the changes that occurred in the Oobleck and those
     that occur in your organizations alike? How are they different?
   • How did the Oobleck react to change? How do you personally
     react to change?
   • Do you think quick changes or slow changes are best for you as
     an individual? For your company? For your colleagues? Why?
   • How do changes within a team impact the group as a whole?
     What about individual members of the group?
   • What recommendations would you make to a group that is
     undergoing change?

Variation   Provide each group with only one cup of Oobleck and
have the members of the group share it during the investigation.

*Notes to the Facilitator   1. While things may be a little messy
during the investigation of Oobleck, the clean-up is easy because any
excess can be cleaned with running water. WARNING: Oobleck will
clog sinks if you pour it directly down the drain! Dispose of the
mixture by placing in a trash receptacle. If any spills, it vacuums
or sweeps up easily once it dries.*

*2. The mixture will flow like a liquid, will break into pieces like a
solid, will powder when rubbed, and will withstand shocks but not
support weight.*

*3. It is not necessary to discuss how the cornstarch and water work
together. There have been numerous scientific models competing to
explain this behavior. The models would have to explain why the
particles of cornstarch behave as both a solid and a liquid. Perhaps it
has to do with the time it takes the particles to move when you poke
them rapidly as opposed to poking them slowly.*

Source: Sneider, C.I., Baker, L.H., & Bergman, L. (Eds.). (1999). *Oobleck: What do scientists do?* GEMS
(Great Explorations in Math and Science).

➤ Organizational Pulse

Goals
1. To assess current conditions within an organization.
2. To introduce the concept of systems thinking.
3. To examine the influence of organizational factors on group performance.
4. To identify ways to counter negative organizational culture.

Group Size   Several groups of four to six persons each from an intact work group, or from the same organization.

Time Required   Approximately 1 hour.

Materials
1. A copy of the Organizational Pulse Survey and a pencil for each participant.
2. Two newsprint sheets and felt-tipped markers for each group.
3. Masking tape.

Physical Setting   A room large enough for groups to work without disturbing one another. Writing surfaces should be provided. Wall space is required for posting newsprint sheets.

Process
1. Begin the session by explaining that groups need to take a "systems" approach when examining their own effectiveness, that is, how the organizational environment influences a work group. Tell the participants:

   "Organizations are very complex systems with a wide variety of interacting components. Systems thinking is a way of looking at the whole by seeing the interrelationships of the many dynamic components. An important part of systems thinking, then, is the examination of the organizational culture, which can be defined as a psychological state strongly affected by conditions within the organization. It includes the values, norms, beliefs, and practices that govern how an organization functions. You will now have an opportunity to look at some dimensions of your own organization."

2. Distribute a copy of the Organizational Pulse Survey and a pencil to each participant. Review the instructions at the top of the sheet and ask individuals to complete the survey.

3. When everyone has completed the survey, direct the participants to form groups of four to six persons each. Ask the groups to discuss their overall ratings of the statements. Allow approximately 10 minutes.

4. Explain that the results of the survey will help identify those areas of the organization that are perceived to show a negative trend. Distribute two newsprint sheets and felt-tipped markers to each group. Ask the group members to identify the statements that they agree occur *frequently* (indicated by a circled number) and to list these on a sheet marked "Frequent." The groups will then identify the statements that they agree occur *moderately* (indicated by an X) and to list these on a sheet marked "Moderate." Groups will have 20 minutes to complete the task.

5. Time the activity for 20 minutes, giving a 2-minute warning before time expires. Provide masking tape and instruct the groups to post their sheets. Ask each group in turn to present its two lists.

6. Lead a concluding discussion based on the following questions:
   • How do these negative organizational factors influence your own work group? How does this fit into the view of "systems thinking"?
   • What are the most critical conditions within your organization that need to be improved?
   • What do you think is the single most influential organizational characteristic? Why? How does this impact the functioning of your own group?
   • In general, how can a group counter some of the negative effects of its organizational culture? In working with other groups within the organization, what can your own group do to improve organizational conditions?

Variation   Ask groups to make a list of specific things the
organization can do to improve conditions in terms of the
"frequently" and "moderately" occurring statements identified
in step 4.

*Note to the Facilitator   This activity requires a higher level of
facilitation skills and an overall understanding of the organizational
culture. The debriefing session may uncover sensitive or controversial
issues and you should have sufficient skill in opening up and closing
down such discussions. This activity can be a powerful tool in opening
up a discussion of topics in an environment that is currently
experiencing a lot of negativity, but it should be conducted with care.*

Organizational Pulse Survey

Instructions: Carefully consider each of the following factors as they pertain to your organization. The word "group" can apply at any level appropriate to your situation, from a project team or department to the company as a whole. Follow these directions:

- Circle the number of the statement if it occurs *frequently.*
- Place an X in front of the statement if it occurs *moderately.*
- Do nothing to the statement if it occurs *infrequently.*

1. Rivalry when one person or group gets closer to a common goal.
2. One person or group obstructs or sabotages the progress of another person or group.
3. Criticism and putdowns that show individuals and their contributions are not valued highly.
4. Less coordination of efforts and less teamwork.
5. Many individuals doing things their own way.
6. Decreased group solidarity and loyalty among members.
7. Organizational rigidity during times of change.
8. Direction of group energy and activity is scattered and less organized.
9. Communication breakdowns among group members.
10. Conflicts, power jockeying, bickering, and insistence on being right.
11. Decreased friendliness and increased suspicion; people feel they need to be on their guard.
12. Difficulty in reaching consensus and moving toward goals.
13. Expectation of receiving hostility or rejection from others in the work setting.
14. "Goofing off" or working on personal business during available work time.
15. Creativity, innovation, and risk taking are not encouraged.

➤ Our Song

Goals
1. To provide an opening activity that predicts group performance for the entire session.
2. To provide a closing activity that evaluates group performance for the entire session.
3. To identify internal and external factors that influence group performance.
4. To apply creative thinking skills.

Group Size   Several groups of four to seven persons each.

Time Required   Approximately 10 minutes at the beginning of a session and 20 minutes at the end of the session.

Materials   Paper and a pencil for each participant.

Physical Setting   A room large enough for groups to work without disturbing one another. Writing surfaces should be provided.

Process
1. Direct the participants to form groups of four to seven persons each. (These groups will work together in terms of activities and discussions for the remainder of the session.) Distribute paper and a pencil to each participant.
2. Explain that the members of each group are to think of the title of a song that represents how they predict they will perform as a group for the remainder of the session. Allow approximately 5 minutes for discussion, and then ask each group for its song title. Instruct the participants to write the song title on the paper provided and to place it aside until the end of the session.
3. Run the planned activities for the remainder of the session.
4. At the end of the session, ask the groups to evaluate their overall performance by reflecting on the feelings, behaviors, and outcomes for the various activities and discussions. Each

member of the group is to think of a new song title that represents how that individual felt the group actually performed. Direct the participants to record the title of the song on the paper that contained the original song title selected by the group. Allow approximately 5 minutes for individual work.

5. Instruct group members to share their song titles with one another and to give a brief explanation of why they chose these songs.

6. Lead a concluding discussion based on the following questions:
   - Did individuals share perceptions of the group's expected performance? Did individual group members share similar perceptions of the group's overall performance? If not, why was that?
   - Did your group's actual performance during the session match the original expectations, as evidenced by the song chosen earlier? If not, in what way(s) did the performance differ?
   - What factors within a group influence its ability to perform? What external factors influence performance?
   - What could your group have done differently to improve its overall performance?

Variations

1. After individual group members share their song titles in step 5, ask each group to select the one title it feels best represents the group's actual performance for the session and share it with the larger group.

2. At the end of the workshop, have each group compose customized lyrics to the chosen song and then sing the final song to the larger group.

➤ Patent Pending

Goals
1. To apply creative thinking skills by developing an invention.
2. To improve problem-solving skills.
3. To examine participant roles and group dynamics.
4. To demonstrate group interdependence by sharing resources.

Group Size   Several groups of four to seven persons each.

Time Required   1 to 1½ hours.

Materials
1. A variety of materials, such as milk cartons, paper clips, modeling clay, Popsicle® sticks, foil, spools of thread, pipe cleaners, pins, brass fasteners, washers, buttons, hooks, yarn, rope, toothpicks, tape, clothespins, washers, rubber bands, plastic tubing, film canisters, screws, boxes, scissors, and so forth.
2. Paper and a pencil for each participant.

Physical Setting   A room with separate tables for each group and a table for holding the materials.

Process
1. Prior to the session, set up a supply table containing all the materials.
2. At the session, direct the participants to form groups of four to seven persons each. Distribute paper and a pencil to each person.
3. Referring to the supply table, explain that the groups are to use any of the materials they wish to create something useful. They are to name their inventions and to make note of their functions on the paper provided. After completion of the projects, each group will give a report on its invention by telling or demonstrating how it is to be used. Allow 30 to 40 minutes for group work.

4. Have each group in turn show its invention, give its name, and tell or demonstrate how it is to be used.
5. Lead a concluding discussion based on the following questions:
   * How would you describe this activity in a step-by-step fashion?
   * How did your group decide on its invention? Did you select materials and then develop the idea, or did you develop an idea and then select the materials? Why? Was this an effective process? Why or why not?
   * Did your group encounter any problems while working on the invention? If so, what kind and how were they resolved?
   * How well did members of your group work together? What behaviors occurred? Did everyone participate equally in the task? If not, why not? How were various group roles "assigned"?
   * How well did you work with members of other groups in sharing resources? What behaviors occurred?
   * If you were to go through the same activity again, what would be a reasonable course of action?

Variations

1. Have each group develop a written sales advertisement for their invention and present it on a newsprint sheet.
2. Have each group develop a 2-minute "television" commercial about its invention and act it out for the class (see *Infomercial* in "Communication").

➤ Personal Links

Goals
1. To give and receive compliments within a group.
2. To build cohesion within a group.
3. To provide a closing activity at the end of a session.

Group Size   Several groups of five or six participants each who know one another or who have worked together previously.

Time Required   15 to 20 minutes.

Materials
1. Five or six paper strips (approximately 1 inch by 11 inches) and a felt-tipped pen for each participant.
2. A dispenser of transparent tape for each group.

Physical Setting   A room large enough for the groups to work without disturbing one another. Writing surfaces should be provided.

Process
1. Direct the participants to form groups of five or six persons each.
2. Distribute five or six paper strips and a felt-tipped pen to each participant. Provide each group with a dispenser of transparent tape.
3. Instruct each participant to take one of the paper strips and write his or her name in large letters. Next, the participant is to form a link by taping both ends of the strip together to form an "O." Each individual will then pass the circle link to the person on his or her right. That person will take another strip of paper and write something positive about the individual whose name is on the first link. The new paper strip is to be inserted through the last link and taped to form a new link so that it begins to form a chain. This process is to be repeated until the chain passes

around to everyone in the group and finally ends up with the original owner.

4. When all the chains are complete, ask the group members to read silently the positive statements about them.

5. Lead a concluding discussion by asking the following questions:
   - How did you feel about giving compliments to others in your group? Why did you feel this way?
   - How did you feel about receiving the compliments? Why was that?
   - Why is it important to share "positive strokes" with team members?

Variation   Provide colored markers, crayons, stickers, and other materials so that individuals can decorate their original name links before passing them around the group.

➤ Piecing It All Together

Goals

1. To stress the importance of each member's individual contributions to the group effort.
2. To explore the importance of working together effectively as a group.
3. To provide an icebreaker activity at the beginning of a session.

Group Size   Ten to twenty participants.

Time Required   20 to 30 minutes.

Materials

1. A picture puzzle (approximately 75 to 100 pieces, depending on the number of participants).
2. An envelope for each participant.
3. A clock with a second hand or a stop watch.

Physical Setting   A room with table space for each participant to assemble five to seven puzzle pieces and a centrally located table with space large enough to assemble the entire puzzle.

Process

1. Prior to the session, prepare one puzzle subset for each participant by breaking the puzzle into equal subsets of approximately five to seven *connectable* pieces each. Note that some participants may have an additional piece, depending on the total number of pieces in the puzzle and the number of participants. Place each puzzle subset into an envelope.
2. At the session, distribute an envelope of puzzle pieces to each participant. Explain that the group as a whole will be putting together a picture puzzle, but each person needs to assemble his or her own section of the puzzle first. Allow enough time for all individuals to complete the task.

3. Explain that the participants now will have 5 minutes to connect all the subsets appropriately until the total puzzle is solved. Designate the location where the puzzle will be assembled.

4. Time the activity for 5 minutes, giving a 2-minute warning. End the task when time has expired.

5. If the entire puzzle was not completed in the allotted time, explain to the participants that they will be allowed to continue until the puzzle is finished, but that you will be timing how long it takes to complete the task.

6. Time the activity until the puzzle is complete, noting the amount of time that elapses. Announce the additional time that was required.

7. Lead a concluding discussion based on the following questions:
   - What reactions did you have when you realized your individual importance to the overall group effort?
   - What impact did the time deadline have on your effectiveness?
   - What was the impact of having others available during the group activity to help you with your individual efforts? Did group members participate equally or did some people take control of the task? How does this reflect your past experience regarding how individuals actually work together as a team?
   - How does this activity relate to group efforts back in the workplace?
   - What are some specific ways that groups can improve the coordination of their individual efforts?

Variations

1. Play some energizing music (for example, the "William Tell Overture") during the group assembly task to create an additional sense of urgency. Add the following question to the discussion: What impact did the music have on your actions?

2. When preparing the envelopes with the puzzle subsets, make sure that participants receive different amounts of puzzle pieces to solve. Add the following questions to the discussion: How did you feel about group members who had more (or fewer) puzzle

pieces to put together? How did you react? How does this relate to individual workload assignments back on the job?

3. Don't tell participants that their pieces connect to form a whole. Let them discover that on their own and then discuss the dynamics later.

➤ Rapid Fire

Goals

1. To evaluate individual comprehension of content matter as a closing activity.
2. To gauge individual concerns and interests about the session topic as an opening activity.
3. To gain insight into personal opinions on aspects of a specific content area.

Group Size   Six to thirty participants.

Time Required   5 to 15 minutes.

Materials   Prepared question(s) to be asked of the participants.

Physical Setting   Any room in which the group regularly meets.

Process

1. Prior to the session, prepare question(s) that pertain to specific aspects of the training content (for example, "What is one indicator of shared leadership?"); that ask for topics to be covered within the session (for example, "What aspects of leadership would you like to discuss in this session?"); or that ask for personal opinions (for example, "What one quality would you want in a leader?").
2. Explain to the participants that you will be asking a question (or set of questions) to which they will respond as quickly as possible. They should keep their answers brief and to the point, although some background information may be provided if necessary.
3. Pose the same general content question to each group member or ask a different question of each individual, allowing only a few moments for participants to think about their answers. Move from person to person around the room until everyone has had

an opportunity to answer the question. Depending on the amount of time and the purpose of the activity, repeat the procedure as many times as desired.

4. Lead a concluding discussion based on the following questions:
   - What were your personal reactions to responding to the question(s)? How did others seem to react to the process?
   - Was this an effective technique to gain information? Why or why not?
   - What new insights and ideas on the topic did you gain from the responses given?

Variation   Rather than workshop content, focus on individual self-awareness by posing questions such as:
- What is one word that describes you best?
- What do you want to be doing five years from now?
- What animal do you think best represents your personality?

Note to the Facilitator   *Allow individuals to pass on a question if they seem reluctant or unable to answer it.*

➤ Role Out

Goals
1. To observe how roles play out in a group situation.
2. To examine a variety of functional roles within a group.
3. To identify the positive and negative aspects of group roles.
4. To use creative thinking skills.

Group Size   Several groups of five to seven persons each.

Time Required   Approximately 1 hour.

Materials
1. Paper and a pencil for each participant.
2. A set of the Role Out Cards in an envelope for each group.
3. A newsprint flip chart with the following information:
   TASK:
   Provide information
   Offer new ideas
   Ask for information
   Ask for opinions
   Give your opinion
   RELATIONSHIP:
   Encourage others
   Mediate conflicts
   Equalize participation
   SELF-ORIENTED:
   Reject ideas
   Dominate discussion

Physical Setting   A room large enough to allow groups to work without disturbing one another. Writing surfaces should be provided.

Process

1. Direct the participants to form groups of five to seven persons each. Provide paper and a pencil to each participant.

2. Tell the groups that their assignment is to brainstorm ideas for a fun and innovative fundraising event. They will accomplish this task by following certain directions.

3. Distribute a set of Role Out Cards in an envelope to each group. Instruct the groups to pass the envelope so that each person can remove one card, keeping the information concealed from others. The envelope of remaining cards should be set aside.

4. Signal for the brainstorming discussion to begin and allow approximately 10 to 15 minutes for discussion. When the groups have stopped, instruct the members of each group to disclose the roles assigned and to spend a few minutes sharing reactions to the experience.

5. Allow approximately 10 minutes, and then address the groups. Explain that there are a variety of different functional roles individuals take on within a group and that they fall into three categories: task, relationship, and self-oriented functions. Ask:
   • Were you able to discern the various roles exhibited in your group? Why or why not?
   • What are some examples of the task-oriented roles used? Examples of relationship roles?
   • Do you think there were any self-oriented roles that occurred in your group? If so, what were they?

6. Referring to the prepared flip chart, reveal the range of functional roles that were assigned for this discussion.

7. Lead a concluding discussion based on the following questions:
   • How did your assigned role affect your participation in the group? How did it affect the group's ability to think creatively?
   • How did the self-oriented roles impact the group process? Besides the two identified on the flip chart, what other self-oriented roles can occur within a group? (*nonparticipation or avoidance, seeking recognition*)

- Besides the task roles listed on the chart, what are some others that can occur in groups? *(give examples, point out relevance, measure quality of methods or facts, take notes)*
- Besides the relationship roles listed on the chart, what are some others that can occur in groups? *(give alternatives to help gain compromise, strive for acceptance of ideas, reflect back on group dynamics)*
- Within your actual work groups, what are the most common roles played out? Are there any roles that are lacking? If so, which ones?

Role Out Cards

PROVIDE INFORMATION	OFFER NEW IDEAS
ASK FOR INFORMATION	ASK FOR OPINIONS
GIVE YOUR OPINION	ENCOURAGE OTHERS
EQUALIZE PARTICIPATION	MEDIATE CONFLICTS
REJECT IDEAS	DOMINATE DISCUSSION

➤ Rules

Goals
1. To identify reasons why groups need rules.
2. To list group rules for effective functioning.
3. To set boundaries for newly formed groups.

Group Size   Several groups of four or five persons each, preferably from an intact work group.

Time Required   Approximately 1 hour.

Materials
1. Paper and a pencil for each participant.
2. A newsprint flip chart and felt-tipped markers for recording.
3. Masking tape.
4. A newsprint sheet and a felt-tipped marker for each group.

Physical Setting   A room large enough for the groups to work without disturbing one another. Writing surfaces should be provided. Wall space is required for posting newsprint sheets.

Process
1. Direct the participants to form groups of four or five persons each. Distribute paper and a pencil to each participant.
2. Explain that the groups will answer the question, "Why do groups need rules?" Each group should identify at least five reasons. Allow approximately 15 minutes for discussion, and then ask each group in turn to share its reasons. Record each new reason on a flip chart sheet and then post it with masking tape.
3. Distribute a newsprint sheet and a felt-tipped marker to each group. Ask each group to identify ten to twelve rules that they think are necessary for a group to function effectively. Allow approximately 20 minutes for the task.
4. Instruct the groups to post their sheets with masking tape. Ask each group in turn to review its rules.

5. Ask the groups to review all the lists and to narrow down the rules by combining similar ones. Allow approximately 10 minutes for discussion.

6. Use a round robin format to ask each group for one narrowed group rule until all have been identified. Record these on a flip chart sheet.

7. Lead a concluding discussion by asking the following questions:
   - How do you feel about the set of group rules that was established? Why are these rules important?
   - Would your group be willing to commit to this list as a functioning set of rules? Why or why not? What can group members do to gain commitment to rules?
   - What is the difference between rules and guidelines?
   - Why is it important for groups to examine their rules or guidelines at periodic intervals?

Variation   After a set of group rules has been established, assign one or more rules to each group. Provide poster boards and various art supplies, and ask the groups to make display signs for posting in the workplace.

➤ Rummage Sale

Goals
1. To provide an icebreaker activity at the beginning of a session.
2. To build cohesion within a group.
3. To introduce the concept of synergy.
4. To use creative thinking skills.

Group Size   Several groups of five to eight persons each.

Time Required   20 to 30 minutes.

Materials
1. A copy of the Rummage Sale List for the facilitator.
2. A prepared set of numbered point slips.
3. A newsprint flip chart and felt-tipped markers for recording.
4. A prize for the winning group (optional).

Physical Setting   A room with separate tables for each group.

Process
1. Prior to the session, use small pieces of card stock or paper and a felt-tipped pen to prepare point slips to be awarded to groups for finding the stated articles. You will need to make ten slips each of the numbers "5" and "3" and enough slips of the number "1" to equal approximately eight to ten times the number of participating groups. Keep the numbers separate.
2. At the session, direct the participants to form groups of five to eight persons each.
3. Explain that you will be reading a list of items that each group will try to locate from among the possessions of its members at the table. After each item is announced, the first group to have a representative stand *with the item in hand* will be awarded 5 points, the second group will receive 3 points, and all the other

groups will receive 1 point each. The group with the most points at the end of the game will be the winner.

4. Using the Rummage Sale List, announce each item and award a 5-point slip to the first group to produce the item, a 3-point slip to the second, and a 1-point slip to all other groups who have the item. Repeat the process for each of the remaining items. Make a point of acknowledging to the whole group any creative interpretations of an announced item *(see Note to the Facilitator)*.

5. After the point slips have been awarded for the last announced item, instruct the groups to tally their point slips and record the final count for each group on the flip chart. Announce the winning group, and present a prize if you desire.

6. Ask the following questions and record the responses on the flip chart:

    • What made this activity difficult? *(limited resources, time pressure, unclear or variable definitions, need to think creatively)*
    • How did working together as a team impact your performance?

7. Using the recorded responses, lead a general discussion on "synergy." Explain that synergy occurs when a team uses its combined resources to create a "whole that is greater than the sum of its parts." That is, the group process offers results in gains in energy and effectiveness that go beyond what would be expected from the combined efforts of separate individuals. What energy is to the individual, synergy is to the group.

Note to the Facilitator   *Some of the items in the Rummage Sale List can represent different items or be interpreted in creative ways. For example, a "match" could be two items that are the same; a "hat" could be a fedora or a dunce cap made of paper; a "magnifying glass" could be eyeglasses or a beveled drinking-glass bottom; and a "picture of a man with a beard" could be a $5 bill. The final item, "a sock with a hole in it," is any sock, since there must be a hole in it where the foot goes in.*

Rummage Sale List

Award the following numbered point slips for producing each item listed:

1st = 5   2nd = 3   all others = 1

1. Calendar
2. Stamp
3. Mirror
4. Ruler
5. Hat
6. Tie
7. Picture of a man with a beard
8. Magnifying glass
9. Match
10. Sock with a hole in it

➤ Scrambler

Goals
1. To show the connection of individuals to the team effort.
2. To provide an icebreaker activity at the beginning of a session.
3. To practice giving verbal directions.
4. To apply problem-solving skills.

Group Size   Several groups of seven or more persons each.

Time Required   20 to 30 minutes.

Physical Setting   A large open space for groups to perform the activity without disturbing one another.

Process
1. Direct the participants to form groups of seven or more persons each, with two participants designated as "Unscramblers" for each group. Ask these participants to leave the room at this point.
2. Instruct the remaining members of each group to hold hands in a circle. Without letting go, the group members should twist about and step over and under arms to form a scrambled band of participants. When the groups are well mixed, call the "unscramblers" back into the room to do their work. Tell them to verbally direct the group members to move in ways to unscramble without having anyone let go of anyone else's hand.
3. Lead a concluding discussion based on the following questions:
   • What was the outcome of the activity? How can we describe it in objective terms?
   • As an "umscrambler," how difficult was it to uncouple the group? Why? What process did you use to unscramble the group? Was this process effective? Why was that?
   • How well were directions communicated to group members? What was ineffective? How could the directions have been improved to produce more effective results?
   • What skills did you learn that could help you in the future with challenges you encounter?

➤ Secret Service

Goals

1. To coordinate the efforts of group members in performing a task.
2. To discuss the effects of intergroup competition.
3. To follow written instructions.

Group Size   Six groups of three to five persons each.

Time Required   20 to 30 minutes.

Materials

1. Eighteen large envelopes and masking tape or tacks for posting.
2. Masking tape or tacks.
3. Six sets of 2-inch by 3-inch Secret Service Message Cards, made from 4-inch by 6-inch index cards.
4. One set of Secret Service Hazard Cards.
5. One small envelope for each group.

Physical Setting   A large open-space room so that the participants can move about freely while carrying out their instructions. Wall space is required for posting the large envelopes.

Process

1. Prior to the session, prepare the large envelopes by printing on the backs of the envelopes (flap side) the names of the towns/countries shown in the chart below:

SUITA Japan	SERGIPE Brazil	SETUBAL Portugal
SURAT India	SHAOXING China	SERPUKHOV Russia
SPOLETO Italy	SZCZECIN Poland	SUVA Fiji
SOKOTO Nigeria	SPIEZ Switzerland	SEMARANG Indonesia
SUNDSVALL Sweden	SZOLNOK Hungary	STOLP Germany
SHIRAZ Iran	STEYR Austria	SALTA Argentina

2. Use masking tape or tacks to attach the envelopes in various places about the room, to act as receptacles for receiving the Secret Service Message Cards. Try to have them cover as wide an area as possible.

3. Prepare the Message Cards by cutting 4-inch by 6-inch index cards in half to create 4-inch by 3-inch sections. Print each town name (without the countries) on a separate card. Produce six copies of each town and shuffle the cards. Duplicate the Secret Service Hazard Card page on card stock and cut into separate cards. Place eighteen Message Cards plus two Hazard Cards intermixed among them for a total of twenty cards in each small envelope, and then seal the envelope. Prepare six envelopes.

4. At the session, direct the participants to form six groups of three to five persons each. Distribute one small envelope of cards to each group.

5. Explain that the participants are members of Secret Agent groups that will be required to carry dispatches to all parts of the world. Inside the envelopes are the Message Cards with the destination listed on each.

6. Referring to the large envelopes posted around the room, tell the participants that each group can deliver only ONE message at a time, placing it in the appropriate envelope. The group will decide which agent is in "play" at any one time, but the next message cannot be removed from the envelope until that person has been seated back in the group. Say that, in addition to the Message Cards, the envelopes also contain Hazard Cards that have instructions to be carried out by the player during the delivery of a message. When a Hazard Card is pulled from the envelope, the player also will select the next Message Card and faithfully carry out the conditions of the Hazard Card while the message is being delivered. The players must carry out the hazard without any explanation to the other agents in play. The winner will be the first group to deliver all of its Message Cards and submit its empty envelope to you.

7. Signal for the groups to open their envelopes and start the game. Stop the activity when the first group completes the task, or

allow all the groups to deliver their cards before announcing the
winning team.

8. Lead a concluding discussion based on the following questions:
   - What were your personal reactions to this activity? How did
     others react to it?
   - How did you feel about competing against the other groups?
     How did you feel about performing the conditions on the
     Hazard Cards? Why did you feel that way?
   - What factors affected your ability to complete the task?
   - How did your group coordinate its efforts? Was this an
     effective approach? Why? Would your group have done
     anything differently? If so, what?
   - How can we relate what occurred during the activity to what
     occurs in the workplace?

Variation   Play the game with individuals delivering the Message
Cards: Give each participant a message, on the back of which
each must write his or her name before delivering it to the
destination. Issue new cards after participants return. The winner
is the one who correctly delivers the most messages (checked
later by their signatures). Every now and then hand out a Hazard
Card together with a message. The player returns the Hazard
Card when collecting the next assignment, and the Hazard Cards
can be reused as often as you wish. When all the messages are
delivered (or whenever you decide to stop), appoint two
participants to help check the contents of the envelopes to
find the winner.

Secret Service Hazard Cards

HAZARD NO. 1	HAZARD NO. 2
You are endeavoring to contact another Agent who is unknown to you by using a password. Whisper to the female you know *least* well: "There is a ladder in your shoe."	At lunch your coffee was drugged by an enemy agent. Stagger sleepily to your destination, bumping into at least three people on the way.
HAZARD NO. 3	**HAZARD NO. 4**
You bail out from a plane, land in the water, and have to swim to your final destination. With the arm movements of the breaststroke and blowing out through puffed cheeks, carry on until your message is delivered.	*Before delivering the message:* FEMALE: Select a male and whisper: "Are you Popoff?" If Yes, shake his hand and say "Good luck." If No, try again. MALE: Select a female, and ask "Are you Mata Hari?" If Yes, shake her hand and say "Good luck." If No, try again.
HAZARD NO. 5	**HAZARD NO. 6**
Disguised as a doctor, take the pulse of every member of the opposite sex you pass on the way to your destination. Also ask each one to put out his or her tongue; then shake your head and say: "Tut-tut!"	You have crossed a desert and are suffering heatstroke from the sun and are not really responsible for your actions. Take three steps forward, turn a complete circle, and howl like a dog. Continue like this to your destination.
HAZARD NO. 7	**HAZARD NO. 8**
Due to a transport breakdown, you are obliged to cycle. Proceed to your destination holding imaginary handlebars, raising your knees high, and say "ting-a-ling" again and again.	You must pass through a high-tech research laboratory that emits a constant blinding light. Make your way to your destination with your eyes closed, only opening them to take very quick looks at your whereabouts.
HAZARD NO. 9	**HAZARD NO. 10**
You are disguised by wearing a giant pickle costume, but it limits your ability to walk. You must proceed to your destination while shuffling your feet the entire way.	You are being followed by a barking dog. You decide the best way to discourage him is to bark back. Continue to do this until you have delivered your message.
HAZARD NO. 11	**HAZARD NO. 12**
Your car has jammed in reverse gear. Continue to your destination *backwards*, sounding your horn as you go.	You must make your way through a small tunnel. Place your right hand on your left knee and your left hand on your right knee. Proceed like this to your destination.

➤ Shake It Up

Goals

1. To coordinate individual efforts with other group members.
2. To examine the advantages and disadvantages of working with people who are similar to you.
3. To provide an icebreaker activity at the beginning of a session.
4. To divide participants into subgroups.

Group Size   Twelve to thirty participants.

Time Required   10 to 15 minutes.

Physical Setting   A room large enough that participants can move about in an unrestricted fashion.

Process

1. Direct the participants to each count off consecutively as numbers one, two, or three.
2. Explain that the participants will walk around shaking hands with whomever they meet. If your number is "one" you will shake the other player's hand once. If you are a "two" you will shake two times, and as a "three" you will shake three times, but NO TALKING is allowed. When you meet others with the same number, you will become "psychic teammates" and proceed through the game together, looking for other players with the same number. The game will end when everyone locates his or her number group.
3. Signal for the task to begin and observe the interactions that take place. Note what happens when different numbers meet and shake because each player will be shaking a different number of times, with one player wanting to stop shaking while the other player will want to continue. Stop the task when all participants have found their appropriate number groups.

4. Lead a concluding discussion based on the following questions:
   - How did you feel during this activity? How did others react to it?
   - What happened when you met someone with a different number? How did you resolve this "conflict"? What happens when group members have conflicting goals in the workplace? How does that apply to interdepartmental groups?
   - What are the advantages of working with people who are the same as you? What are the disadvantages?

Note to the Facilitator   *If this activity is used to form subgroups, you can choose to have all the members of the same number group work together (three subgroups; emphasis on similarity) or you can have one member from each number group work together (three-member groups; emphasis on diversity).*

➤ Spin Off

Goals
1. To demonstrate the importance of each individual for the team effort.
2. To build cohesion within a group.
3. To provide an icebreaker activity at the beginning of a session.

Group Size   Several groups of five to ten persons each.

Time Required   10 to 15 minutes.

Materials
1. A Frisbee® (or heavyweight plastic plate) for each group.
2. Prizes (optional).

Physical Setting   A room large enough for each group to work at a separate round table.

Process
1. Direct the participants to form groups of five to ten persons each and to be seated in a circle around the tables. Ask the participants to count off so that each person has a number within the group. Place a Frisbee (or plate) in the center of each table.
2. Explain that the goal of the exercise is to keep the Frisbee (or plate) spinning at all times. The first player (#1) will stand, then turn the Frisbee on its edge and spin it as you would a coin. As the player sits down, he or she will call out the number of another player. The player whose number is called stands, gets to the Frisbee before it stops, gives it another spin, then calls out another player's number before sitting down. Players continue calling one another's numbers, keeping the Frisbee spinning. If the Frisbee stops spinning completely, a player starts it again, but the group is fined one penalty point for each restart. Assign one player in each group to keep track of any penalties.

3. Emphasize that the object is to cooperate in keeping the Frisbee spinning, not to trick other players. Signal for the groups to begin and allow approximately 5 minutes before stopping the activity.

4. Ask the groups how many penalties they were charged, if any. You may choose to award a prize to any group with zero penalties or to the group(s) with the lowest penalty score.

5. Lead a concluding discussion by asking the following questions:
   • How does group size affect doing this task?
   • Were the same people selected to perform repeatedly or were all members equally chosen to participate? Why did this occur?
   • How does this exercise relate to teamwork in general?

➤ Splits

Goals

1. To overcome perceptual sets and accept change.
2. To examine the roles of time pressure and mental flexibility in change management and problem solving.
3. To identify ways for groups to become more flexible.

Group Size   Several groups of three to five persons each.

Time Required   30 to 45 minutes.

Materials

1. An envelope of twenty-four Splits Cards for each group.
2. A prepared newsprint flip chart sheet with completed words (*see Answers in Note to the Facilitator*).
3. A clock or timer.
4. Masking tape.

Physical Setting   A room with a separate table for each group. Wall space is required for posting newsprint sheets.

Process

1. Prior to the session, duplicate the Splits Cards page onto card stock, cut the sheet into twenty individual cards, and place the cards in an envelope. Prepare one set for each participating team. Record the completed words on a newsprint flip chart sheet; post the sheet, but keep it concealed.
2. At the session, direct the participants to form groups of three to five persons each.
3. Distribute a prepared envelope of Splits Cards to each group. Explain that the envelope contains twenty-four three-letter words that can be arranged so as to produce twelve six-letter words. The groups will have exactly 5 minutes in which to complete the task.

4. Time the activity for 5 minutes. Referring to the prepared flip chart sheet, reveal the correct answers.
5. Lead a discussion based on the following questions:
   • Were some words more difficult to arrange than others? Which ones? What made them more difficult?
   • What role did perception play in this?
6. Explain that the pronunciation and visual presentation of the three-letter words may have either helped or hindered the formation of the new words in this activity. For example: PEA-LED and RED-ONE may have been more difficult because the split did not occur where it was expected; whereas ROT-TEN and SON-NET may have been more obvious because of the double letters that joined them together. Perceptual sets are a person's tendency to see things in a certain way, do things a certain way, and stick to the familiar because it is more comfortable than changing. Ask:
   • How willing was your group to change its initial card combinations to get a more appropriate match as the activity progressed? Why was that?
   • Was the amount of time you had in which to complete the task a factor? Why or why not? How does time pressure impact change management issues in the workplace? How does time pressure impact a group's ability to solve problems? In general, what steps can a group take to facilitate changes when time is a factor?
   • What role does mental flexibility play in accepting change? How does mental flexibility influence problem solving within a group?
7. Lead a concluding discussion on what a group can do to become more flexible. Record the important issues on a flip chart.

Note to the Facilitator *Answers:* ACT-ION,   BAR-BED, CAR-TON, FOR-EGO, MAR-GIN, PAL-ACE, PEA-LED, PER-SON, RAT-HER, RED-ONE, ROT-TEN, SON-NET

Splits Cards

ACT	ION
BAR	BED
CAR	TON
FOR	EGO
MAR	GIN
PAL	ACE
PEA	LED
PER	SON
RAT	HER
RED	ONE
ROT	TEN
SON	NET

➤ Style

Goals
1. To compare two styles of leadership (participative and directive).
2. To examine the effects of leadership style on the group process.
3. To discuss factors influencing the choice of leadership style.

Group Size   Several groups of five to seven persons each.

Time Required   Approximately 1 hour.

Materials
1. A set of building supplies (3 feet of masking tape, twenty index cards, twenty paper clips, two rubber bands) for each group.
2. A copy of the Style Resource Sheet 1 or 2 for each group (alternate between groups).

Physical Setting   A room with a separate table for each group.

Process
1. Explain that participants will become part of an architectural team to design and build a project.
2. Direct the participants to form groups of five to seven persons each and assign a number to each group. Distribute a set of building supplies to each group.
3. Select one member from each group to be the leader and call these individuals aside. Distribute a copy of the Style Resource Sheet 1 to some of the leaders and a copy of the Style Resource Sheet 2 to the others. Emphasize that they are not to reveal their roles to their group members.
4. After the leaders return to their groups, explain that each group is to build something using ALL the materials provided. They will have 30 minutes to plan and construct the design. Signal for the groups to begin.
5. Time the activity for 30 minutes, giving a 5-minute warning before time expires. Ask each group to give a brief presentation describing its project.

6. After all groups have made their presentation, ask:
   - How did your group decide what to build? How do you feel about the final product? Why is that?
   - Did you feel that your individual suggestions were supported? Why or why not?
   - Were you encouraged to participate? What behaviors supported this? How did you feel about your role in the group process?
   - How did the group leader affect the overall group process?
7. Reveal that the group leaders played the roles of two different leadership styles. Ask leaders to read aloud the instructions from Resource Sheet 1 and Resource Sheet 2. Tell the participants: "Directive leaders inform group members what is expected of them, give specific guidance as to what is to be done, and show how to do it. Participative leaders consult with group members, solicit their suggestions, and take their ideas into consideration before making a decision."
8. Lead a concluding discussion by asking the following questions:
   - Are different leadership styles appropriate for certain situations? Why or why not?
   - What factors contribute to the choice of a leadership method? *(type of decision or task involved, amount of time, amount of group acceptance required, information available, group structure and performance level, organizational climate)*
   - How did these factors influence the effectiveness of the leadership style during the activity?
   - What is the preferred leadership style in your organization? Give some examples of when this style works well and examples of when it doesn't work.

Variation Set specific criteria (for example, height, sturdiness, attractiveness, creativity) for the construction projects and have each groups rate the other designs.

Style Resource Sheet 1

You are to be a *PARTICIPATIVE* (democratic) leader.

Your main purpose is to *encourage* the performance of the group.

1. Make certain that the entire group discusses all activities.
2. Encourage participation by all members, during both planning and construction.
3. Accept and support decisions promoted by the rest of the group members.
4. Promote an atmosphere of equality and participation.

DO NOT REVEAL YOUR LEADERSHIP STYLE TO OTHER GROUP MEMBERS.

Style Resource Sheet 2

You are to be a *DIRECTIVE* (autocratic) leader.

Your main purpose is to *control* the performance of the group.

1. Take the dominant role during group discussion.
2. Take little or no input from group members into consideration and make your own decisions.
3. Assign tasks to individual group members.
4. Give specific directions and demonstrate exactly how things should be done throughout the activity.

DO NOT REVEAL YOUR LEADERSHIP STYLE TO OTHER GROUP MEMBERS.

➤ Taking the Lead

Goals
1. To experience being a group leader.
2. To introduce the concept of shared leadership.
3. To build cohesion within a group.

Group Size   Several groups of five to seven persons each.

Time Required   15 to 20 minutes.

Physical Setting   A room large enough that participants can move about in an unrestricted fashion.

Process
1. Direct the participants to form groups of five to seven persons each. Select one member from each group to act as the leader, with all members standing in a line behind that person.
2. Explain that the group members are to follow their leader, who may move about in any fashion (for example, skipping, bending, or hopping). The leader can choose at any time to rotate to the end of the line, to allow the next person in line to become the leader.
3. Signal for the groups to begin, and allow approximately 5 minutes for the activity to run before stopping the action.
4. Lead a concluding discussion based on the following questions:
   - Did each person have a chance to be leader of the group? Why did that happen? How did you feel when you were the leader?
   - How long did each leader of your group perform? Was the length of time fairly consistent? Was this a longer or shorter duration than that of the leaders of other groups? What factors may have contributed to how long the leaders chose to perform?
   - As a leader, did you model your behavior in terms of the leaders of other groups? Why or why not?

- Why is participative or shared leadership an important factor in the group process? In what situations might this kind of leadership be a hindrance?
- What things can a group do to support shared leadership in the workplace?

➤ Tale of the Tape

Goals
1. To utilize individual group member input for a collective product.
2. To examine the factors impacting the completion of a group project.
3. To explore the importance of communication and information sharing in group work.
4. To provide an icebreaker activity at the beginning of a session.

Group Size   Six to twelve participants.

Time Required   15 minutes.

Materials
1. A pencil for each participant.
2. A roll of business machine paper (calculator, cash register).

Physical Setting   A room with a long table or a series of smaller tables pushed together to create a continuous writing surface for all participants.

Process
1. Arrange players in a single line, side by side, along the length of a table or other continuous writing surface. Distribute a pencil to each participant. Roll out a ribbon of the paper in front of the players.
2. Explain that group members will be combining their efforts to create a story. Each person is limited to adding three words to the story line during each turn. One by one, participants will add their words, connecting them to the words of the last person. Players can read the last few words before making their additions, but they cannot go back to look at the previous story line.

3. Instruct the first person to begin the story and facilitate the addition of words by the other participants as needed in order to keep the task moving along.
4. When the last person in line has added three words, pull the next portion of blank tape back to the beginning and ask the group members to continue the story. Continue this process until the story is as long as you wish it to be. The last player to add something should make the last few words finish the sentence.
5. Several readers can take turns reading the story out loud.
6. Lead a concluding discussion based on the following questions:
   • What were your personal reactions to this activity? What approach did you take to accomplish your individual part of the task? How well did your efforts as an individual mesh with those of other group members?
   • Did the final story make sense? What factors influenced this outcome?
   • What can happen when only a linear line of communication exists within a group? How does this impact the sharing of information? How does it hinder a group's ability to complete a project?
   • How does this activity relate to the accomplishment of a group project in the workplace?

➤ Team Report Card

Goals
1. To identify characteristics of an effective team.
2. To assess a team's past performance in terms of the identified characteristics.
3. To create a basic plan to improve team performance.

Group Size
An intact team or work group of up to twelve members.

Time Required
45 minutes.

Materials
1. A newsprint flip chart and felt-tipped markers for recording.
2. Masking tape.
3. A Team Report Card Worksheet and a pencil for each participant.
4. A calculator.

Physical Setting
Any room in which the group regularly meets. Writing surfaces should be provided. Wall space is needed for posting newsprint sheets.

Process
1. Ask the participants to brainstorm a list of characteristics that they feel are important to the effective functioning of a group. Record the answers on the flip chart and use masking tape to post the sheet(s).
2. Distribute a copy of the Team Report Card Worksheet and a pencil to each participant.
3. Explain that the group will have 10 minutes to identify the six most important team characteristics (for example, communication, leadership, goal setting, decision making, problem solving, creativity, trust) that are agreed on by all members. These are to be listed on the worksheet in the section marked "Characteristics."

4. Allow approximately 10 minutes for the group to complete the task and then stop the discussion.

5. Record the six characteristics chosen by the group on the flip chart. Ask for some examples of how each characteristic is portrayed in the team setting.

6. Explain that individuals will now have the opportunity to rate the team's performance for each of the six characteristics in the past six months. Referring to the worksheet, explain the following grading system:

   5 = Exceptional: Always outperforms
   4 = Good: Usually high-performing, but some improvement can be made
   3 = Average: Meets basic requirement
   2 = Deficient: Needs improvement to meet basic requirement
   1 = Failing: Does not meet basic requirement

7. Allow approximately 5 minutes for individual participants to perform the task and then call time.

8. Collect the worksheets and record the grades for the six characteristics, using the flip chart page produced in step 5. Use a calculator to determine the average score (total of all scores divided by the number of group members) for each characteristic. Record the average score for each and circle the numbers on the flip chart.

9. Lead a concluding discussion based on the following questions:

   • Were your personal scores in line with the rest of the group members' scores? What are some factors that might have contributed to whether they were or not?

   • What area requires the most attention to improve the team's effectiveness?

   • What are some specific actions that the team can make to improve its future performance?

   • What factors outside the team must be addressed in order to improve its performance?

Team Report Card Worksheet

Instructions:

1. As a group, select the six most important of the team characteristics you came up with previously and list each one under the Characteristics heading. (10 minutes)

2. As an individual, use the scale provided to rate the team's performance in the past 6 months. Place the appropriate number in the Grade column. (5 minutes)

TEAM PERFORMANCE

5 = Exceptional
4 = Good
3 = Average
2 = Deficient
1 = Failing

CHARACTERISTICS   GRADE

_____   _____

_____   _____

_____   _____

_____   _____

_____   _____

_____   _____

⟩ Where Are You?

Goals

1. To assess the feelings and reactions of individual members during a group session.
2. To relate the concept of perception to the outcomes of task and relationship processes.

Group Size   Eight to twenty participants.

Time Required   5 to 15 minutes.

Materials   A 5-inch by 8-inch index card and a felt-tipped marker for each individual.

Physical Setting   Any room in which the group regularly meets. Writing surfaces should be provided.

Process

1. At the beginning of the session, distribute an index card and a felt-tipped marker to each participant. Explain that the materials will be used at a later time.
2. Sometime during the group session, stop and ask each individual to write on a card, in large letters, *one word* that describes how he or she is feeling right then. Next ask the participants to hold up their cards and to look around at the variety of responses.
3. Point out how rare it is for different people to bring the same feelings or reactions to an experience or situation. Invite the participants to share why they wrote down the words that they did.
4. Lead a discussion on perception in terms of how it defines an individual's concept of reality. Ask for examples of situations in which differing perceptions can impact the outcome of an event (for example, court trials, victim accounts, accident reports).

Direct the discussion to why it is important to be aware of individual feelings, reactions, and perceptions in order to facilitate the overall group process.

5. After continuing with the remainder of the session, relate the content topic to the issue of perception and its impact on both task and relationship processes.

Variation   Keep an ongoing assessment of an extended group session by distributing several index cards and a felt-tipped marker to each participant at the beginning. Stop at desired intervals and ask the participants to write one word that describes a personal feeling or reaction at that time.

➤ Why's Guise

Goals
1. To review previous group performance, as a closing activity.
2. To identify performance improvement strategies.

Group Size   Any previously formed groups.

Time Required   Approximately 1 hour.

Materials
1. Three index cards and a pencil for each participant.
2. A prepared flip chart sheet with the following statement: "I wonder WHY the group . . ."
3. A newsprint flip chart and felt-tipped markers for recording.
4. Masking tape.

Physical Setting   A room large enough for groups to work without disturbing one another. Writing surfaces should be provided. Wall space is required for posting newsprint sheets.

Process
1. Following a previously conducted group task or activity, explain that participants will have the opportunity to review their group's performance in terms of actions and outcomes.
2. Distribute three index cards and a pencil to each group member. Ask each group to select one member to act as facilitator.
3. Referring to the prepared flip chart, tell the participants: "You are going to reflect on your group's performance during the previous activity. Think about the specific actions of the group members as well as what occurred in terms of the final results. Think about areas in which the group was not as effective as it could have been. Next, on each index card, write a phrase that completes the statement, 'I wonder why the group . . .'; for example, 'I wonder why the group did not get everyone's input before making a decision' or 'I wonder why

the group members argued.' When you are finished, please pass the completed cards to your group's facilitator."

4. When all participants have completed this task, ask group members to review the statements on the cards and have the facilitators lead a discussion within their groups on the various topics. After approximately 15 minutes, give a 2-minute warning, and then stop the group discussions.

5. Ask the groups to select one member to act as recorder for the next task. Distribute a newsprint sheet and a felt-tipped marker to each group. Explain that groups will now make a list of the *top three* (if time is limited, top one or two) general topics that were identified (for example, "communication," "decision making," and "teamwork"). These topics are to be listed at the top of the newsprint sheet. For multiple topics, each group should circle the topic that is MOST significant or use the single topic chosen. Group members should list suggested strategies that the group could use to improve its performance in this area.

6. Allow approximately 25 minutes, and then instruct the groups to post their sheets using the masking tape provided. Ask each group in turn to present its list.

7. Lead a concluding discussion based on the following questions:
   • What impressions and insights did you get from this closing activity?
   • What were some of the factors that influenced your group's performance today? How do similar factors in the workplace influence a group's ability to be effective?
   • How could the performance improvement strategies you identified be implemented in a workplace setting?

Variation   Prepare a flip chart sheet with the statement, "I wonder WHY I . . ." and have individual participants review their personal actions and behaviors following an activity. Each person is to create and commit to an individual action plan for improved personal performance.

➤ Section 2

Task-Oriented Process

Introduction to Task-Oriented Process

The activities in the Task-Oriented Process category examine those functions within the group that contribute to accomplishing a job, including planning, goal setting, problem solving, creativity, risk taking, decision making, and resource use.

Task-oriented processes, along with relationship-oriented processes, balance together to create an effectively performing group. The task dynamic refers to what a group must do to achieve its goal. It constitutes the "what" and "why" issues of the group's work. Goals literally define the very reason for a group to exist. They provide the group with a sense of direction and a source of motivation; they align the energy and actions of members of a group. Work groups also need some structured and disciplined approaches to their tasks. These procedures help to plan, schedule, budget, set goals, share information and other resources, make decisions, identify and resolve problems, and evaluate progress. The process includes activities that facilitate the completion of the group's task-defined goals.

Activities that deal with *planning* functions examine the use of strategies, objectives, and specifications that precede an action or set of actions taken by a group. This can include developing a strategic plan for the group by reviewing past actions, assessing current conditions, identifying solutions to problems, envisioning future needs, and action planning. It can also refer to individual action planning in meeting personal goals.

Goal-setting activities are based on the establishment of a direction for action or a specific quantity of work to be accomplished. Goal setting also allows individuals to judge the effort requirements of tasks. This can apply to a particular task or to the combined goals of the group.

Problem-solving activities involve the objective examination of issues to arrive at a solution. The problem-solving process is a set of steps by which problems are examined and solved. A key component in this process is the ability to recognize patterns that can be applied to other situations. A variety of techniques can be used to solve problems, including brainstorming and rank ordering. For the problem-solving process to succeed, individuals must be free to express their ideas and opinions in an atmosphere of openness and sharing.

Activities in *creativity* promote the ability of an individual or a group to be inventive, imaginative, or original. During problem solving, a group needs to suspend judgment and create alternative strategies and approaches to address the problem it is attempting to solve. It is in assessing such alternatives that the issue of risk taking is addressed.

Risk-taking activities explore the degree to which an individual or group is willing to perform an action that is deemed to result in negative or risky consequences.

Decision-making activities examine the procedures by which individuals or groups arrive at a decision, judgment, or conclusion through a process of deliberation. Decision making is actually the final step in the problem-solving process, at which time action is required to implement a solution. Consensus is the ideal decision-making method because it promotes commitment by all group members. It takes longer to reach a consensus decision, but the quality of the decision is generally higher than one made by an individual member of the group. However, decisions made by an authority figure or majority voting may be necessary for less important or urgent issues.

➤ Animal Appeal

Goals
1. To apply creative thinking skills.
2. To identify unique traits among common items.
3. To discuss the relationship between creativity and group diversity.

Group Size   Several groups of three to five persons each.

Time Required   30 to 40 minutes.

Materials
1. A copy of the Animal Appeal Worksheet and a pencil for each participant.
2. A newsprint flip chart and felt-tipped markers for recording.

Physical Setting   A room large enough for groups to work without disturbing one another. Writing surfaces should be provided.

Process
1. Begin the session by explaining that although a group of items may share many common traits, it is good to look for the unique features of the individual items that comprise the whole.
2. Distribute a copy of the Animal Appeal Worksheet and a pencil to each participant. Read aloud the instructions at the top of the sheet. Allow approximately 5 to 8 minutes for individual work, and then stop the activity.
3. Direct participants to form groups of three to five persons each. Explain that the group members will work together to pool their resources in completing the task. Allow approximately 15 minutes for discussion, and then stop the groups.
4. Ask the groups for feedback on their answers to the puzzle. Record the responses on a flip chart. Some possible answers

include: *Deer* is the only one with antlers. *Dolphin* is the only marine mammal. *Possum* is the only marsupial. *Puma* is the only feline. *Rabbit* is the only one that hops. *Rat* is the shortest word; it's the only word that can be used as a slang verb (to betray). *Snake* is the only word that doesn't start with the same letter as any of the others; it is the only reptile and only egg-laying animal.

5. Lead a concluding discussion based on the following questions:
   • How did creative thinking play a role in this activity? Did working in groups help or hinder the creative process? Why did it help or hinder?
   • In a group situation, why is it important to identify the unique characteristics (strengths and weaknesses) of each individual member?
   • How do creativity and group diversity logically relate to each other? *(variety of ideas can be generated because of the wide range of experience of diverse members; as we search for alternatives through creative thinking, we can begin to expand personal views and ideas)*
   • How can we relate these insights to situations in the workplace environment? How can a group more effectively draw on the unique characteristics of its members?

Animal Appeal Worksheet

Instructions: The following seven words and what they represent have many properties in common, but they do not share all the same traits. Find seven (or more!) different reasons for determining what makes one or more of these words distinct from the rest.

POSSUM   RABBIT   DOLPHIN

SNAKE   PUMA   RAT   DEER

Reasons:

1. _____

2. _____

3. _____

4. _____

5. _____

6. _____

7. _____

More:

8. _____

9. _____

10. _____

11. _____

12. _____

➤ Appearances Can Be Deceiving

Goals
1. To evaluate various group problem-solving approaches.
2. To examine the role of competition on group performance.
3. To consider the influence of making errors on the inclination to take risks.

Group Size
Several groups of three to five persons each.

Time Required
20 to 30 minutes.

Materials
1. A copy of the Appearances Puzzle Sheet and a pencil for each participant.
2. A prize for the winning group (optional).
3. A transparency of the Appearances Solution Sheet or a copy of the sheet for each group.
4. An overhead projector.

Physical Setting
A room large enough for groups to work without disturbing one another. Writing surfaces should be provided.

Process
1. Direct the participants to form groups of three to five persons each.
2. Distribute a copy of the Appearances Puzzle Sheet and a pencil to each participant.
3. Refer the participants to the instructions on the puzzle sheet and read them aloud.
4. Explain that the first group to arrive at the solution will be the winner (show the prize, if you chose this option). Say that when a group completes the puzzle, a member of the group is to stand. Signal for the groups to begin.

5. Acknowledge when the first group completes the puzzle, and stop the activity. Ask the winning team to reveal the solution, which follows:

   NOBODY SEEMS TO BE LISTENING EXCEPT WHEN YOU MAKE AN ERROR.

6. Display the Appearance Solution Sheet transparency showing the correct path on the grid using the projector (or distribute a copy of the Solution Sheet to each group).

7. Lead a concluding discussion based on the following questions:
   - What approach did your group use to solve the puzzle?
   - How did competition to be the winning group influence performance?
   - If you were going through the same activity again, would your group change its problem-solving approach? If so, how? If not, why?
   - Looking at the solution, how does this statement apply to what happens in the work environment? How does this influence your inclination to take risks? Give some examples of situations in which this was the case.
   - How does the element of competition influence your inclination to take risks? Give some examples.

Appearances Puzzle Sheet

Instructions: A statement is coiled in the 7 by 7 grid below. To spell it out, start with one letter and move to an adjacent letter in any direction. Each letter is used only once and one letter is null. (*HINT:* Start with the letter N.)

C	P	T	W	U	O	Y
E	X	A	M	H	E	N
I	N	E	K	R	O	T
N	G	E	N	R	O	R
E	T	A	T	E	B	N
I	S	O	S	O	D	S
L	E	B	M	E	E	Y

Appearances Solution Sheet

Solution: NOBODY SEEMS TO BE LISTENING EXCEPT WHEN YOU MAKE AN ERROR.

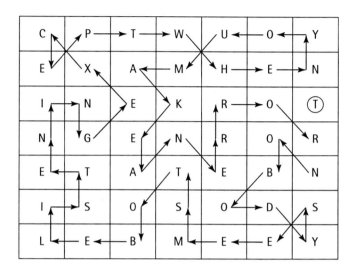

⊒ Cite Unseen

Goals

1. To apply problem-solving and decision-making skills in a group situation.
2. To identify basic steps in the problem-solving process.
3. To examine the process of problem solving in groups.

Group Size   Several groups of four or five persons each.

Time Required   30 minutes.

Materials

1. A copy of the Cite Unseen Worksheet and a pencil for each participant.
2. A prepared newsprint flip chart with the following quotation solution: "The human mind once stretched by a new idea never goes back to its original dimensions."

Physical Setting   A room large enough for groups to work without disturbing one another. Writing surfaces should be provided.

Process

1. Prior to the session, conceal the quotation on the prepared newsprint flip chart.
2. At the session, direct the participants to form groups of four or five persons each. Distribute a copy of the Cite Unseen Worksheet and a pencil to each participant.
3. Tell the groups that they will work together to solve a puzzle that reveals a quotation. Referring to the worksheet, read aloud the instructions at the top.
4. Signal for the groups to begin working on the task. Allow approximately 10 minutes, and then ask a volunteer from one

of the groups to provide the solution. Reveal the previously concealed solution on the prepared newsprint flip chart. Ask:
- What steps did your group take to solve the puzzle?
- Was this approach effective? Why or why not?

5. Emphasize that to be an effective problem solver, you need to think about all the possibilities available and then narrow them down to the best one. In the puzzle, you were given the possibilities from which to choose (the letters) to get to the solution. This is only one part of the basic problem-solving process. Ask:

   In workplace situations, what additional steps in the basic problem-solving process do you need to take before this step and after it? (*Before: describe or define the problem, determine the cause or causes, generate possible solutions, evaluate alternatives; After: plan action steps and follow-up, implement the actions, evaluate*)

6. Lead a concluding discussion by asking the following questions:
- How did working on the puzzle as a group help the problem-solving process? How did it hinder the process?
- What are some examples of situations in the workplace in which problems were effectively solved by a group of people?
- How does the quotation apply to problem solving in general? What are some examples of how it applies to situations in your organization?

Cite Unseen Worksheet

Instructions: Place the letters over each vertical column into the open spaces below them, but not necessarily in the originally listed order. A black square indicates the end of a word; a word is continued on the next line if a black square does not appear at the end of a line. After all the letters have been placed correctly, a quotation by Oliver Wendell Holmes will be revealed when the words are read from left to right, line by line.

B	V	C	M	E	S	M	I	R	I	B	H	N	D	N
O	D	I	E	T	N	O	O	O	N	C	I	A	K	L
T	H	E	R	H	G	T	W	S	I	D	A	N	D	
T	O	E	I		U	E	A	E	T	G	I	C	A	
E	N		A		N	S	R	N		M	E	E		
	Y				S		E			S				

Solution:

➤ Close Resemblance

Goals

1. To examine how people reason by analogy in solving problems.
2. To identify how poor reasoning by analogy can lead to problems.
3. To compare individual efforts to group efforts.

Group Size Several triads.

Time Required 45 minutes to 1 hour.

Materials

1. A copy of the Close Resemblance Worksheet and a pencil for each participant.
2. A clock or timer.
3. A prepared newsprint flip chart with the following numbered word sets:
   - (1) NOTE – SCALE
   - (2) FAN – BREEZE
   - (3) INCH – FOOT
   - (4) SCHOOL – FISH
   - (5) WATCH – HAND
   - (6) EYE – HURRICANE
   - (7) CUBE – DIE
   - (8) ICE – SKATE
   - (9) WIND – WOUND
   - (10) TEA – EWE

Physical Setting A room large enough for triads to work without disturbing one another. Writing surfaces should be provided.

Process

1. Distribute a copy of the Close Resemblance Worksheet and a pencil to each participant.

2. Indicate that individuals will have 5 minutes to try to solve the analogy statements presented on the worksheet. Explain that an analogy involves making a connection between two things that otherwise seem dissimilar. Read aloud the directions at the top of the worksheet:

   "You are asked to complete ten analogies in which the first set of items bears a similar relationship to that shared by the second two items. For example, 'CAT is to KITTEN as DOG is to PUPPY.' The twenty words that go in the blanks to complete the given statements are arranged alphabetically at the end of the page. Each word is used only once. Keep your mind open—some of the relationships are completed in unexpected ways!"

3. Signal for the individual task to begin. Time the task for 5 minutes, giving a 2-minute warning, and then stop the activity. Ask the following questions:
   • How well did you do as an individual in completing the task?
   • What made this task difficult?
   • How did you approach the solutions?

4. Indicate that participants will now have an additional 5 minutes to work together in small groups to complete the task. Direct the participants to form triads.

5. Signal for the group task to begin. Time the task for 5 minutes, giving a 2-minute warning, and then stop the activity.

6. Referring to the prepared newsprint flip chart, review the correct answers to the analogies. Ask groups to provide the reasoning that supported each analogy.

7. Lead a discussion by asking the following questions:
   • How well did the group do in completing the task? How did the group's performance compare to the performance of the individuals?
   • What factors helped the group's performance? What factors hindered the group's performance?
   • What could have been done to make your group's efforts more effective?

8. Explain that an analogy is also a form of logical inference based on the assumption that if two things are known to be alike in

some respects, then they must be alike in other respects. However, there is variation from one analogy to another in the extent to which the relationships being compared are similar.

9. Discuss the usefulness of reasoning by analogy. For example, just as studying leads to a good test grade in school, so spending time to research data helps to make a good decision in buying a car. Remind participants that failing to recognize *differences* in analogous relationships can lead to problems; for example, deciding that medicine that made your dog better will also make your cat better.

10. Lead a concluding discussion using the following questions:
    • What are some specific workplace examples of how using analogous reasoning helped?
    • What are some specific workplace examples of how using analogous reasoning led to problems?
    • What guidelines can groups incorporate to make the best use of analogous reasoning?

Variation   Providing paper and pencils, ask groups to create stories or cartoon strips that show how problems or humorous situations may be caused by faulty reasoning by analogy. Have the groups share their products.

Note to the Facilitator   *Prior to the session, familiarize yourself with the reasoning behind the presented analogies.*

Close Resemblance Worksheet

Instructions: You are asked to complete ten analogies in which the first set of items bears a similar relationship to that shared by the second two items. For example, "CAT is to KITTEN as DOG is to PUPPY." The twenty words that go in the blanks to complete the given statements are arranged alphabetically at the end of the page. Each word is used only once. Keep your mind open—some of the relationships are completed in unexpected ways!

1. LETTER is to ALPHABET as _____ is to _____

2. LAMP is to SUNSHINE as _____ is to _____.

3. MONTH is to YEAR as _____ is to _____.

4. HERD is to CATTLE as _____ is to _____.

5. COMPASS is to NEEDLE as _____ is to _____

6. HUB is to WHEEL as _____ is to _____.

7. GLOBE is to SPHERE as _____ is to _____.

8. WATER is to SWIM as _____ is to _____.

9. LIE is to LAY as _____ is to _____.

10. OWE is to PEA as _____ is to _____

BREEZE	FAN	ICE	SKATE
CUBE	FISH	INCH	TEA
DIE	FOOT	NOTE	WATCH
EWE	HAND	SCALE	WIND
EYE	HURRICANE	SCHOOL	WOUND

➤ Connectable

Goals
1. To apply creative problem-solving skills.
2. To examine how perception affects problem solving.

Group Size Several groups of three or four persons each.

Time Required 20 to 30 minutes.

Materials
1. A copy of the Connectable Puzzle Sheet and a pencil for each participant.
2. A clock or timer.
3. A copy of the Connectable Answer Sheet for each group.

Physical Setting A room large enough for groups to work without disturbing one another. Writing surfaces should be provided.

Process
1. Direct the participants to form groups of three or four persons each. Distribute a copy of the Connectable Puzzle Sheet and a pencil to each participant.
2. Referring to the worksheet, read the instructions aloud. Tell the participants that they will have 8 minutes to complete the activity.
3. Allow approximately 8 minutes, and then signal for the groups to stop. Distribute a copy of the Connectable Answer Sheet to each group and instruct the groups to review their answers. Allow several minutes, and then ask the groups if they came up with any different connection words from the ones listed on the Answer Sheet.

4. Lead a concluding discussion based on the following questions:
   - Was the "connectable" word for each set easy to identify? Which ones were more difficult? Why?
   - What role did perception play in making the connections?
   - How did this activity use both logical and creative thinking?
   - How does this process apply to problem solving in general? *(You need both types of thinking to get the full picture.)*
   - What specific things can a group do to increase the creative thinking skills of its members?

Connectable Puzzle Sheet

Instructions: For each set of three words below, find the common fourth word that's not given. The linking word should appear *before or after* each of the three words to form well-known compound words or phrases. Here's an example:

> MAKER—TENNIS—STICK

What word links these three? The correct answer for the set above is MATCH, as in matchmaker, tennis match, and matchstick. Here are twenty more sets for you to solve.

1. SMOKE—COMPUTER—PLAY
2. FIRE—ARTIST—NARROW
3. GUN—SLOT—TIME
4. BURGLAR—CLOCK—FIRE
5. HEAD—PLANT—ROTTEN
6. CRIER—DOWN—GHOST
7. PAN—MIX—CHEESE
8. HERRING—CROSS—TAPE
9. EVIL—GLASSES—WITNESS
10. ORANGE—INSURANCE—SECRET
11. BABY—SHOW—DOUBLE
12. BOMB—LINE—FATHER
13. BODY—CHANNEL—MUFFIN
14. STOP—PEACH—BULL
15. FIRE—WRESTLING—CHAIR
16. PIE—CRAB—CARAMEL
17. ELECTRIC—CROSS—WHISTLE
18. RED—BOTTLE—BLOT
19. MAIL—AMERICAN—LANE
20. SILENT—MARE—CLUB

Connectable Answer Sheet

1.	SMOKE–COMPUTER–PLAY	SCREEN
2.	FIRE–ARTIST–NARROW	ESCAPE
3.	GUN–SLOT–TIME	MACHINE
4.	BURGLAR–CLOCK–FIRE	ALARM
5.	HEAD–PLANT–ROTTEN	EGG
6.	CRIER–DOWN–GHOST	TOWN
7.	PAN–MIX–CHEESE	CAKE
8.	HERRING–CROSS–TAPE	RED
9.	EVIL–GLASSES–WITNESS	EYE
10.	ORANGE–INSURANCE–SECRET	AGENT
11.	BABY–SHOW–DOUBLE	TALK
12.	BOMB–LINE–FATHER	TIME
13.	BODY–CHANNEL–MUFFIN	ENGLISH
14.	STOP–PEACH–BULL	PIT
15.	FIRE–WRESTLING–CHAIR	ARM
16.	PIE–CRAB–CARAMEL	APPLE
17.	ELECTRIC–CROSS–WHISTLE	TRAIN
18.	RED–BOTTLE–BLOT	INK
19.	MAIL–AMERICAN–LANE	EXPRESS
20.	SILENT–MARE–CLUB	NIGHT

➤ Counter Attack

Goals
1. To practice strategic decision making.
2. To identify factors that impact strategic planning.
3. To determine ways to improve the planning process.

Group Size   Any number of pairs.

Time Required   30 to 40 minutes.

Materials   A Counter Attack Worksheet and a pencil for each pair.

Physical Setting   Any room in which the group regularly meets. Writing surfaces should be provided.

Process
1. Direct the participants to form pairs. Distribute a Counter Attack Worksheet and a pencil to each pair.
2. Referring to the worksheet, explain that the participants will be playing a strategy board game. Players will take turns drawing one of the five shapes in the squares of the playing board. The player who draws a shape next to or at a diagonal to the same shape *loses*. Review the example given on the sheet.
3. Instruct the participants to play two games, first on Board One and then on Board Two, then to await further instructions. Stop the task when all the pairs have completed their games.
4. Lead a discussion by asking:
   - How difficult was it to play the game? What factors had an impact on your decisions?
   - Were you able to improve your strategic moves when playing the second game? Why or why not?
5. Instruct the participants to now play two more games, first on Board Three and then on Board Four, using only the first three shapes. Stop the task when all the pairs have completed their games.

6. Lead a concluding discussion based on the following questions:
   - Was the second set of games easier or harder to play than the first set? In what way?
   - What factors in the real world impact a group's ability to incorporate a strategic plan?
   - How can a group improve its overall planning process?

Counter Attack Worksheet

This is a game of strategy. Players take turns drawing one of the following five shapes in the squares of a 5 by 5 board. The player who draws a shape *next to or at a diagonal to the same shape* LOSES.

The FIVE SHAPES are: # O X ∩ Θ

Example: Examine the board below that shows a game in progress. Three squares are labeled for identification. In square 1, any shape except ∩ would lose. In square 2, any shape would lose. In square 3, any shape except ∩ would be safe.

	X	1		
	#	O	Θ	
		2		
	X		∩	
			3	

First play two games with all five shapes on Board One and Board Two. Next, play two games using only the first three shapes on Board Three and Board Four.

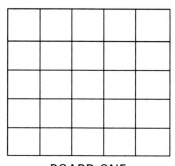

BOARD ONE

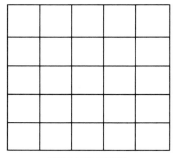

BOARD TWO

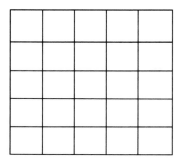

BOARD THREE

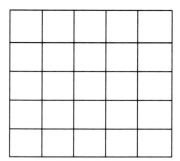

BOARD FOUR

➤ Fab Five

Goals

1. To apply creative thinking skills.
2. To discuss the concepts of creativity and innovation within the work environment.
3. To relate innovation to risk taking.
4. To identify factors influencing the accomplishment of goals.

Group Size   Several groups of four or five persons each.

Time Required   30 to 40 minutes.

Materials

1. A copy of the Fab Five Worksheet and a pencil for each participant.
2. A clock or timer.
3. A newsprint flip chart and felt-tipped markers for recording.
4. Masking tape.

Physical Setting   A room large enough to allow groups to work without disturbing one another. Writing surfaces should be provided. Wall space is required for posting a newsprint sheet.

Process

1. Direct the participants to form groups of four or five persons each. Assign a group designation to each (for example, number, letter, color).
2. Distribute a copy of the Fab Five Worksheet and a pencil to each participant. Read the instructions aloud. Stress that the goal is to brainstorm imaginative answers. Groups will have 5 minutes to complete the task.
3. Time the activity for 5 minutes and then stop the groups. Instruct the groups to determine how many points they expect to score. Record these goals on a sheet of the newsprint flip chart and post with masking tape.

4. For each item on the worksheet, ask each group in turn to read its list of answers. Use the flip chart to list group designations and record 1 point for each unique response made by a group.

5. Lead a concluding discussion based on the following questions:

- In terms of points, did your group reach its goal? What factors influenced this? *(number of participants, participant diversity, time limit, individual perspectives and background, willingness to share ideas)* Do goals help or hinder the creative process? Why is that?

- What impact did time pressure have on creativity? What other factors influenced the creative flow? How does this relate to what occurs in the workplace?

- What role does innovation play in the functioning of a group? How does it support an organization's ability to be competitive? *(solve problems, make decisions, generate new ideas, product breakthroughs)*

- How do innovation and risk taking relate to one another? To what extent does your organization support innovation and risk taking?

- What specific things can a group do to "think outside the box"?

Fab Five Worksheet

Instructions: List four things that share the described quality for each item below. Your group will earn 1 point for each one that supports the category and is *not* mentioned by any other group. Therefore, think creatively!

1. Things that keep you dry in the rain:

2. Things you can throw:

3. Things that have wings:

4. Things that are yellow:

5. Things that can fly:

Out of the 20 possible points, how many do you think your group will score?

➤ Favorable Outlook

Goals
1. To identify expected group milestones.
2. To compare and contrast group and organizational goals.
3. To discuss ways to align group and organizational goals.

Group Size   Several groups of three or four persons each from an intact work group.

Time Required   Approximately 1 hour.

Materials
1. A newsprint sheet and two colors of felt-tipped markers for each group.
2. Masking tape.
3. A newsprint flip chart and felt-tipped markers for recording.

Physical Setting   A room large enough for groups to work without disturbing one another. Writing surfaces should be provided. Wall space is required to post newsprint sheets.

Process
1. Direct the participants to form groups of three or four persons each.
2. Explain that common goals are the foundation of well-functioning groups. Support for those goals comes from aligning the expectations of the group and the organization.
3. Distribute a newsprint sheet and two felt-tipped markers in different colors to each group.
4. Ask the groups to draw a time line, starting with today and extending out one year from now. Using one of the felt-tipped

Adapted from Ukens, L. L. (1996). Great expectations. In *Pump them up! 35 workshops to build stronger teams.* King of Prussia, PA: HRD Press.

markers, they should mark the dates and note the specific milestones that they expect the group to accomplish. These milestones can consist of particular outcomes (for example, completed project or new process) or reflect growth and development issues (for example, new skills or role changes). Allow approximately 15 minutes to complete the task.

5. Ask the groups to use the second color felt-tipped marker to mark the dates and note the specific milestones that the organization expects the group to accomplish. Allow approximately 15 minutes to complete the task.

6. Provide masking tape, and ask the groups to post the time lines. Instruct the participants to review the various time lines. Allow approximately 5 minutes.

7. Ask the participants to identify both common and varying themes among the groups as well as between the groups and the organization. Record responses on a flip chart.

8. Lead a concluding discussion based on the following questions:
   - What similarities exist among the goals identified? What differences exist? Why would different expectations exist?
   - What can the group do to promote and sustain a set of common goals?
   - How can the group work with management to align their goals?
   - In what ways did the group work well together to accomplish the tasks today?

Variations

1. Ask the entire group to develop a list of specific group goals for the next six months.
2. Facilitate a discussion on group standards and procedures that exist or can be instituted to support the achievement of goals.

⊒ For Shore

Goals

1. To assess a situation in terms of strategic planning.
2. To solve a problem through consensus decision making.
3. To apply creative thinking skills.
4. To resolve disagreements through collaboration.

Group Size   Several groups of five or six persons each.

Time Required   Approximately 1 hour.

Materials

1. A newsprint sheet and a felt-tipped marker for each group.
2. Masking tape.

Physical Setting   A room large enough for groups to work without disturbing one another. Writing surfaces should be provided. Wall space is required for posting newsprint sheets.

Process

1. Direct the participants to form groups of five or six persons each. Ask each group to select a recorder.
2. Distribute a newsprint sheet and a felt-tipped marker to each group.
3. Tell the participants:

   "Imagine that you were sailing on an old-time schooner in the Pacific Ocean when you were suddenly hit by an unexpected storm. Shipwrecked with no radio, radar, or any modern aids, your only hope is to cast off in the ship's dinghies for the shores of a nearby deserted island. You have navigational information that the island has plenty of trees, water, some wildlife, wild fruits and root crops, and a cave for shelter. Each group of five can take ten things with them in the boat and must avoid overcrowding. Your group will have 20 minutes to make a consensus decision on what things it will take and the reasons why. List the items on the newsprint sheet for posting."

4. Allow approximately 20 minutes for group work, giving a 2-minute warning before time expires. Provide masking tape and instruct the groups to post their sheets.
5. Ask each group in turn to read its list and describe the reasons for their selections.
6. Lead a concluding discussion based on the following questions:
   - What similarities, if any, are there among the various items selected by all groups? Were the reasons for their selection the same? Why do you think this occurred?
   - How did your group decide on what items to take? What role did creative thinking play? What underlying values influenced your decisions?
   - How difficult was it for all group members to reach agreement on the items? How were disagreements handled? What role did collaboration play?
   - What factors did your group consider in order to plan strategically? How does this relate to strategic planning in the workplace?
   - Overall, how did your experience reflect current conditions in your work environment?

Variation   If there are no more than four groups, you can have all the participants come to consensus on a final set of ten items that are selected from the previous lists.

➤ Goal Mining

Goals

1. To negotiate expectations within a group.
2. To identify clear group goals.
3. To build cohesion within a group.

Group Size   Up to twelve members of an intact work group.

Time Required   1 to 1½ hours.

Materials

1. A newsprint flip chart and felt-tipped markers for recording.
2. A newsprint sheet and a felt-tipped marker for each participant.
3. Masking tape.

Physical Setting   Any room in which the group regularly meets. Writing surfaces should be provided. Wall space is required for posting newsprint sheets.

Process

1. Explain that the participants will be establishing goals and priorities for the group. Remind the group that goals should be Specific, Measurable, Achievable, Relevant, Timely, and reasonably Challenging (SMART/C).
2. Ask the group members for feedback to create a list of basic goals for the next twelve months. Record the items on a flip chart, assigning a letter of the alphabet to each goal. Be sure that the goals follow the SMART/C guidelines; ask participants to clarify any goal that does not.
3. Distribute a newsprint sheet and a felt-tipped marker to each participant. Ask members of the group to set their individual priorities for the goals by ranking them from first to last using the appropriate letters. Provide masking tape and direct the participants to post their ranking sheets.

4. After all the participants have posted their sheets, ask them to check the individual rankings to see what particular issues emerge as the most important. Record these issues on a flip chart sheet and post it.

5. Using the original list of goals, lead a discussion on the goals within the context of the individual rankings. First ask the group if they would like to eliminate any of the goals, and then have the group come to consensus on the priority of the remaining goals. Record the final group ranking on a flip chart sheet. Using these final rankings, ask the group to identify any resources that it will need to meet each goal.

6. Lead a concluding discussion based on the following questions:
   • What role do goals play in creating a cohesive team? What role does teamwork play in supporting group goals?
   • How important is individual commitment to the achievement of group goals? Why is this true?
   • Did any particular values emerge as guiding principles for the group's goals? If so, what were these?
   • Was it difficult to write the goals in terms of making them measurable? Why do you think that was?
   • How do clear goals influence the accomplishment of tasks?
   • What are some specific things the group can do to increase the likelihood that it can accomplish these goals?

Variation   Have participants identify individual and/or corporate goals in addition to group goals. Follow the ranking and discussion procedures for each category.

➢ How Sweet It Is!

Goals
1. To specify criteria of excellence.
2. To develop and apply a test based on these criteria.
3. To explore the impact of group dynamics on task performance.

Group Size   Several groups of five or six persons each.

Time Required   Approximately 1 hour.

Materials
1. Two or more prepared bags of cookies for each group (small plastic bags and marking pen required).
2. Paper and a pencil for each participant.
3. A newsprint flip chart prepared with the following information:
   TASK: to develop a taste test for cookies
   • specify standards of excellence
   • decide how to assess quality based on these standards

Physical Setting   A room with a separate table for each group.

Process
1. Prior to the session, obtain the same type of cookie (for example, chocolate chip) from two or more *different* manufacturers. For each participating group, prepare one set of cookie bags: place approximately three cookies from one manufacturer in a small plastic bag and label it #1; repeat for each manufacturer, numbering the bags sequentially. As an example, if you selected chocolate chip cookies from three different manufacturers, each group would receive three bags of cookies, with the bag containing the first manufacturer's cookies marked #1, the second manufacturer's cookie bag marked #2, and the third manufacturer's bag marked #3.
2. At the session, direct the participants to form groups of five or six persons each. Distribute paper and a pencil to each participant.

3. Referring to the prepared flip chart, explain that the groups are to develop a taste test for cookies. Each group must (1) specify *standards* of excellence among cookies and (2) decide how to *assess* cookie quality based on these standards. Groups will have approximately 20 minutes for the task. To help the participants focus on the task, tell them that they should try to answer the following questions:

   • *To establish criteria:* What qualities does a good cookie possess? Think about your favorite cookie. What is there about this cookie that makes it your favorite?

   • *To develop the test:* How can these qualities be measured? Describe any scales used. Develop at least one objective and one subjective test.

4. Allow approximately 20 minutes, giving a 5-minute warning before time expires. Explain that each group will now apply the taste test it developed, making note of its application and the results. Distribute one set of prepared cookie bags to each group. Allow approximately 10 minutes for the task.

5. Ask each group to present feedback on the following:

   • Describe the criteria developed by the group.

   • Describe the taste test, its application, and results.

6. Lead a discussion based on the following questions:

   • What problems, if any, arose with respect to the task? Was it easy or difficult to specify the criteria and develop the test? Why?

   • Did all groups agree on what makes the best cookie? If not, what are the implications when different groups have different standards for their work?

   • How can a work group develop standards of excellence for the tasks it must perform? Why is it important to develop standards that can be measured (tested)?

7. Explain that the way in which people work together (group process, dynamics) is as important as what people work toward (desired outcomes, goals, objectives). Awareness of how a group

is functioning can lead to improving group performance of its tasks. Ask:

- What did the group actually do while performing the tasks (criteria development and testing)? How were decisions made? How was discussion carried forward? What roles did individuals take upon themselves?
- How can a group improve its functioning so that it can perform tasks more effectively?

Variations

1. Instead of cookies, substitute some other food or an object (for example, photographs, poems, music, and so forth).
2. Have each group apply the taste test developed by another group; that is, for two groups, A would use the test developed by B, and B would use the test developed by A. This can be done in place of the groups doing their own taste tests or it can be done in addition to the group's own taste test to assess how effectively the measurements hold across different groups.

➤ Idea Shuffle

Goals
1. To search for a variety of solutions to a stated problem.
2. To evaluate proposed solutions.
3. To provide a closing activity that reviews information gained during a training session.

Group Size   Five to seven groups of three to five persons each. This activity works best for members of an intact work group or from the same organization.

Time Required   Approximately 1 hour.

Materials
1. A newsprint flip chart containing a problem statement.
2. A deck of standard playing cards affixed with 2-inch by 3-inch labels.
3. Paper and a pencil for each participant.
4. A copy of the Idea Shuffle Resource Sheet for each group.
5. A newsprint sheet and a felt-tipped marker for each group.
6. Masking tape.

Physical Setting   A room large enough for groups to work without disturbing one another. Writing surfaces should be provided. Wall space is required for posting newsprint sheets.

Process
1. Prior to the session, determine a problem statement for the participants to work on. This can be a general problem or something specific to the intact work group or to the organization. Write the statement on a newsprint flip chart for participants to view. Prepare the deck of playing cards by placing a label on the back of each card so that the card face still shows.

2. At the session, direct the participants to form five to seven groups of three or four persons each. Explain that this activity is designed to help the participants look at possible problem solutions that they might not ordinarily consider.

3. Distribute paper and a pencil to each participant. Referring to the prepared flip chart with the written problem statement, explain that the participants are to think of possible ways to solve the problem. Allow approximately 5 minutes for the task, and then ask the participants to rank order their solutions.

4. Shuffle the prepared playing cards and deal a card to each participant in sequence until all the cards are distributed (two to four cards each, depending on the size of the group).

5. Instruct the participants to use their top-ranked solutions and write one idea on the label of each playing card they received (that is, two cards will use the top two ideas, one written on each card). The information should be concise but contain enough detail to sufficiently explain the idea.

6. When everyone has completed the task, collect all of the cards and shuffle them. Deal seven cards to each group. Place any extra cards aside.

7. Distribute a copy of the Idea Shuffle Resource Sheet to each group. Ask each group to select five of the seven cards that comprise the best poker hand, disregarding the labels. Collect the two discards from each group and place these with the extra cards from the previous deal. Shuffle these cards together and distribute two to each group, placing any extra cards from this deal aside.

8. Ask the groups to once again select five of the seven cards that comprise the best poker hand. Collect the two discards from each group and place these aside.

9. Distribute a newsprint sheet and a felt-tipped marker to each group. Explain that each group is to look at the backs of their cards for the problem solutions. Each group is to discuss these five alternatives for solving the original problem, looking at both the advantages and disadvantages of each. The groups are to

decide on a rank order for the solutions and record the ranked ideas on the newsprint sheets provided.

10. Allow approximately 20 minutes, giving a 2-minute warning before time expires. Provide masking tape and instruct the groups to post their sheets.
11. Ask each group in turn to present its list and explain the reasoning.
12. Lead a concluding discussion based on the following questions:
    - What do the top-ranked ideas from the various groups have in common? How do they differ?
    - How did this problem-solving approach help expand the range of possible solutions?
    - How difficult was it to evaluate someone else's idea? Why was that?
    - How can we use what we learned in this activity back in the workplace?

Variation   Rather than address a problem statement, this activity can be used as a closing review activity. Ask participants to write statements on the cards that address information gained from the training session. The cards selected for the poker hand then become the concepts discussed in the group.

Idea Shuffle Resource Sheet

The following list contains possible poker hands in ascending order.

One pair
Two pairs
Three of a kind
Straight (any five cards in sequence)
Flush (all cards of the same suit)
Full house (three of a kind and one pair)
Four of a kind
Straight flush (all cards of the same suit in sequence)
Royal flush (straight flush comprising 10, J, Q, K, A)

➤ It Figures

Goals

1. To apply problem-solving skills.
2. To make connections between concepts and numbers.
3. To combine the knowledge of individual group members into a collective effort.
4. To examine the interdependence of task and relationship outcomes.

Group Size   Several groups of three or four persons each.

Time Required   20 to 30 minutes.

Materials

1. A copy of the It Figures Puzzle and a pencil for each participant.
2. A copy of the It Figures Solution Sheet for the facilitator.
3. A newsprint flip chart with the letters A through P listed.

Physical Setting   A room large enough for groups to work without disturbing one another. Writing surfaces should be provided.

Process

1. Direct the participants to form groups of three or four persons each. Distribute a copy of the It Figures Puzzle and a pencil to each participant.
2. Explain that each clue in the puzzle is presented in the form of a two-part equation. The group should determine the answers to both parts, perform the appropriate calculation, and then write the answer in the box corresponding to the letter of the clue. After all the boxes are correctly filled in, each horizontal line and each vertical line will total one key number. Groups will have 10 minutes to complete the task.
3. Time the activity for 10 minutes, and then reconvene the groups. Review the answer to each block A through P by using

participant feedback and referring to the It Figures Solution
Sheet. Record the information on the prepared flip chart sheet.

4. Lead a concluding discussion by asking the following questions:
   • How did your group approach this task? Was it effective? Why
   or why not? What, if anything, would you have done
   differently?
   • How well did group members work together? What factors
   contributed to this?
   • What significance did working with numbers have on the task
   as a whole? How difficult was it to assign quantities to
   conceptual ideas? Were any special problems encountered? If
   so, what kind? How were these problems resolved?
   • In what ways are task and relationship outcomes interdependent in the workplace?

Variation   Introduce the concepts of competition and time pressure
by having the groups stand when they solve the puzzle, noting
the order of completion. Discuss how these factors influenced a
group's performance.

It Figures Puzzle

A	E	I	M
B	F	J	N
C	G	K	O
D	H	L	P

KEY NUMBER =

A) Baker's dozen + Blackjack

B) Ali Baba's Thieves − Duet

C) February days / Horsemen of the Apocalypse

D) Inches in a foot / Pecks in a bushel

E) Alphabet letters − Nickels in a dollar

F) "Days of Christmas"− Single

G) Sawbuck + Days in a week

H) One gross / Trio

I) "Little Indians" + Spider legs

J) Octopus legs + Deadly sins

K) Piano keys / "Calling Birds"

L) Ounces in a quart − Olympic rings

M) Feet in a fathom × Seasons in a year

N) Dyad × Baseball innings

O) Minutes in an hour − Two dozen

P) Months in a year / Sides to a triangle

It Figures Solution Sheet

A	E	I	M
34	6	18	24
B	F	J	N
38	11	15	18
C	G	K	O
7	17	22	36
D	H	L	P
3	48	27	4

KEY NUMBER = 82

A) 13 + 21

B) 40 − 2

C) 28 / 4

D) 12 / 4

E) 26 − 20

F) 12 − 1

G) 10 + 7

H) 144 / 3

I) 10 + 8

J) 8 + 7

K) 88 / 4

L) 32 − 5

M) 6 × 4

N) 2 × 9

O) 60 − 24

P) 12 / 3

➤ It's in the Mail

Goals
1. To combine individual resources in accomplishing a task.
2. To identify tasks requiring high levels of accuracy.
3. To examine the importance of a "big picture" approach to planning.

Group Size   Eight to twenty participants.

Time Required   30 minutes.

Materials
1. Several dozen envelopes with a wide variety of addresses.
2. A large map of your country (or an overhead transparency of the map).

Physical Setting   A room with a large rectangular conference table and sufficient space for the participants to move around freely. Wall space is needed for posting the map.

Process
1. Prior to the session, collect several dozen envelopes showing addresses from a wide variety of locations within your country. You may use old envelopes with return labels or prepare your own by printing an assortment of addresses on new envelopes. Post a map of your country on the wall in a location that will be visible to all participants. Keep the map concealed until needed.
2. Begin the session by explaining that the participants are to imagine that a map of the country is on the table. Using this imaginary map, they will work as a group to place envelopes with a variety of addresses in their correct geographic locations. The group will have 10 minutes to complete the task.
3. Distribute several envelopes to each participant and signal for the activity to begin. Give a 2-minute warning before time

expires and then reveal the posted map. Ask the participants to use the map to check the accuracy of their placement of the envelopes.

4. Lead a concluding discussion based on the following questions:
   - How accurate were your placements of the envelopes? Did you perform better or worse than expected? What factors were your personal expectations based on?
   - How did the group approach this task in general? Was it an effective approach? Why or why not?
   - How were individuals able to pool their knowledge? Was the size of the group a factor? Why or why not?
   - What are some examples of tasks you perform in the workplace that require high levels of accuracy? How do you check your accuracy?
   - Why is it important to have a clear view of the "big picture" while accomplishing a task? How does this impact the overall planning process?

Variations

1. Use envelopes with addresses from locations around the world. Have the participants visualize an imaginary globe and place the envelopes in a circular pattern, from the nearest to the farthest distance in relation to where they are currently located. Be sure that the starting location is marked prominently. Have a map of the world or globe available to check the accuracy of the envelope placement at the end of the group work.
2. Use addressed boxes instead of envelopes and have the participants imagine the map placement on the floor.

➤ Making Contact

Goals

1. To practice creative problem solving.
2. To examine the process and factors involved in problem solving.
3. To discuss how individuals make interpersonal connections in a variety of situations.

Group Size   Several groups of three to five persons each.

Time Required   30 to 45 minutes.

Materials

1. A copy of the Making Contact Worksheet and a pencil for each participant.
2. A clock or timer.
3. A copy of the Making Contact Answer Sheet for each group.

Physical Setting   A room large enough for groups to work without disturbing one another. Writing surfaces should be provided.

Process

1. Direct the participants to form groups of three to five persons each.
2. Distribute a copy of the Making Contact Worksheet and a pencil to each participant.
3. Explain that the purpose of this exercise is to find the appropriate word for each blank provided that will result in creating a compound word or well-known, two-word phrase when that new word is connected with the preceding word, and then again with the word that follows. Refer to the example at the top of the worksheet: cat → fish → hook. Explain that "cat" connects to "fish" to form "catfish" and that "fish" then connects to "hook" to form "fish hook." Each column, when the blanks have been filled, will present an interconnected series of word

pairs. Announce that groups will have 10 minutes in which to
complete the task.

4. Time the task for 10 minutes, giving a 2-minute warning, and
   then stop the activity.

5. Distribute a copy of the Making Contact Answer Sheet to each
   group. Instruct the groups to review their answers against those
   provided. Allow sufficient time for the groups to discuss the
   answers.

6. Lead a discussion based on the following questions:
   - How difficult was this task? What factors impacted your ability
     to complete the task?
   - What steps did your group take in completing this task? Was
     this an effective approach?
   - How can you relate this activity to creative problem solving,
     which combines logical thinking with creativity?
   - How did working as a group help in completing the task? How
     did it hinder the task?

7. Explain that this activity involved making connections between
   words. Lead a discussion on how individuals make interpersonal
   connections in a variety of situations: between group members,
   across groups, with customers, and so forth.

Variation   Before the groups begin to solve the problems, ask each
group to predict how many of the twenty answers it will be able
to complete in the time allotted. Record the predictions on a
newsprint flip chart, and then compare these goals with the
actual numbers of completed answers for each group after the
Answer Sheet review. Add the following questions to the final
discussion:

- How close did your group come to its predicted results?
- What considerations did your group take into account when
  setting its goal?

Making Contact Worksheet

Instructions: Find the appropriate word for each blank that will connect with the preceding word as well as with the word that follows. Each pair of connected words will form a compound word or a well-known, two-word phrase. For example: cat *fish* hook

The word "cat" connects to the word "fish" for "catfish," and then the word "fish" also connects to "hook" to form "fish hook."

Completing each column below will result in an interconnected series of word pairs. Your group will have 10 minutes to complete the task.

#1	#2	#3	#4	#5
match	color	close	hot	stop
↓	↓	↓	↓	↓
↓	↓	↓	↓	↓
car	side	back	leg	house
↓	↓	↓	↓	↓
↓	↓	↓	↓	↓
hole	mother	hand	shop	up
	↓	↓	↓	↓
	↓	↓	↓	↓
	slide	mark	off	bed
		↓	↓	↓
		↓	↓	↓
		wind	board	bottom
			↓	↓
			↓	↓
			way	man
				↓
				↓
				bar

Making Contact Answer Sheet

#1	#2	#3	#4	#5
match	color	close	hot	stop
↓	↓	↓	↓	↓
BOX	BLIND	CALL	DOG	LIGHT
↓	↓	↓	↓	↓
car	side	back	leg	house
↓	↓	↓	↓	↓
PORT	STEP	STAGE	WORK	HOLD
↓	↓	↓	↓	↓
hole	mother	hand	shop	up
	↓	↓	↓	↓
	LAND	BOOK	LIFT	STREAM
	↓	↓	↓	↓
	slide	mark	off	bed
		↓	↓	↓
		DOWN	SPRING	ROCK
		↓	↓	↓
		wind	board	bottom
			↓	↓
			WALK	LINE
			↓	↓
			way	man
				↓
				HANDLE
				↓
				bar

➤ Mind Benders

Goals
1. To encourage creative thinking.
2. To work collaboratively as a group on a problem-solving task.
3. To discuss the role of perception in communication and problem solving.

Group Size   Several groups of three or four persons each.

Time Required   30 minutes.

Materials
1. A copy of the Mind Benders Worksheet and a pencil for each participant.
2. A clock or timer.
3. A copy of the Mind Benders Answer Sheet for each group.

Physical Setting   A room large enough for groups to work without disturbing one another. Writing surfaces should be provided.

Process
1. Direct the participants to form groups of three or four persons each.
2. Distribute a copy of the Mind Benders Worksheet and a pencil to each participant.
3. Referring to the worksheet, read aloud the instructions at the top of the page. Tell the groups that they will have exactly 10 minutes to complete the task and reach one group solution. Time the activity for 10 minutes, giving a 1-minute warning before time expires.
4. Distribute a copy of the Mind Benders Answer Sheet to each group and ask them to review their answers.
5. Lead a concluding discussion based on the following questions:
   • How well did your group do in solving the puzzle? What factors influenced your ability to complete the task?

- How did you decide which answers were correct? Who took the lead in your group? How did that happen?
- How does perception affect the communication process? What happens when there is a perceived "hidden meaning" behind our words?
- How does perception affect an individual's ability to look at things in new and different ways? What effect do our preconceived notions have on our ability to solve problems quickly?
- Why is it important to improve our mental flexibility to adapt to new situations and conditions?

Variation   Provide the groups with index cards and have them create one or more of their own paired words to exchange with other groups to solve.

Mind Benders Worksheet

Instructions: The object of this puzzle is to match the ten words on the left with the ten on the right, based on their having similar or related meanings. The relationships are disguised by the use of puns, double meanings, or altered spacing within the words. For example, "engaged" can be matched to "towed" (to wed). Be creative! You'll need to "bend" your mind a little in order to see some of the relationships.

_____	1. gored	A. lesson
_____	2. headdresses	B. adverse
_____	3. automate	C. blush
_____	4. pungent	D. orator
_____	5. diet	E. carpooler
_____	6. comeback	F. dugout
_____	7. understands	G. jokester
_____	8. jingle	H. rehabilitation
_____	9. constraining	I. chieftain
_____	10. clanking	J. laterally

Mind Benders Answer Sheet

C	1.	gored = GO RED	(BLUSH)
D	2.	headdresses = HE-ADDRESSES	(ORATOR)
E	3.	automate = AUTO-MATE	(CARPOOLER)
G	4.	pungent = PUN-GENT	(JOKESTER)
A	5.	diet	(LESS-ON)
J	6.	comeback	(LATE-RALLY)
F	7.	understands = UNDER-STANDS	(DUGOUT)
B	8.	jingle	(AD-VERSE)
H	9.	constraining = CON'S-TRAINING	(REHABILITATION)
I	10.	clanking = CLAN-KING	(CHIEFTAIN)

➤ Mirror Image

Goals

1. To identify a problem-solving rule based on personal observation.
2. To apply the rule in making predictions for a similar problem.
3. To discuss the impact of past experiences in the problem-solving process.

Group Size   Several groups of three or four persons each.

Time Required   20 to 30 minutes.

Materials

1. A copy of Mirror Image Worksheet 1 for each group.
2. A pocket mirror for each group.
3. A copy of Mirror Image Worksheet 2 and a pencil for each participant.

Physical Setting   A room large enough for groups to work without disturbing one another.

Process

1. Explain that this activity will allow the participants to make some observations and then to use this information to make predictions.
2. Direct the participants to form groups of three or four persons each.
3. Distribute a copy of Mirror Image Worksheet 1 and a pocket mirror to each group. Read aloud the instructions at the top of the page. Emphasize that each person in the group should have a turn with the mirror so as to make individual observations. Allow several minutes, and then collect the mirrors.
4. Distribute a copy of Mirror Image Worksheet 2 and a pencil to each participant. Read aloud the instructions at the top of the

page. Allow approximately 5 to 10 minutes for the groups to make their predictions.

5. Distribute a mirror to each group, and ask the participants to check their predictions. Ask for feedback on the unchanged words *(see Note to the Facilitator below)*. Ask the following questions:

    • How accurate were the predictions made by your group?
    • Based on your observations from Worksheet 1, what "rule" did you apply to make your predictions on Worksheet 2? Was the rule correct in every case?

6. Explain that some letters are formed so that upside down they are mirror images of themselves. Thus looking at their reflections in a mirror makes them appear normal. The words on Worksheet 1 that follow this "rule" are OBOE and DIED.

7. Lead a concluding discussion based on the following questions:

    • How do individual past experiences impact the problem-solving process? What implications does this have for the workplace?
    • Why is it important to "test" information that results from personal observations?
    • How can we improve our ability to make accurate observations?

Notes to the Facilitator   1. *Seven words on Worksheet 2 remain unchanged: CHOICE, CHECKED, ICE BOX, HIDE, DECIDED, BOOK, ECHO.*

    2. You can make a reflective device to use in place of the mirror by covering an index card with aluminum foil. It is important to smooth the foil as flat as possible for best results.

Mirror Image Worksheet 1

Instructions: Place a pocket mirror on the line below, facing toward you. Look at the reflection of the words. Some change and some do not. Using these observations, you will be asked to guess which words on the next worksheet you see will remain unchanged.

OBOE   DIED   ROSE

Mirror Image Worksheet 2

Instructions: As a group, predict which of the following words will remain UNCHANGED when reflected in a mirror. Underline those words, and then wait for further instructions from the facilitator.

CHOICE	SLEEP
PURPLE	HIDE
SQUARE	DECIDED
WATER	LARGE
CHECKED	TURTLE
ICE BOX	BOOK
TIGER	ECHO
ZOO	TABLE

➤ Name Game

Goals
1. To use logical thinking in solving a problem.
2. To examine factors that can affect the problem-solving process.
3. To discuss roles within the group and their influence on task and relationship processes.
4. To identify ways for groups to improve the analysis and solution of problems.

Group Size   Several groups of three or four persons each.

Time Required   45 minutes to 1 hour.

Materials
1. A copy of the Name Game Worksheet and a pencil for each participant.
2. A clock or timer.
3. A newsprint flip chart and felt-tipped marker for recording.
4. A copy of the Name Game Answer Sheet for each group.
5. Prizes for the winning group (optional).

Physical Setting   A room large enough for the groups to work without disturbing one another. Writing surfaces should be provided.

Process
1. Direct the participants to form groups of three or four persons each.
2. Distribute a copy of the Name Game Worksheet and a pencil to each participant.
3. Explain that the groups are to complete the solution chart by analyzing the clues given. Announce that the first group to complete the assignment correctly will be the winner, but that all groups are expected to continue until finished. A group

representative is to stand when the group has finished. Signal for the task to begin.

4. Time the activity; as each group finishes, note the time elapsed from the beginning of the task. (The task should last approximately 10 minutes.) Use the flip chart to record the completion times for all groups.

5. When all the groups have finished, ask the winning group to provide the answers for its solution chart. Ask the remaining groups for feedback on the accuracy of the solution. (If desired, provide a prize to the winning group.) Ask: What was your group's approach to solving the problem?

6. Distribute a copy of the Name Game Answer Sheet to each group. Instruct the groups to discuss the explanation of the solutions. Allow approximately 5 minutes for discussion.

7. Explain that solving a logic problem is similar to solving a job-related problem because it involves using available information, whether directly or indirectly. Because the information is often sketchy, it is necessary to draw some inferences by analyzing the basic facts. The resulting conclusions enable us to collect additional data in order to arrive at a final solution.

8. Lead a concluding discussion by asking the following questions:

   • What are some factors that can affect the problem-solving process? *(for example, time, group size, amount of information available, analysis of data, conflicts)*

   • How did the time pressure affect your problem-solving skills in this activity? How did group size affect the outcome? What do you think would happen if the size of the group doubled?

   • Did everyone participate equally in the task? Why or why not? What roles emerged within the group? *(for example, leader, negotiator, recorder, and so forth)* How did this influence the task process? How did it influence the relationship process?

   • What are some ways in which a group can improve its process of analyzing and solving problems in the workplace? What are some sources of information that are available?

Name Game Worksheet

The director of Human Resources at Central Corporation discovered that six of the applicants for open positions have unusual names: each whole name sounds like a familiar word or phrase. For example, the applicant from Sea Valley is named John Quill (jonquil). From the following clues, determine the full names of the other five applicants, the word or phrase each name forms, the city where each resides (one is Blair), and the position for which each has applied (one is Research).

Use the chart provided to fill in the information as you discover it from the clues.

1. In addition to Quill, the other surnames are Hangor, King, Ott, Dwyer, and Matick. All the first names are Barb, Carl, Cliff, John, Karis, and May. All come from different cities and each applied for a different job.
2. Cliff wants to be in Sales. His application was received before the one from the applicant from Trent, but later than that of the person from Crestview.
3. Barb is from Tall Palms, and Matick is from Hillsdale. Neither wants to be in Marketing.
4. May was the last one to apply.
5. King wants a Finance position. Ott wants to be in Training.
6. Karis is not interested in a Production job.

First Name	Last Name	Word/Phrase	City	Position

Name Game Answer Sheet

"Jonquil" is the word formed phonetically by John Quill and he is from Sea Valley (intro). By clue 1, we can form the following connections: Cliff and Hangor equal "cliff hanger"; May and King together form "making"; Carl and Ott form "car lot"; Barb and Dwyer sound like "barbed wire"; and Karis and Matick form "charismatic." By clue 2, Cliff applied for a Sales position. By clue 3, Barb is from Tall Palms and Matick is from Hillsdale. Cliff's city is not Trent or Crestview (clue 2), so he is from Blair. May was the last one to apply (clue 4), so she isn't from Crestview (clue 2); she is from Trent and Carl is from Crestview. By clue 5, King applied for Finance, and Ott applied for Training. Neither Barb nor Matick wanted Marketing (clue 3), so, by elimination, John applied for Marketing. By clue 6, Karis wasn't interested in Production, so, by elimination, Barb was applying for Production and Karis for Research. In sum:

First Name	Last Name	Word/Phrase	City	Position
John	Quill	Jonquil	Sea Valley	Marketing
Cliff	Hangor	Cliff hanger	Blair	Sales
May	King	Making	Trent	Finance
Carl	Ott	Car lot	Crestview	Training
Barb	Dwyer	Barbed wire	Tall Palms	Production
Karis	Matick	Charismatic	Hillsdale	Research

➤ On Top of Things

Goals
1. To examine the implications of individual expectations for group performance.
2. To discuss the influence of goal setting on the group process.
3. To work collaboratively on a group problem-solving task.

Group Size   Several groups of three to five persons each.

Time Required   30 to 40 minutes.

Materials
1. A copy of the On Top of Things Worksheet and pencil for each participant.
2. A clock or timer.
3. A prepared newsprint flip chart with the following words, to be concealed prior to the session: Coat, Dog, Drawer, Hat, Heavy, Knot, Most, Notch, Side, Soil.

Physical Setting   A room large enough for the groups to work without disturbing one another. Writing surfaces should be provided.

Process
1. Direct the participants to form groups of three to five persons each.
2. Distribute a copy of the On Top of Things Worksheet and a pencil to each participant.
3. Referring to the worksheet, read the directions at the top of the page aloud. Ask the participants to write down the number of words that they expect their group to locate within the 5-minute time allotment.
4. Signal for the groups to begin. Time the task for 5 minutes, giving a 1-minute warning, and then stop the activity when time expires.

5. Reveal the list of words on the prepared flip chart and direct group members to count the number of correct responses and record the total at the top of the worksheet. Ask the group members to compare their original goal expectations with one another and to discuss factors that influenced their expectations.

6. Lead a concluding discussion based on the following questions:

   • How closely did the goal expectations of individual group members match? What factors were considered in determining the estimate?

   • How did the individual estimates within your group compare with its actual performance? What were your personal reactions to your group's performance in terms of your expectations?

   • Why might the goal expectations of individual group members differ in the workplace? What implications can this have for the group?

   • Why are common goals important to the performance of a team? What role does personal goal setting play in the accomplishment of overall team goals? How does this impact group member relationships?

   • What strategy did your group use to accomplish the task? How does this compare to the way in which a group approaches a problem-solving situation in the workplace?

   • Were there particular roles for different members of your group? If so, how did they evolve?

   • If given the opportunity, would your group have done anything differently? If so, what?

   • How does this activity relate to the team problem-solving process in the workplace?

   Note to the Facilitator *It is possible that participants will provide additional words that are not listed on the prepared flip chart. Determine their acceptance as common terms that follow the word "top," stressing that this was the rule presented in the directions on the worksheet.*

On Top of Things Worksheet

Instructions: Your group will be working on a collaborative task. Within the puzzle square below, there are ten words that are commonly found following the word "TOP." To find the words, start with any letter and move horizontally, vertically, or diagonally to any neighboring letter. A letter cannot be used twice consecutively, but it can be used more than once to connect a word. Each word is at least three letters or more.

Before your group begins its task, estimate how many of the ten words you expect your group to locate in a 5-minute time period.

Wait for the signal from your facilitator before your group begins to solve the puzzle.

Y	G	O	L	E
V	D	M	K	D
A	R	N	O	I
W	E	T	S	L
H	C	O	A	H

1. _____
2. _____
3. _____
4. _____
5. _____
6. _____
7. _____
8. _____
9. _____
10. _____

➤ Opposites Attract

Goals

1. To examine a problem or issue on which a group is divided.
2. To reach a consensus on the group's position on the problem or issue.
3. To develop an action plan that addresses how to resolve the problem or issue.

Group Size   Two equal-sized groups of four to eight persons each from an intact work group or the same organization.

Time Required   2 to 2½ hours.

Materials

1. A newsprint flip chart and felt-tipped markers for recording.
2. Three newsprint sheets and two felt-tipped markers for each group.
3. Masking tape.
4. Paper and a pencil for each participant.

Physical Setting   A room large enough for two groups to work without disturbing one another. Writing surfaces should be provided. Wall space is needed for posting newsprint sheets.

Process

1. To begin the session, explain that this activity will start by everyone working together to identify a problem or issue that pertains to the group or the organization and that allows for opposing viewpoints ("for" or "against"). Using the newsprint flip chart, record the responses, and then have the group select *one issue* to discuss. Write a clear but brief description of the selected issue on the flip chart.
2. Direct the participants to form two equal-sized groups and assign a group to each of the two positions. Explain that

although participants have been assigned to a particular stand on the issue, the activity will require group members to examine the problem or issue from both points of view.

3. Distribute two newsprint sheets and two felt-tipped markers to each group. Instruct the groups to prepare two lists using separate sheets of newsprint paper: (1) *key points* for their side, and (2) their *concerns* regarding the opposing view. Allow approximately 20 minutes for the task.

4. Ask each group to select a spokesperson who will present the group's arguments based on the two lists they have generated. Explain to the participants that they should listen carefully and withhold comments regarding the opposing side's statements. Have both groups post their sheets using masking tape and present their lists of key points and concerns.

5. Distribute paper and a pencil to each participant. Explain that now each group is to prepare a response or rebuttal to the opposing group's arguments, which is to last approximately 3 to 5 minutes. The groups may make any necessary notes on the paper provided. Allow approximately 15 minutes for the task. Ask each group to select a new representative to present the response.

6. After both responses have been presented, instruct the groups to write a short summary listing the *best points* of the opposing group's position. Distribute a newsprint sheet to each group for this purpose. Allow approximately 15 minutes for the task.

7. Ask each group to post its sheet and select a new spokesperson to read and explain the summary list.

8. Using the newsprint flip chart to record responses, have the entire group brainstorm ways to improve or expand the areas of agreement. Both groups should reach a consensus of the work group's position on the problem or issue.

9. Lead a discussion by asking the following questions:
   - How did you personally feel about being assigned to a particular stand on the issue? Was it difficult to "see things the other way" if you were not originally committed to that stance? Why or why not?

- How did the overall process influence your ability to examine the issue more fully?
- How can this approach to problem solving be used to prevent conflicts in the workplace?

10. *Optional*: Lead the work group in developing an action plan to resolve the problem or issue based on the identified areas of agreement. Record key issues of the plan on the newsprint flip chart.

Variation   This activity can be conducted with participants who are not from the same work group or organization by selecting a general topic of discussion that allows for opposing viewpoints (such as gun control, tax increases, and so forth) and omitting the optional final step.

➤ Paying Your Dues

Goals
1. To experience individual decision making.
2. To examine how individual values affect decision making.
3. To practice consensus decision making in groups.
4. To resolve conflict arising from differences of opinion in a group.

Group Size   Several groups of five or six persons each.

Time Required   1 hour.

Materials
1. A copy of the Paying Your Dues Scenario for each participant.
2. A copy of the Paying Your Dues Worksheet for each participant.
3. A pencil for each participant.
4. A clock or timer.
5. A newsprint flip chart and felt-tipped markers for recording.

Physical Setting   A room large enough that groups can work without disturbing one another. Writing surfaces should be provided.

Process
1. Begin the session by explaining that the activity will explore how decisions are made within a group. These decisions are often influenced by the values held by individuals. Values are principles or standards considered worthwhile and desirable.
2. Distribute one each of the Paying Your Dues Scenario, the Paying Your Dues Worksheet, and a pencil to each participant. Instruct the participants to follow along as you read the Scenario out loud.
3. Referring to the worksheet, have individuals rank order the four characters according to the instructions listed. Allow approximately 5 minutes for individual work, then stop the task.
4. Direct participants to form groups of five or six persons each.

5. Explain that groups will have approximately 20 minutes to discuss the scenario and reach a consensus on how to rank order the four characters. Refer to the section headed Group Ranking and review the consensus rules. Signal for the discussion to begin. Give a 5-minute warning before time has expired, then stop the discussion at the end of 20 minutes.
6. Record each group's ranking decisions on the flip chart.
7. Lead a concluding discussion by asking questions such as:
   • How did your individual rankings compare with your group's decision?
   • Why did you rank the characters as you did?
   • Did individuals feel that their opinions were listened to attentively? Why or why not?
   • How were individual thoughts and opinions accepted by the group?
   • How did individual opinions affect the group's ability to make a decision?
   • How were conflicts resolved within the group?
   • How different were the decisions that were made from group to group?
   • How does this activity relate to decision making in the workplace?

Note to the Facilitator   You may wish to provide a short presentation on consensus decision-making components prior to having the groups rank order the characters in step 5 above. The presentation might include information on such issues as using active listening skills, keeping an open mind, no "one-for-one" trading, digging for facts, listing benefits and limitations, fully exploring ideas and opinions, monitoring interactions among people, and so forth.

Paying Your Dues Scenario

MRS. MARTIN has recently taken over her late husband's meat market. Business has been poor because a large supermarket opened down the street. For the past few months, she has been unable to pay all of the rent. In the past, her landlord, MR. GRAYSON, has accepted the partial payments and extended her more time to come up with the difference, but now he is out of work and needs the money for his large family. He tells Mrs. Martin that she has two weeks to pay the rent or he must force her to move out.

Mrs. Martin becomes desperate. She knows that she cannot earn the full rent payment in two weeks, so she decides to go to the bank for a loan. The bank manager, MR. LONG, turns down her request for a loan because he doesn't think that she can be successful with the business. Mrs. Martin pleads with him, saying, "If I have enough time, I know my market will make money." Mr. Long replies, "I'm sorry, Mrs. Martin, but I have to protect the people who put their savings in this bank. You are not a good risk."

Mrs. Martin became so distressed by her predicament that she couldn't eat her dinner that night. When she burst into tears, her 12-year-old son JOHNNY begged to know what was wrong. His mother broke down and told him the whole story, and added, "Don't worry, dear. I'll take care of everything."

The next morning, Mrs. Martin decided that the only way she could earn enough money was by placing her thumb on the scale while weighing the meat so that it would appear that the meat weighed more than it actually did. That way, she could make more money for each piece of meat. Mrs. Martin knew her plan meant that she would be cheating all of her customers, many of whom were her friends and neighbors, but she was determined to keep the meat market at any cost.

Meanwhile, Johnny had a plan also. One of his classmates had just been given a new ten-speed bike for his birthday. That afternoon, while the basketball team was at practice in the gym, Johnny cut the lock on the new bike and stole it. He planned to sell the bike and give the money to his mother.

Paying Your Dues Worksheet

The four characters in this story made certain decisions: MRS. MARTIN,
MR. GRAYSON, MR. LONG, and JOHNNY.

Individual Ranking

Think about what each person did in this predicament. In your opinion, decide
which person did the *most wrong*, and list that person in the space below as
the "#1 Offender." Then decide whom you would rank as the #2 Offender, and
so forth for each character.

#1 Offender: _____

#2 Offender: _____

#3 Offender: _____

#4 Offender: _____

Group Ranking

Discuss as a group what each person did. Using the rules of consensus listed
below, decide as a team how to rank the four characters as #1 Offender, then
#2, #3, and #4.

Rules of Consensus

1. All members of the group should participate.
2. No voting is allowed.
3. The final decision must be acceptable to everyone.

#1 Offender: _____

#2 Offender: _____

#3 Offender: _____

#4 Offender: _____

➤ Prospect–Us

Goals
1. To identify individual expectations of group goals.
2. To identify resources for accomplishing group goals.
3. To increase open communication among group members.
4. To build team cohesion through values clarification.

Group Size   Six to twelve persons from an intact work group.

Time Required   2 hours.

Materials
1. Two newsprint sheets and a felt-tipped marker for each participant.
2. Masking tape.
3. Paper and a pencil for each participant.
4. A newsprint flip chart and felt-tipped markers for recording.

Physical Setting   Any room in which the group regularly meets. Writing surfaces should be provided. Wall space is required for posting newsprint sheets.

Process
1. Begin the session by explaining that the activity is intended to reveal hidden agendas and, by working through them, to increase open communication. Distribute a newsprint sheet and a felt-tipped marker to each participant. Ask the group members to make individual lists of what they would like the work group to achieve within the next six months. Emphasize that these should be specific plan actions that may be achieved realistically and not deal in generalities or abstractions. Allow approximately 15 minutes for the task.
2. Ask participants to rank their lists according to which performance should be accomplished first, second, and so on.

They are to write the rank number to the left of each idea and circle it. Allow approximately 10 minutes for the task.

3. Provide masking tape and instruct the participants to post their lists on the wall. Distribute paper and a pencil to each participant and ask group members to compare the lists, evaluating them in terms of the direction for the group and what roles individuals play in working toward that direction. Allow approximately 10 minutes for the task.

4. Using a newsprint flip chart to record responses, lead a discussion by asking the following questions:
   • In terms of meeting the goals listed, what are the group's current strengths? What are the group's current weaknesses?
   • What skills, if any, does the group need to acquire or increase in order to meet the goals listed?

5. Lead the group members in clarifying their overall vision for the group and in describing what they mean by such terms as open communication, collaboration, accountability, and so forth.

6. Distribute another newsprint sheet to each participant. Ask each group member to list his or her talents, skills, and experience. Allow approximately 10 minutes for the task.

7. Ask participants to rank their lists according to which are their favorites. They are to write the rank number to the left of each point and circle it. Allow approximately 10 minutes for the task.

8. Instruct the participants to post their lists on the wall next to or below their original "what to do" lists.

9. Ask the group to examine the lists to discover previously unknown assets. Lead a concluding discussion based on the following questions:
   • After viewing the lists of talents, how well did the group assess its strengths and weaknesses as previously identified?
   • What talents did you discover within the group that you were not aware of? How might group members gain from others who have talents that they personally are not interested in pursuing?
   • How can the group make the best use of its available resources? How can the group stay aware of its resource base as time goes on?

➤ Rhyme Time

Goals

1. To apply creative thinking skills.
2. To discuss the advantages and disadvantages of group problem solving.
3. To examine the relationship of problem solving to creativity.

Group Size   Several groups of three or four persons each.

Time Required   20 to 30 minutes.

Materials   A copy of the Rhyme Time Worksheet and a pencil for each participant.

Physical Setting   A room large enough for groups to work without disturbing one another. Writing surfaces should be provided.

Process

1. Direct the participants to form groups of three or four persons each.
2. Distribute a copy of the Rhyme Time Worksheet and a pencil to each participant. Read aloud the instructions at the top of the sheet. Explain that the groups will have approximately 5 minutes to complete the riddle.
3. Allow approximately 5 minutes, and then ask the groups for the solution to the riddle (*see Note to the Facilitator*).
4. Explain that the group members are now going to create their own rhyming riddles, which will be presented to another group to solve. Refer to the section on the worksheet titled "Create Your Own" and read the instructions aloud. Instruct the participants to work within their groups to first decide on a word, writing it on the Solution line, and then to create the rhyme for the letters in the word, ending in a two-line riddle that refers to the word in some context.

5. Allow approximately 10 minutes. When all groups have completed the task, instruct them to tear off the lower portion (dotted line) of one copy of the worksheet that contains the new poem. Direct each group to exchange its copy with another group. Tell the group members to work together to solve the new rhyme.

6. Allow approximately 5 minutes, and then ask each group to read the rhyme it received and provide the solution. The original group that wrote the rhyme can confirm the solution.

7. Lead a concluding discussion based on the following questions:

   • Did working as a group help or hinder the solution or the riddle? What were the advantages? What were the disadvantages?

   • What problem-solving approach did your group take to solve the first riddle? Did your group use the same method for the second riddle? Why or why not?

   • How did your group approach the task of creating the new rhyme?

   • What similarities existed between your problem-solving approach and your creativity approach? Were there any differences? If so, what? How are these factors logically related to one another?

Note to the Facilitator   *Solution is YOURSELF. This answer is based on the riddle clue and the only sensible combination of the following letter possibilities: 1st is Y or V; 2nd is O or W; 3rd is U or N, O; 4th is R or E, D; 5th is S or T, E; 6th is E or V; 7th is L or A; 8th is F or I.*

Rhyme Time Worksheet

Instructions: Working together as a group, choose the correct letter from each clue in the rhyme below. When put in order, the letters will spell the solution to the riddle.

Solution

My 1st in every but not in remain.
My 2nd in grown but not in grain.
My 3rd in undo but not die.
My 4th in reside but not in sigh.
My 5th in test you'll always find.
My 6th in even but not in mind.
My 7th in least but not in nest.
My 8th in first but not in rest.
Never practice to deceive
If in this you do believe.

Create Your Own

Instructions: As a group, create your own poem for a six- to eight-letter word to be solved by another group.

Solution:

Rhyme:

➤ Risky Business

Goals
1. To explore the conditions for and implications of taking risks.
2. To learn to assess the level of risk and its impact on decision making.
3. To provide an opportunity for groups to identify the risk level of current problems or decisions that require resolution.

Group Size   Several groups of five to ten persons each, preferably from intact work groups.

Time Required   Approximately 2 hours.

Materials
1. A copy of the Risky Business Quotations Sheet for each participant.
2. A pencil for each participant.
3. A transparency of the Risky Business Quotation Tally Sheet.
4. A transparency projector and screen and washable transparency markers for the facilitator.
5. A copy of the Risky Business Worksheet for each participant.
6. A newsprint flip chart and felt-tipped markers for recording.
7. Five prepared newsprint sheets, each with one of the following headings: "Reward," "Support," "Resources," "Expectations," and "Experience."
8. Masking tape.
9. Another newsprint sheet with the following prepared headings, dividing the page into four parts: (1) Level of Risk Involved; (2) Likelihood of Making a Mistake; (3) Probable Consequences for Project, Team, or Organization; and (4) Benefits vs. Risk.

Source: Ukens, L. (1999). Risky business: Assessing risk. In E. Biech (Ed.), *The 1999 Annual: Volume 2, Consulting* (pp. 67–73). San Francisco: Pfeiffer. This material is used by permission of John Wiley & Sons, Inc.

Physical Setting   A room large enough so that participants can work in groups without disturbing one another. Writing surfaces should be provided. Wall space is needed for posting newsprint sheets.

Process

1. Explain that this session will focus on a team's ability to take risks. Summarize by giving the following background information before continuing:

   "People hesitate to take risks to different degrees. Every decision that one makes contains some element of risk, perceived differently by different people. Obviously, some risks are worthwhile; others should be avoided. Work groups must also weigh the benefits against the risks when they make decisions. An important factor that must be considered with teams is how well individual members of the team are in alignment in their risk orientation. The organizational environment also plays a large part in a team's willingness to take risks. It follows that organizations that expect individuals and teams to 'go the limit' must create an environment that supports and fosters risk taking and that individuals must strive to identify, understand, and accept the level of risk associated with the decisions they must make."

2. Direct the participants to form groups of five to ten persons each, preferably as members of a natural work group.

3. Distribute a copy of the Risky Business Quotations Sheet and a pencil to each participant. Ask participants to select the one quote from the list that best describes their individual philosophy about taking risks and mark it with an "I." Next, ask participants to select the quote that they think best represents the current risk-taking practices of their work team as a whole and mark it with a "T." Finally, ask participants to select a quote that best represents what they perceive to be their organization's approach to risk taking and mark it with an "O." Tell them to discuss their choices for a few minutes in their groups.

4. Record the number of participant responses, by a show of hands, for each quotation, for the Individual, Team, and Organization. Record responses on the Risky Business Quotation Tally Sheet transparency and show them using the projector.

5. Lead a discussion with the total group by asking the following questions:
   - What reasons did you have for choosing particular quotes?
   - In general, do the quotes people chose reflect a willingness to take risks or avoid them?
   - Can you give some examples of past team or organizational actions or decisions that reflect this view?
   - How well do the quotes you chose as individuals mesh with those chosen for your team?
   - How well do the quotes you chose for your team reflect the ones chosen for your organization?
   - How do you think that this affects how your team approaches risks?

6. After the discussion, distribute one copy of the Risky Business Worksheet to each participant. Announce that the groups will have approximately 15 minutes to discuss the questions on the worksheet and to take notes.

7. Allow 15 minutes, call time, reconvene the total group, and discuss each question. Record responses on the appropriate prepared newsprint sheet as the discussion proceeds, then use masking tape to post the sheet before moving on to the next topic.

8. Ask the participants to again form into their groups and to identify two specific examples of current problems or decisions they are facing that involve some risk. Give them a few minutes, and then turn to the final newsprint sheet you prepared. Ask each group to use the chart to identify the following for each example: (1) level of risk involved; (2) likelihood of making a mistake; (3) probable consequences (project, team, organization); (4) benefits versus risk.

9. Reconvene the large group. Ask each group, in turn, to present one of its examples and to share a summary of its discussion.

10. Lead a closing discussion by asking the following questions:
    - What have you learned about your own orientation toward risk?
    - What have you learned about the effect that risk can have on teams?
    - How can teams learn to take appropriate risks?
    - What does your team need to do more of or less of in the future in regard to taking risks?

Risky Business Quotations Sheet

"Just do it."

"Seize the moment."

"Look before you leap."

"Opportunity knocks but once."

"Strike while the iron is hot."

"Nothing ventured, nothing gained."

"Better to be safe than sorry."

"Slow and steady wins the race."

"When in Rome, do as the Romans do."

Risky Business Quotation Tally Sheet

Quotation	Individual	Team	Organization
Just do it.			
Seize the moment.			
Look before you leap.			
Opportunity knocks but once.			
Strike while the iron is hot.			
Nothing ventured, nothing gained.			
Better to be safe than sorry.			
Slow and steady wins the race.			
When in Rome, do as the Romans do.			

Risky Business Worksheet

REWARD
What is the payoff for taking a risk?

SUPPORT
What backing will the team receive for taking a risk?

RESOURCES
What are the resources required to make taking a risk successful?

EXPECTATIONS
Does the organization assume that this time you will take risks?

EXPERIENCE
How has the organization responded to risk taking in the past?

➤ Roman Candles

Goals
1. To apply creative thinking skills.
2. To investigate the role of creativity in problem-solving situations.
3. To examine how the group process impacts creativity.

Group Size   Several triads.

Time Required   45 minutes.

Materials
1. A copy of the Roman Candles Puzzle and a pencil for each group.
2. A newsprint flip chart prepared with the six equations from the Roman Candles Puzzle sheet.
3. A newsprint sheet prepared with these answers:

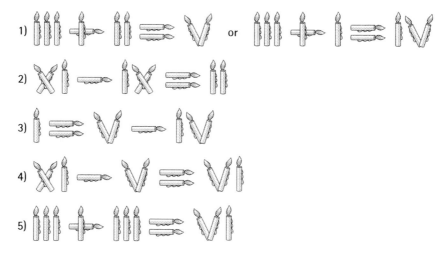

4. Masking tape.

Physical Setting   A room large enough for groups to work without disturbing one another. Writing surfaces should be provided. Wall space is required for posting the prepared newsprint sheet.

Process

1. Prior to the session, post the prepared newsprint sheet of answers and conceal its contents.
2. At the session, direct the participants to form triads. Ask each group to select a recorder.
3. Distribute a copy of the Roman Candles Puzzle and a pencil to each group. Read aloud the instructions at the top of the sheet.
4. Allow approximately 20 minutes for group work, and then stop the activity. Refer to the prepared flip chart of equations from the puzzle sheet, and ask the groups for possible solutions to the first equation, visually pointing out each suggested move. Ask the participants for consensus on the correct answer and indicate the appropriate move on the chart. Repeat this procedure for each of the next four equations. Reveal the answers on the prepared newsprint sheet and compare to the suggested solutions.
5. Refer to the final "trick" equation on the puzzle sheet. Ask the groups for feedback on how to solve the problem, and then reveal the answer that it can be solved by turning the paper and looking at the equation upside-down.
6. Lead a concluding discussion based on the following questions:
   • How well did you feel you did in finding the solutions to these equations? Why was that?
   • What was difficult about doing this activity? What role did creativity play?
   • Did working in a group help or hinder problem solving? Why was that?
   • Why should groups think "outside the box" when trying to solve problems?
   • How does your experience relate to problem-solving situations in the workplace?

Variation Provide each group with a package of small birthday candles and have them physically work out possible alternatives to each equation.

Roman Candles Puzzle

Instructions: Correct these Roman-numeral equations by moving only *one* candle in each puzzle. Show your correction by crossing out the candle that is to be moved and drawing it in its new location.

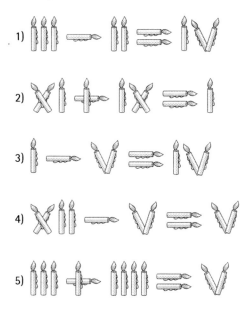

How can you correct this super-tricky equation *without moving a single candle?*

➤ Team Time

Goals
1. To use creative problem-solving skills.
2. To practice consensus decision making.
3. To explore factors used for selecting among alternatives.
4. To discuss the advantages and disadvantages of teamwork.

Group Size   Several groups of four or five persons each.

Time Required   Approximately 1 hour.

Materials
1. A copy of the Team Time Worksheet and a pencil for each participant.
2. A clock or timer.
3. A newsprint flip chart and felt-tipped markers for recording.
4. Masking tape.

Physical Setting   A room large enough for the groups to work without disturbing one another. Writing surfaces should be provided. Wall space is required for posting newsprint sheets.

Process
1. Direct the participants to form groups of four or five persons each.
2. Distribute a copy of the Team Time Worksheet and a pencil to each participant. Read aloud the situation and the instructions at the top of the page.
3. Time the activity for 20 minutes and then stop the discussion.
4. Ask each group in turn to disclose its final solution to the problem and the reasoning behind the idea. Record the ideas on the flip chart. When all the groups have reported, post the newsprint sheets using masking tape. Ask for some examples of other ideas generated during the group discussions.

5. Lead a concluding discussion based on the following questions, using the flip chart to record responses:
   - How difficult was it to generate a variety of solutions to this problem? Why was it difficult or not? Did your group withhold initial judgment of an idea until it had been discussed? If not, why? How did this impact the generation of ideas?
   - What are your personal reactions to the various solutions? Is there only one right answer to this situation? Why or why not?
   - How did your group decide on a "best solution"? Did you consider various risk factors before making your decision? Why or why not?
   - How does group problem solving increase an individual's ability to think creatively? Are there occasions when it might be a hindrance to creativity? If so, when?
   - What insights did you gain regarding problem solving and decision making in general?
   - What factors influenced the behaviors and outcomes in this activity? What do you think your group did well during the exercise? Why do you think that? Could your group have done anything differently to improve its functioning? If so, what?
   - Overall, what are the advantages of working together as a group? What are some disadvantages?
   - What are some examples of a past experience in which you wish there had been better teamwork? Would the outcome have been different? If so, how?
   - What guidelines can a group establish to help facilitate better teamwork?

Team Time Worksheet

Situation

The first pair of paramedics arrived at the accident at 6:15 P.M. It was already dark. Three adults were standing at the edge of the pond. Twenty-five feet out, there was a hole in the ice. A young boy was in the water and holding onto a fallen tree. When the medics called for assistance, they were told everyone was at a fire across town. They could expect no backup for at least 15 minutes.

Instructions

Your group has 20 minutes to generate *at least* five solutions to the problem and to agree on the BEST solution. Use the chart below to record your ideas.

IDEA	REASON
1.	
2.	
3.	
4.	
5.	
6.	
7.	

➤ Weekend Getaway

Goals

1. To encourage groups to share available resources.
2. To explore how one group may need to rely on other groups for necessary resources.
3. To practice creative problem solving.
4. To examine ways to increase the level of creativity used in the problem-solving approach.

Group Size   Four groups of four to seven persons each.

Time Required   1 to 1½ hours.

Materials

1. A Weekend Getaway Situation Card for each group.
2. Six Weekend Getaway Resource Cards for each group.
3. Paper and a pencil for each participant.

Physical Setting   A separate table should be provided for each group, with sufficient room for participants to move between tables.

Process

1. Prior to the session, prepare the Weekend Getaway Situation Cards and Resource Cards (two sheets) by cutting each sheet into individual cards.
2. At the session, direct the participants to form four groups of four to seven persons each.
3. Randomly distribute a Weekend Getaway Situation Card and six Weekend Getaway Resource Cards to each group. Provide paper and a pencil for each participant.
4. Explain that each group is on a weekend trip and has encountered a dilemma, as designated by the Situation Card. Using only the resources provided, the group will have

10 minutes in which to begin to devise a detailed rescue plan. The plans will be judged on their originality and effectiveness.

5. Signal for the task to begin, allow approximately 10 minutes for group work, and then stop the activity.

6. Explain that groups now will have an additional 15 minutes in which to refine their rescue plans by having the opportunity to exchange resources with other groups. However, they must observe the following two rules:
   - The Situation Card must remain with the original group.
   - No group may have more than six Resource Cards at any one time.

7. Signal for the task to resume, allow approximately 15 minutes for group work, and then stop the activity.

8. Ask each group to report on its situation, the resources used, and the final escape plan.

9. Lead a discussion by asking the following questions:
   - How did your group coordinate the exchange of Resource Cards with other groups?
   - How many of the original Resource Cards did your group use in the final rescue plan?
   - Were some resources more valuable to your group than others? Why was that? Did they hold the same value for all groups? Why or why not?
   - How does the exchange of resources with other groups in the workplace help meet team goals? How does resource sharing help meet organizational goals?

10. Explain that this activity required that groups use both creativity and logical reasoning. Ask:
    - In your opinion, which group devised the most effective or logical plan? Why?
    - Which group devised the most creative plan? What made it seem the most creative to you?
    - How difficult was it to be creative in using the available resources while still focusing on analytical or logical reasoning? Why was it difficult?

- What are some things that a work group can do to add more creativity to their problem-solving efforts?

Variation   If you are working with intact work groups, distribute newsprint sheets and felt-tipped markers and have each group record suggestions for guidelines that address the following issues:

- Situations in which the group must rely on resources from outside the group.
- Kinds of resources necessary.
- Ways in which resources could be obtained.
- Resources within the group that can be provided to other groups.

Weekend Getaway Situation Cards

The group is caught in a snowstorm while hiking in the mountains.	The group is caught in the cave-in of an abandoned mine.
The group is being held hostage in a remote cabin by escaped convicts.	The group is accidentally locked in an abandoned warehouse.

Weekend Getaway Resource Cards—1

COMPASS	4 BALLOONS
8 CANDLES	BUCKET
FLASHLIGHT	100 PAPER CLIPS
STRAW BASKET	HAMMER & NAILS
MASKING TAPE	10-FT. ROPE
SAFETY MATCHES	BOX OF STRAWS

Weekend Getaway Resource Cards—2

ALUMINUM FOIL	100 THUMB TACKS
BACK PACK	NECKTIE
FLASHLIGHT	STYROFOAM COOLER
CAN OF COLA	RUBBER BANDS
100 TOOTHPICKS	50-FT. FISHING LINE
SCISSORS	POCKET KNIFE

Relationship-Oriented Process

Introduction to Relationship-Oriented Process

The activities in the Relationship-Oriented Process category explore ways to maintain good working relationships within the group, including group cohesiveness, trust, collaboration, conflict management, and negotiation.

Even if every group member knows and understands the goals, member roles, and responsibilities, and there are effective group procedures in place, the group could become ineffective and dissatisfying if group members do not get along well enough with one another. Relationship-oriented processes, along with task-oriented processes, balance together to create an effectively performing group. This dynamic of the group refers to the personal and social needs of group members that contribute to group cohesion. It is the "how" dynamic that the group uses to facilitate task accomplishment. Some key elements that identify good relationships include trust, mutual respect, reliability and dependability, adequate interaction with one another, efforts to resolve conflicts constructively, an understanding and acceptance of one another's roles and goals, a sense of fairness, efforts to build commitment rather than compliance, and recognition of mutual interests.

Group cohesiveness activities emphasize the sense of belonging that an individual feels by being a member of the group. They present situations in which participants explore their links to other members of the group and to the group as a whole.

Trust activities assess the level of confidence that a group member has in the integrity, ability, character, and truth of another individual or a particular process. For a group that is in the stage of forming or one that has been faced with ongoing disagreement, confrontation, and escalating conflict, mutual trust becomes much more elusive. To further establish or regain trust, communication, consistency, and cooperative initiatives can be introduced.

Activities that support *collaboration* deal with situations in which group members are asked to work together to produce an integrated joint effort, such as that found in the concept of teamwork. It integrates and builds on the mutual interests of all members of the group, and it simultaneously shows concern for both task and relationships. Collaboration is also the most difficult but potentially most rewarding approach to conflict resolution.

Conflict is a natural phenomenon in groups; it is merely the result of having the benefit of people with different perspectives. It has certain advantages as well as disadvantages. *Conflict management* activities look at the process of managing differences among the ideas, perceptions, beliefs, and goals of individuals within a group. Conflict situations are basically dealt with in five different ways: *avoidance, accommodation, competition, compromise,* or *collaboration. Cooperative competition* (co-opetition) is a concept that recognizes that competing groups can cooperate with one another to meet the needs of each group.

Negotiation activities involve a reciprocal communication process that is used to identify a basis of agreement between two parties with conflicting interests. Through discussion the conflicting parties examine specific issues, explain their positions, and exchange offers and counteroffers.

➤ All Tied Up

Goals
1. To explore the concept of teamwork.
2. To demonstrate the cohesiveness of team members.
3. To use as an icebreaker activity at the beginning of a session.

Group Size   Several groups of five to eight persons each.

Time Required   15 minutes.

Materials   A ball of soft string or yarn for each team (with the same length of string on each).

Physical Setting   A room large enough that the groups can form lines and move freely while carrying out their instructions.

Process
1. Direct the participants to form groups of five to eight persons each. Instruct the groups to form a line, standing side by side.
2. Provide the first player on each team with a ball of string. Explain that, upon your signal, the first player is to hold onto the end of the string and hand the ball to the next player. The next player is to hold onto the string and unwind enough so that he or she can pass the ball along the *front* of the line to the third player, and so on. When the ball of string reaches the person at the far end of the line, that player then hands the ball of string *behind* his or her back to the player it just came from, then on down the line to once again return to the front of the line. This process is repeated until all the string is used. The first group to be wrapped up using all the string wins. Repeat the instructions if necessary.
3. Signal for the task to begin. Stop the activity when a group uses all its string and announce the winner. Direct the groups to carefully unwind the string.

4. Lead a discussion based on the following questions:
   - How does this activity demonstrate the concept of teamwork in general?
   - What impact did the size of the group have on your ability to accomplish this task? How does group size influence a group's ability to perform in the workplace?
   - How did the activity demonstrate aspects of group cohesiveness?
   - What are some ways to increase group cohesiveness in the workplace without "binding" the roles of individual members?

Variation Have an untying relay with the same rules, as each group tries to untie itself first.

➤ At Issue

Goals
1. To identify subjective elements involved in conflict.
2. To discuss the influence of personal biases on group member relationships, conflict, and decision making.
3. To develop ways to identify and overcome bias.

Group Size   Several groups of three or four persons each.

Time Required   1½ to 2 hours.

Materials
1. A copy of each of the At Issue Resource Sheets (1 and 2) for the facilitator.
2. Paper and a pencil for each participant.
3. A newsprint flip chart and felt-tipped markers for recording.
4. A copy of a conflict story or article for each participant.

Physical Setting   A room large enough for groups to work without disturbing one another. Writing surfaces should be provided.

Process
1. Prior to the session, obtain a story or article from a current newspaper, magazine, or work source that describes a "conflict" situation or controversial issue.
2. Begin the activity by reading aloud the situation printed on the At Issue Resource Sheet 1. Solicit responses to the question posed at the end of the story. *(Some possible answers: the point of view, the accuracy of information, the completeness of the information, and the training of the person.)*
3. Ask participants to identify all the possible elements involved in a conflict; in other words, factors that create subjective influence. Distribute paper and a pencil to each participant. Record responses on the flip chart. *(Some possible answers: age, experience, education, values, upbringing, interests and hobbies, expectations, politics, geographic location, class status.)*

4. Facilitate a general discussion on these factors that affect individual perceptions and ideas, and then lead the discussion to the identification of bias *(a preference or an inclination, especially one that inhibits impartial judgment).*

5. Referring to the flip chart, tell the participants that they now will have an opportunity to discuss these elements in terms of a current situation.

6. Direct the participants to form groups of three or four persons each and assign a number to each group. Distribute a copy of the conflict article or story to each participant.

7. Ask the participants to read the story and to use the list of conflict elements identified earlier to discuss how they relate to the story, keeping in mind the concept of bias. Allow approximately 15 minutes for the discussion.

8. Explain that the groups will be assigned questions relating to the story according to their group designations. Using the At Issue Resource Sheet 2, assign one or two questions to each group, depending on the amount of time and the number of groups involved. Allow approximately 10 minutes of discussion time for each assigned question.

9. Ask each group to share its question(s) and group responses. Use the group responses to facilitate a class discussion by inviting other participants to challenge responses, stating whether they agree or disagree and giving reasons for their choices.

10. Lead a concluding discussion by asking the following questions:
    - In what ways can bias influence the climate of an organization? How does this impact the behaviors and feelings of its member groups? How does it affect the perception of the organization by others?
    - How does personal bias affect the working relationships among group members?
    - How can personal biases lead to conflict situations? Give some real-world examples.
    - How does bias impact our ability to make valid decisions? Give some examples.

• What are some ways for individuals to overcome bias in order to manage or resolve conflict? What can be done to eliminate bias in order to make more valid decisions? How can the group process support these actions?

Variations

1. Have the group as a whole determine a possible solution to the conflict discussed in the article.
2. Have the groups or group as a whole offer a solution to the conflict based on a unique point of view; for example, as a fish in the Lake Erie story on Resource Sheet 1.

At Issue Resource Sheet 1

You have recently moved into an area surrounding Lake Erie. In the mail you receive a notice of a community meeting that concerns the pollution of Lake Erie and its potential health hazards. As the parent of two young children, you are concerned and decide to attend the meeting.

A panel of persons has been assembled to address the concerns of the community regarding the situation. The panel consists of a housewife, a farmer, the president of the Save Lake Erie Club, and a government ecologist. Each person speaks in turn.

You have to decide who you will believe so that you can take a stand on the issue.

WHAT DO YOU HAVE TO CONSIDER BEFORE YOU DECIDE WHO YOU WILL BELIEVE?

At Issue Resource Sheet 2

1. How valid is the information used by each element involved in the conflict?

2. What additional information do you need to help you make an informed decision?

3. What are three facts and three opinions in the story?

4. What are three causes and three effects in the story?

5. What are the proposed solutions to the problem?

6. What is an alternative solution to the problem discussed in the story?

7. Whom will you believe regarding this issue and why?

⊒ Big Pushover

Goals
1. To examine the effect of competition on group dynamics.
2. To discuss ways of resolving conflict.
3. To build team cohesion through a physical group activity.

Group Size   Twelve to twenty participants, who will work in two
   equal-size teams.

Time Required   15 minutes.

Materials
1. Masking tape.
2. Rope (approximately 20 to 25 feet long).

Physical Setting   A large open area.

Process
1. Prior to the session, use the masking tape to mark three small
   parallel lines on the ground, each about 10 feet apart. Lay the
   rope on the ground so that it lies along the middle tape and is
   parallel to the two outer tape lines.
2. At the session, direct the participants to form two equal-size
   teams. Instruct members from each team to line up behind the
   outer tape lines, side by side, with one group facing the other.
3. Explain that this game is played the exact opposite way from
   "Tug of War." At a given signal, the groups will pick up the rope
   and try to PUSH it over the tape line behind the opposing team.
4. Signal for the groups to begin. Make note of each group's actions
   and interactions. Stop the activity after one group has pushed
   the rope behind the opposing team or after approximately
   8 minutes.

5. Lead a discussion based on the following questions:
   - What insights and impressions did you gain from the activity?
   - How did the competitive nature of the activity influence behaviors and outcomes?
   - How well did your team work together during the activity? What behaviors were displayed? In what ways could the team have improved its effectiveness?
   - How does your experience relate to what happens in the workplace? Give some examples.
   - Conflicts can involve both pushing (like this game) and pulling (like Tug of War). What are some ways in which a group can help resolve conflicts in the workplace? What can individual members of the group do to help resolve conflicts?

➤ Blind Faith

Goals

1. To place individual trust in other members of the group.
2. To practice giving clear and precise directions to others.
3. To build cohesion within a group.

Group Size   Several groups of four or five persons each.

Time Required   20 to 30 minutes.

Materials

1. A blindfold for each group.
2. Several beanbags, sheets of paper, cardboard squares, books, Frisbees®, and other stationary objects for each group.

Physical Setting   A large open space that allows each group to carry out the instructions.

Process

1. Direct the participants to form groups of four or five persons each. Designate a particular work area for each group.
2. Provide a blindfold to one member from each group and ask him or her to secure it in place. Distribute several stationary objects to each group and ask group members to place the objects in various locations within the designated work area, each one approximately three or four large paces apart from the others.
3. Explain that the blindfolded person in each group must step on each object by taking directions from other members of the group. Group members can call only one direction at a time and then must allow the blindfolded participant to carry out the whole direction before calling out another one.
4. Allow approximately 5 to 10 minutes for the task, observing the interactions and making note of the directions given.

5. Lead a concluding discussion based on the following questions:
   - What impressions and insights did you gain from the activity?
   - For those blindfolded, what role did trust take during the task? How did trust influence your behavior?
   - For those giving the directions, how did you feel about the trust placed in you? How did this influence your behavior?
   - What kinds of directions were more helpful? Which were less helpful? How could the communication process have been improved? How do clear and precise instructions impact our ability to perform effectively?
   - How does this exercise relate to what is happening in your own work group? How can group trust be increased?

Variation   Time the first event. Select a new group member to be blindfolded and direct the groups to move the objects into different locations. Repeat step 3 and time the second event to see if the groups can better their initial records.

⊃ Bouncers

Goals
1. To examine the concept of collaboration.
2. To show the interdependent nature of teamwork.
3. To build cohesion within a group.
4. To provide an icebreaker activity at the beginning of a session.

Group Size   Several groups of four or five persons each.

Time Required   15 to 20 minutes.

Materials   Two large round inflated balloons for each group.

Physical Setting   A room large enough that the groups can move around freely in an unrestricted fashion.

Process
1. Direct the participants to form groups of four or five persons each. Instruct the members of each group to hold hands and stand in a circle.
2. Explain that group members will bounce a balloon in the air without letting go of one another's hands. If the balloon lands on the ground, they must pick it up and start it bouncing in the air again without letting go of anyone's hands.
3. Provide each group with a balloon and signal for the task to begin. Allow several minutes and then ask the groups to stop.
4. Explain that this time, the group members are to follow the same rules with two balloons. Distribute an additional balloon to each group and signal for the task to begin. Allow several minutes and then ask the groups to stop.
5. Lead a concluding discussion based on the following questions:
   • What were your personal reactions to this activity? How did others seem to be reacting?
   • How well did your group do with bouncing one balloon?

- How well did your group do with bouncing two balloons? What factors contributed to the outcome? What, if anything, could your group have done differently?
- What would you predict would happen if your group tried to bounce three balloons? Why?
- How does this activity relate to the concept of collaboration?
- How can you relate this activity to the interdependent nature of teamwork? How does this relate to what happens in the workplace?

Variation   Mark off a section of the room for each group. Explain that the group members must remain in this area while accomplishing the two tasks. Discuss how restrictions in the workplace can impact the effectiveness of teams.

➤ Bumper-Idiom

Goals

1. To examine individual perceptions of teamwork.
2. To communicate characteristics of teamwork through a bumper sticker slogan.
3. To create cohesiveness among group members.
4. To provide an icebreaker activity at the beginning of a session.

Group Size   Several groups of three to five persons each.

Time Required   30 to 45 minutes.

Materials

1. Three 3-inch by 5-inch index cards and a pencil for each participant.
2. One 4¼-inch by 11-inch sheet of card stock for each group.
3. Several felt-tipped markers in a variety of colors for each group.

Physical Setting   A room large enough for groups to work without disturbing one another. Writing surfaces should be provided.

Process

1. Prior to the session, cut a sheet of 8½-inch by 11-inch card stock in half lengthwise, creating two 4¼-inch by 11-inch strips.
2. At the session, direct participants to form groups of three to five persons each.
3. Distribute three index cards and a pencil to each participant. Tell participants that they will have approximately 2 minutes to write on each card a single word that expresses something related to the concept of "teamwork."
4. After approximately 2 minutes, collect all the cards. Shuffle the cards and redistribute them by giving each group six cards and placing the excess cards aside. Distribute one cut card-stock strip and several felt-tipped markers to each group.

5. Explain that after examining their cards, groups will create a group slogan that utilizes all the words. They will use the slogan to design a decorative bumper sticker. Groups will have 15 minutes to design and decorate their bumper stickers.

6. After approximately 15 minutes, stop the task. Ask a member from each group to share the group's bumper sticker with everyone.

7. Lead a concluding discussion based on the following questions:
   - How difficult was it to create a concise slogan for the bumper sticker? Why was that true?
   - What are some common key words or phrases that occurred among the slogans?
   - How did the perceptions of teamwork differ? Were they mostly positive or negative? What factors can influence individual views on teamwork?
   - How can a slogan or motto encourage individuals to work together as a group? In what other ways are slogans and mottoes used in an organization?

Variation Instruct the groups to post the bumper sticker cards around the room for the remainder of a training session.

➤ Button Up

Goals
1. To compete with members of the same group.
2. To discuss the concepts of conflict and competition.

Group Size   Several groups of four persons each.

Time Required   15 to 20 minutes.

Materials   A large button with four holes and four 6-foot lengths of embroidery thread or string for each group.

Physical Setting   A large open-space area in which the groups can carry out the task.

Process
1. Prior to the session, tie one length of thread or string in each of the four holes in the buttons.
2. At the session, direct the participants to form groups of four persons each. Distribute a prepared button to each group and instruct the group members to each hold a string end, standing approximately an equal distance apart.
3. Explain that the object of the game is to capture the button from the other players. When the signal is given, the group members are to try to maneuver their strings by pulling, snapping, loosening suddenly to throw another player off balance, or jerking quickly when another player tries to loosen or take up slack. If a player's string is let go or breaks, that individual is out of the match, while the others continue.
4. Give a signal and allow the groups approximately 5 to 10 minutes for play.
5. Lead a concluding discussion based on the following questions:
   • What were your feelings and reactions while competing with other members of your own group? How did others react?
   • During the activity, who did what to whom? Did people "change position" during play? If they did, what was the result?

- Under what circumstances is competition beneficial? *(for example, motivation to do your best, as in sports)*
- How can we relate what occurred in this activity to conflict situations in general?
- How does your experience relate to what is happening in your workplace?

Variation   To make the play more difficult, have the participants be seated for the game so that they cannot change positions.

➤ Clash Action

Goals

1. To assess personal and organizational methods of dealing with conflict.
2. To identify active and passive approaches to handling conflict.
3. To relate conflict resolution to problem solving.

Group Size   Several groups of four or five persons each.

Time Required   45 minutes to 1 hour.

Materials

1. A copy of the Clash Action Worksheet and a pencil for each participant.
2. A newsprint sheet listing the number and key word(s) for each of the fourteen conflict methods shown on the worksheet.
3. Two felt-tipped markers in different colors for recording data.
4. Masking tape.

Physical Setting   A room large enough for groups to work without disturbing one another. Writing surfaces should be provided. Wall space is required for posting newsprint sheets.

Process

1. Explain that conflict resolution is difficult when individuals are locked into old patterns of thinking or planned solutions. This activity will give the participants an opportunity to open up new ways of thinking and communicating to help deal with conflict.
2. Distribute a copy of the Clash Action Worksheet and a pencil to each participant. Read aloud the instructions at the top of the sheet. Allow sufficient time for all participants to complete the survey, and then collect the unsigned sheets.
3. Direct the participants to form groups of four or five persons each. Tell the groups that they are to conduct a discussion based on the following statement:

"There is a tendency for people to see themselves differently from the way they see others in the organization when it comes to handling conflict."

4. During the discussion time, tabulate the data from the worksheets. On the prepared newsprint sheet, record the totals for each of the fourteen conflict methods, using one color for individual scores and another for organizational scores. Stop the group discussions after you have finished recording all the data. Use masking tape to post the sheet.

5. Referring to the newsprint sheet, review the scores for the conflict methods and compare the number of positive versus negative methods used. Ask:
   • What trends, if any, are revealed by this data?
   • How does the data shown here reflect the input made during your previous group discussion?

6. Using the worksheet, read each statement in turn, having the participants identify the method as being either an "ACTIVE" (2, 3, 6, 8, 10, 12, 13, 14) or a "PASSIVE" (1, 4, 5, 7, 9, 11) way of dealing with conflict.

7. Explain that a passive approach avoids or ignores the conflict and does not reduce its occurrence. In terms of the active methods identified, numbers 6, 8, 10, and 12 are more positive approaches because they are not negative or punitive.

8. Lead a concluding discussion by asking the following questions:
   • What are some general ground rules that a group can establish to help manage conflict?
   • Why are data gathering, listening, and reflection so important to conflict resolution?
   • How is conflict resolution logically related to the overall problem-solving process?

Variation   Use as a carryover activity in a two-day workshop by having participants complete the Worksheets at the end of day one and then revealing the completed flip chart of tabulations at the beginning of day two.

Clash Action Worksheet

Instructions: The following is a list of fourteen statements that describe ways to handle conflict. (1) In the column labeled "YOURSELF," place an X next to the FIVE methods that you truthfully find yourself using MOST OFTEN. (2) In the column labeled "ORGANIZATION," place an X next to the FIVE methods of handling conflict that you believe are used MOST by the majority of others in your organization. *Your answers will be kept confidential, so be honest!*

METHODS FOR HANDLING CONFLICT	YOURSELF	ORGANIZATION
1. Be **indirect** and only hint at feelings or problems that bother you.		
2. Find something **outside your control** to blame the situation on.		
3. Seek a specific **scapegoat.**		
4. Use **sarcasm** when talking about the conflict situation with others.		
5. Make an effort to **smooth** the tension over or to live with the situation.		
6. **Blow up** and let people know just exactly how you feel or how angry the situation makes you.		
7. **Hide your feelings** at the moment and only reveal them later to friends or confidantes in private.		
8. Attempt to get more **information or clarification** on the situation in general.		
9. Work out your feelings by putting energy and attention into other **unrelated activities** or interests.		
10. Listen and gather additional information by **talking** directly with those involved.		
11. Back down under pressure by **yielding or agreeing** rather than dealing with the conflict source.		
12. Make an active attempt to **compromise.**		
13. Complain to others about the **unfairness** of the situation.		
14. Seek out creative **alternatives** to the situation or new ways of approaching the conflict.		

➤ Don't Label Me

Goals
1. To identify ways in which we assign labels to people.
2. To examine the impact of stereotyping on interrelationships.

Group Size   One or more groups of six to ten persons each.

Time Required   20 to 30 minutes.

Materials   An adhesive label for each participant with one of the following phrases, allowing for at least one different phrase for each member of a group: Ignore me; Praise me; Agree with me; Disagree with me; Treat me as though I'm stupid; Treat me as an expert; Correct everything I say.

Physical Setting   A room large enough for groups to work without disturbing one another.

Process
1. Direct the participants to form groups of six to ten persons each.
2. Apply one label to each person's forehead, keeping the instructions on the label concealed from that person. Be sure to use a variety of different labels for each group.
3. Provide the groups with a specific topic of discussion and allow approximately 10 to 15 minutes for the group members to thoroughly discuss the issue.
4. After an appropriate amount of discussion time, stop the activity. Ask group members to try to guess their individual labels.
5. Lead a concluding discussion based on the following questions:
   - Were you able to identify your individual label? What behaviors by others helped you to determine this?
   - What kinds of labels occur in our everyday lives? What impact do these labels have?
   - How does stereotyping affect our ability to interrelate with others?
   - What can be done to eliminate stereotyping in the workplace?

➤ Down to Basics

Goals

1. To identify characteristics of teamwork.
2. To observe how individual efforts contribute to the team effort.
3. To examine the impact of competition on team effort.

Group Size   Several groups of three to five persons each.

Time Required   40 minutes to 1 hour.

Materials

1. A copy of the Down to Basics Worksheet and a pencil for each group.
2. A clock or timer.
3. A newsprint flip chart and felt-tipped markers for recording.
4. Masking tape.
5. Prizes for the winning group (optional).

Physical Setting   A room large enough for groups to work without disturbing one another. Writing surfaces should be provided. Wall space is needed for posting newsprint sheets.

Process

1. Direct participants to form groups of three to five members each.
2. Explain that each group will utilize all its members in a combined effort to accomplish a task.
3. Distribute a copy of the Down to Basics Worksheet and a pencil to each group. Refer to the worksheet and read the directions aloud.
4. Signal for the activity to begin, time it for exactly 10 minutes, and then announce for groups to stop.
5. Ask each group to record on the worksheet the total number of words generated in the time allotment. Identify the group with the highest total as the winner. (As an option, you may choose to present prizes to the group members.)

6. As a group, review the set of words generated for each letter, in turn, by recording the words on the flip chart as the groups present them. Encourage any further additions to the list of words before moving on to the next letter. Use masking tape to post the sheets.

7. Lead a concluding discussion based on the following questions:
   - How well did your group do in accomplishing this task? What factors contributed to this?
   - What role did each individual play in the overall team effort? How does this relate to what happens in the workplace?
   - Did the desire to win have any impact on the task? How does the "spirit of competition" help groups to put forth their best efforts as a unified team? How does competition deter teams from working together with other groups?
   - What are some ways you can incorporate the team characteristics we have identified into your own work group back in the workplace?

Variations

1. Create a team guide by choosing one word for each letter of TEAMWORK. Ask participants to vote on the most popular word for each, and then assign one or more words to each group, which will come up with some phrases or guidelines pertaining to each word. Collect the information and, after the session, duplicate a customized version of the guide for each participant.

2. Create additional worksheets with words relating to other concepts, such as CONFLICT, QUALITY, and so forth.

Down to Basics Worksheet

Instructions: For each letter in the word TEAMWORK, your group is to list as many single words as possible that describe some aspect of teamwork, beginning with each designated letter. For example, the letter "T" might include "trust" as a listed word. This task will be accomplished by starting the worksheet and pencil with one member of the group who must enter a word for the "T" (other than the example), who will then pass the worksheet and pencil to the next member, who must enter a word for the "E," who will pass the worksheet and pencil to the next member, who must enter a word for the "A," and so forth.

The goal is to enter the most words possible for each letter in turn during a 10-minute period. The group with the highest total score will be declared the winner. Select the first player and wait for your facilitator to give the signal to begin.

T	
E	
A	
M	
W	
O	
R	
K	

➤ Drawing on the Group

Goals
1. To communicate group inclusion through visual representations.
2. To examine the impact of physical proximity on group cohesiveness.
3. To build cohesion within a group.

Group Size   Several groups of five to seven persons each.

Time Required   45 minutes.

Materials
1. A newsprint sheet and a set of crayons or felt-tipped markers for each group.
2. Masking tape.

Physical Setting   A room large enough for all groups to each form a standing circle; a chair for each participant is required for group discussion. Writing surfaces should be provided. Wall space is required for posting newsprint sheets.

Process
1. Direct the participants to form groups of five to seven persons each, asking them to stand in a circle without giving any specific information on how far from or how close to stand to one another. After a few moments, tell members of the groups to hold hands. Ask:
   - How do you feel now? Are you more or less comfortable than you were? Why?
   - Do you feel a greater sense of group unity? Why or why not?
   - Do you feel more or less "free"? Why?
2. Tell the group members to let go and, while remaining in approximately the same positions, turn their backs so that they face outward from the circle. Ask:
   - Do you feel more or less comfortable now? More or less "free"? Do you still feel an integral part of the group?

- Is there any difference in the way you now feel about the group? Why is that?

3. Ask the members of each group to sit together for the next part of the activity. Distribute a newsprint sheet and a set of crayons or felt-tipped markers to each group. Instruct each group to draw a visual representation of what the members think is their combined "group identity." (If questions arise asking for more details, prompt the groups to think about how all the members come together to form a group without leading the groups in any one direction.) They will have 15 minutes to complete the pictures.

4. When the groups have finished the pictures, provide masking tape and ask them to post them around the room. Ask each group in turn to describe in words what its picture represents.

5. Lead a concluding discussion based on the following questions:
   - What impressions and insights did you gain from this activity?
   - How important is it for an individual to feel a part of a group? How does this impact the overall relationship process within a group? How does it impact a group's ability to complete tasks?
   - How does physical proximity of group members impact its cohesiveness? What are some unique challenges faced by members of a virtual team?
   - How did your group come to agreement on what to put into its drawing? What basic group values or goals were depicted?

Variation   After the newsprint sheets are posted, ask other groups to make some observations on what they think is being represented in each picture before having the target group describe its picture.

➤ In the Middle

Goals
1. To examine individual responses to conflict.
2. To discuss common factors contributing to conflict situations.
3. To identify ways to manage conflict.

Group Size   Eight to twenty-five participants.

Time Required   10 to 15 minutes.

Physical Setting   A room large enough that the participants can move around freely in an unrestricted fashion.

Process
1. Place yourself in the middle of the room and ask the participants to gather around you.
2. Tell the participants:
   "Imagine that I represent *conflict*. Think about how you usually react when you experience a conflict personally or witness a conflict happening nearby. Then place yourself, in relation to me, somewhere in the room in a way that indicates your *first response* to conflict or disagreement. Think about your body position, the direction that you are facing, and the distance you want to be from conflict."
3. Once the participants have found a position relative to you in the room, ask individuals to explain why they are standing where they are.
4. Next, tell the participants:
   "If this represents your first reaction to conflict, what might your *second* reaction be, after thinking about the conflict? Change your position relative to me if you wish."
   Note whether or not anyone changed position and ask why the change occurred.

5. Lead a concluding discussion by asking the following questions:
   - What insights and impressions did you gain from this activity?
   - In general, how is conflict usually handled in your work environment? Is it effective? Why or why not?
   - What are some common factors that can contribute to conflict situations? (*for example, lack of information, misunderstanding, miscommunication, assumptions, different opinions or values*)
   - What are some specific things a group can do to actively manage conflict?

➤ In the Spirit of Things

Goals
1. To explore perceptions of conflict and cooperation.
2. To use creativity in describing implied concepts.
3. To practice consensus decision making.
4. To develop strategies to improve teamwork.

Group Size   Several groups of five to seven persons each.

Time Required   1 to 1½ hours.

Materials
1. A copy of the In the Spirit of Things Worksheet for each participant.
2. A pencil for each participant.
3. A copy of the In the Spirit of Things Group Worksheet for each participant.
4. A newsprint flip chart and felt-tipped markers for recording.

Physical Setting   A room large enough for groups to work without disturbing one another. Writing surfaces should be provided.

Process
1. Distribute a copy of the In the Spirit of Things Worksheet and a pencil to each participant. Explain that individuals should use their imagination to answer the ten questions with a single word each.
2. Allow approximately 5 minutes for the task and then tell participants to stop.
3. Divide the participants into groups of five to seven persons each. Group members should discuss their answers to the worksheet, giving some reasons as to why they responded as they did. Allow approximately 10 minutes for discussion.
4. Lead a discussion by asking the following questions:
   • Which questions were the most difficult to answer? Why was that?

- How similar were individual answers among the various members of your group?
- Did other members of your group have difficulty making a connection between your imagery and the concept? Why or why not?

5. Distribute a copy of the In the Spirit of Things Group Worksheet to each participant. Explain that groups will have approximately 15 minutes to come to agreement (consensus) on a one-word answer to each question along with a reason.

6. After the time is up, refer to each question in turn and ask groups to provide their answers. Record the answers on the flip chart.

7. Lead a concluding discussion based on the following questions:
   - How similar were the responses from group to group? What may have contributed to their being similar or different?
   - What approach did your group take in order to reach consensus on the answers? Was it a difficult process? Why or why not? What roles did cooperation and conflict play in the decision-making process?
   - What did you learn about cooperation and conflict from this activity? What changes in your work environment can be made to make teamwork more effective?

Variations

1. If time permits, provide each group with a newsprint sheet and felt-tipped marker, and then instruct groups to develop a list of specific strategies or rules that can be used to improve teamwork in terms of cooperation and conflict management. Direct groups to post their sheets and have each group present a verbal report.

2. If the participants are members of intact work groups, provide each group with a sheet of poster board, scissors, glue, and several magazines, and then instruct them to create a collage representing their current group environments in terms of cooperation and conflict.

In the Spirit of Things Worksheet

Instructions: As an individual, you will have 5 minutes to provide a one-word answer to each of the following questions as well as a brief explanation of the reason for your answer.

1. What TEMPERATURE is COLLABORATION?

2. What SEASON is HARMONY?

3. What SOUND is FRIENDSHIP?

4. What SHAPE is AVOIDANCE?

5. What ANIMAL is TEAMWORK?

6. What SMELL is COOPERATION?

7. What SHAPE is CONFLICT?

8. What is VEHICLE is DISAGREEMENT?

9. What COLOR is COMPETITION?

10. What FRUIT is NEGOTIATION?

In the Spirit of Things Group Worksheet

Instructions: You will have 15 minutes to decide on a single answer that represents the opinion of all members of the group and the reasoning for each answer. Do not use voting to arrive at the answers, but fully discuss the responses made by individuals on the first worksheet.

1. What TEMPERATURE is COLLABORATION?

2. What SEASON is HARMONY?

3. What SOUND is FRIENDSHIP?

4. What SHAPE is AVOIDANCE?

5. What ANIMAL is TEAMWORK?

6. What SMELL is COOPERATION?

7. What SHAPE is CONFLICT?

8. What VEHICLE is DISAGREEMENT?

9. What COLOR is COMPETITION?

10. What FRUIT is NEGOTIATION?

➣ Mentoring Memoirs

Goals
1. To identify various mentoring relationships.
2. To identify characteristics of effective mentoring relationships.
3. To discuss how mentoring and coaching efforts support individual and group development.

Group Size   Several groups of four or five persons each.

Time Required   30 to 40 minutes.

Materials
1. Paper and a pencil for each participant.
2. A newsprint flip chart and felt-tipped markers for recording.
3. Masking tape.

Physical Setting   A room large enough for groups to work without disturbing one another. Writing surfaces should be provided. Wall space is needed to post newsprint sheets.

Process
1. Direct the participants to form groups of four or five persons each. Distribute paper and a pencil to each participant.
2. Explain that, according to *The American Heritage Dictionary*, a mentor is defined as "a wise and trusted counselor or teacher." Ask the participants to individually reflect on what comes to mind when considering the characteristics of a mentor. Allow a few moments for reflection, and then ask the groups to create a list of paired fictional characters from literature, film, theater, or television that they think portray mentoring relationships. You may give one or more of the following examples: Yoda and Luke Skywalker, Wizard of Oz and Dorothy, Henry Higgins and Eliza Doolittle.
3. Allow approximately 10 minutes for group discussion, and then ask for at least one example from each group in round-robin

format until all possible examples have been given. Record the
pairs on a newsprint flip chart sheet, and then post the list.

4. Explain that, in the work environment, the definition of a
   mentor can be expanded to identify "an experienced, productive
   senior employee who helps develop a less experienced
   employee." Instruct the groups to discuss some relationships
   they have experienced or observed in the workplace that fit
   this definition of a mentor. Allow the groups approximately
   10 minutes to complete the task.

5. Facilitate a brainstorming session on the characteristics of an
   effective mentoring relationship. List the information on a
   newsprint flip chart sheet and then use masking tape to post
   the list.

6. Lead a concluding discussion based on the following questions:
   - Did the relationships in the fictional examples identified by
     your group support these mentoring characteristics? Why or
     why not? How closely did the relationships in the work
     examples support these characteristics? Give some examples.
   - Are some of the identified relationships stronger examples of
     mentoring than others? Which ones and why?
   - Based on your own life experiences, have you known someone
     who acted as a mentor? Describe the situation.
   - Is there a difference between mentoring and coaching? If so,
     what makes the difference?
   - How can mentors and coaches support the growth and
     development of an individual? How does this strengthen the
     group as a whole?

   Note to the Facilitator   *Mentoring and coaching are two types of
   interpersonal relationships that allow employees to develop skills and
   increase their knowledge about an organization and its customers. As
   stated above, a mentor is generally an experienced, productive senior
   employee who helps develop a less experienced employee. A coach is
   usually defined as a peer or manager who works with an employee in
   terms of motivation, developing skills, and providing reinforcement
   and feedback. Although both mentors and coaches provide assistance
   in terms of individual development, the major difference between the
   two occurs most often in the degree to which the relationship exists.*

Mentoring can include both formal and informal relationships that provide both career support (coaching, protection, sponsorship, and providing challenging assignments, exposure, and visibility) and psychosocial support (friend and role model). Coaching is generally associated with task accomplishment more than interpersonal relationship in which the coach provides feedback and resources and sets up learning experiences.

Resource

Noe, R.A. (2002). Employee development. In *Employee training and development* (2nd ed.), pp. 303–309. New York: McGraw Hill/Irwin.

➤ Model Behavior

Goals

1. To compare conflict and cooperation by building a representative model of each.
2. To examine how conflict can be changed into cooperation.
3. To explore the influence of verbal communication on task accomplishment.

Group Size   Several groups of five or six persons each.

Time Required   45 minutes to 1 hour.

Materials

1. A set of Tinkertoys®, Legos®, or other building materials (minimum of 10 pieces) for each group.
2. A clock or timer.

Physical Setting   A room with separate tables for each group.

Process

1. Direct the participants to form groups of five or six persons each. Distribute one set of building materials to each group.
2. Give the following instructions to the participants:
   "During the next 10-minute period you may not talk. Using the materials you have been provided, you are to make a model of the concept CONFLICT."
   No further instructions or clarification should be given.

   Note to the Facilitator   Repeat the instructions if necessary, but do not answer questions, such as whether the model should be done jointly by the whole group or separately by each member, whether all the materials should be used, and so forth.

3. Time the activity, giving the groups a 5-minute and a 2-minute warning. End the group work when time has expired.

4. Direct the participants to walk around the room to examine the various models. Allow several minutes, and then have the groups reassemble.

5. Give the following directions:

   "During the next 10-minute period you may not talk. Using the materials you have been provided, you are to make a model of the concept COOPERATION."

   No further instructions or clarification should be given.

   Note to the Facilitator   Repeat the instructions, but do not answer questions, such as whether the first model should be disassembled first, who should build the model, and so forth.

6. Time the activity, giving the groups a 5-minute and a 2-minute warning. End the group work when time has expired.

7. Direct the participants to walk around the room to examine the various models. Allow several minutes, and then have the groups reassemble.

8. Lead a concluding discussion based on the questions below.
   - How did you feel personally during this activity? How did others seem to react to it?
   - How did the lack of verbal communication affect the group's ability to carry out the task?
   - What other factors influenced the group's ability to accomplish this task?
   - What differences did you see between the CONFLICT models and the COOPERATION models? What differences were there in how groups approached the task?
   - What are some specific ways you can think of, based on what you have done here, to turn conflict into cooperation in the workplace?

Variation   Create models using any set of opposing concepts, such as TEAM and INDIVIDUAL, TRUST and DISTRUST, WEAK and STRONG, and so forth.

➤ On the Move

Goals

1. To compare competitive and collaborative behaviors.
2. To examine collaboration in terms of conflict resolution and problem solving.
3. To make decisions based on selected criteria.

Group Size   Four groups of four to seven persons each.

Time Required   Approximately 1½ hours.

Materials

1. A copy of the On-the-Move Worksheet and a pencil for each participant.
2. A copy of the On-the-Move Selection Criteria Sheet and several sheets of paper for each of the three volunteer participants.
3. A clock or timer.

Physical Setting   A room large enough for groups to work without disturbing one another. Writing surfaces should be provided.

Process

1. Select three volunteers, and then direct the remaining participants to form four groups of four to seven persons each.
2. Distribute a copy of the On-the-Move Worksheet and a pencil to each participant. Read aloud the situation and the instructions at the top of the sheet.
3. Inform the three volunteers that they will act as the CEOs. Assign a different division designation to each group: Marketing, Sales, Product Development, and Finance.
4. Signal for the groups to begin to prepare for their presentations. Explain that the groups will have approximately 20 minutes to prepare. The CEO volunteers should spend this time defining three criteria (standards) that they will use to judge the presentations. Distribute a copy of the On-the-Move Selection Criteria

Sheet and several sheets of paper to each CEO for taking notes on the discussion and for judging the presentations.

5. Allow approximately 20 minutes, and then ask each group in turn to make its presentation. Explain that you will time the presentations for 20 minutes, giving a signal when the group has 1 minute left. Each CEO volunteer should use the Criteria Sheet to make notes on each presentation.

6. When all groups have finished their presentations, allow a few minutes for the CEO volunteers to make their decision. Ask one volunteer to describe the established criteria on which the decision was based, and then announce the division that will relocate and the reason why.

7. Explain that, although the groups were competing against each other, they still had to maintain an underlying sense of collaboration within the context of working for the same corporation. Competing behavior reflects the extreme example of concern for one's own needs at the expense of others. Collaboration is an integrative method of conflict resolution or problem solving that acknowledges the concerns of all parties involved.

8. Lead a concluding discussion based on the following questions:
   - For those who acted as the CEOs, how difficult was it to establish the criteria for the decision? Did these standards help guide the decision-making process? Why or why not? Did the criteria help the group to work together more effectively? If so, how?
   - How much competitive behavior was evident in the presentations? Was any one group more competitive than the others? What were some examples of this behavior?
   - What are some examples of collaborative behavior that was evident in the presentations?
   - How can we address collaboration in terms of a problem-solving approach?
   - Is a collaborative approach necessary in all situations? Why or why not? What are some examples?
   - How can one accurately assess a situation to determine the most appropriate approach to take in terms of conflict and problem solving?

On-the-Move Worksheet

Situation

A major corporation is moving its headquarters from the East Coast to the West Coast, but plans to move only one of its four major divisions. Each group will represent one of these divisions: Marketing, Sales, Product Development, and Finance. Each group wants very much to be selected for the move. Since only one can be chosen, the company's officers have decided to allow each division an opportunity to present its case about why it should be selected.

Instructions

Each group will have a maximum of 10 minutes to make a presentation, which will then be judged by the criteria the CEOs have listed on the Criteria Sheet. The process will be as follows:

1. Each member of the group is to introduce himself or herself and explain his or her qualifications.
2. The entire group will present what it has accomplished or can accomplish for the company and explain why it should be the division selected to relocate.
3. Following the presentations by all four groups, the CEOs will determine which group will be selected to relocate and why.

On-the-Move Selection Criteria Sheet

Instructions: List below the three criteria (standards) that will be used to make your decision. As CEOs of the organization, it is imperative that you work collaboratively and consider the good of the company in making the final decision. Make notes about each division during the presentations.

CRITERION:
Marketing
Sales
Product Development
Finance
CRITERION:
Marketing
Sales
Product Development
Finance
CRITERION:
Marketing
Sales
Product Development
Finance

➤ Team Totem

Goals

1. To demonstrate the collaboration of individuals within a team.
2. To build cohesion within a group.
3. To identify personal strengths and roles within a group.
4. To use symbols as a form of communication.
5. To provide a closing activity for team members within an extended workshop setting.

Group Size   Five to twenty participants of an intact work group, or team members within a multiple-day workshop setting. If there are more than ten participants, form two groups.

Time Required   1 to 1½ hours.

Materials

1. Several magazines, scissors, colored construction paper, and glue sticks.
2. A small square box for each participant.
3. Several felt-tipped markers in a variety of colors for each participant.
4. A copy of the Team Totem Resource Sheet for each participant.
5. Transparent tape.

Physical Setting   A room with enough tables for all participants to have sufficient work space. A separate table for additional supplies is required.

Process

1. Prior to the session, obtain several magazines containing a variety of different pictures. Place these, along with several scissors, construction paper, and glue sticks, on a table that is easily accessible by all participants.

2. At the session, explain that words are not the only form of communication and that art often presents a detailed story. In the native culture, totem poles are visual statements of the identity of those who erect them. Each symbol shares a piece of information about the person and clan it represents. All the symbol pieces are totems, which are brought together to create the total totem pole.

3. Tell the participants that they will be building their own team totem pole. Distribute a box and several felt-tipped markers in a variety of colors to each participant. Provide each person with a copy of the Team Totem Resource Sheet.

4. Explain that each participant is to create a totem box that contains symbols that represent his or her personal strengths and roles within the team. Participants may draw or cut forms of the animal symbols described on the Team Totem Resource Sheet, design their own symbols, or use pictures cut from the magazines provided (indicate the supply table). Allow approximately 20 to 30 minutes for completion of the task.

5. Have the participants take turns explaining their personal totems.

6. Provide the group with transparent tape and instruct the participants to connect the individual totems into a team totem pole. Allow approximately 5 to 10 minutes, depending on group size. Ask: How did your group determine the position of individual totems in forming the team totem pole?

7. Explain that there is an expression "low man on the totem pole." Although this term is used to indicate someone of low importance, the bottom of the totem pole actually is used for those of highest rank.

8. Lead a concluding discussion based on the following questions:
   - How did you decide what symbols to use on your individual totem? How were these symbols interpreted by others? What kind of "symbols" do we use in the workplace to indicate our personal strengths and roles?
   - How does the team totem pole symbolize collaboration? What are some examples of collaborative situations in the workplace?
   - What insights did you gain about your team during this activity?

Variation   Instead of a box, use a sheet of cardstock or paper as the foundation for creating the individual totems and have the group tape the totems in a vertical line to form the pole.

Team Totem Resource Sheet

Animals on totem poles can represent a certain responsibility role within a clan as well as symbolize the power and characteristics of an individual. Some of these symbols are given below.

Bear = protection and defense; strength and courage
Beaver = strength and resourcefulness; someone who minds his or her own
        business
Bird, crane, or loon = leadership
Buffalo = abundance
Coyote = trickster who educates through humor
Eagle = courage, spirit, and bravery
Fish = healer and scholar
Frog = good fortune
Raven = guardian spirit
Snake = power of magic
Turtle = communication; emissary
Wolf = perseverance and guardianship

➤ Tear It Up

Goals

1. To compare and contrast the concepts of individualism, competition, and cooperation.
2. To explore feelings and reactions during the three types of social interaction.
3. To identify appropriate uses for the three types of interactions.

Group Size   Several groups of three to five persons each.

Time Required   1 to 1¼ hours.

Materials

1. A newsprint flip chart sheet with the following information:
   Tear It Up: Three Types of Interaction
   - *Individualistic:* when one person works alone to reach a goal
   - *Competitive:* when one or more persons work against others toward a single goal
   - *Cooperative:* when two or more persons work together toward a single goal
2. Three blank sheets of paper and a pencil for each participant.
3. A separate newsprint flip chart sheet prepared for *each one* of the following headings: Individualistic Interaction, Competitive Interaction, and Cooperative Interaction.
4. A newsprint flip chart and felt-tipped markers for recording.
5. A pencil for each group.
6. An overhead projector.
7. Masking tape.
8. One sheet of construction paper and a glue stick for each group.

Physical Setting   A room large enough for groups to work without disturbing one another. Wall space is required for posting newsprint sheets.

Source: Ukens, L. (2003). Tear it up: Learning three types of interaction. In E. Biech (Ed.), *The 2003 Annual: Volume I, Training* (pp. 67–72). San Francisco: Pfeiffer. This material is used by permission of John Wiley & Sons, Inc.

Process

1. Introduce the activity by telling participants that they will be exploring three basic types of social interaction: individualistic, competitive, and cooperative. Refer to the prepared flip chart sheet that describes the three types of interaction and read aloud the terms and definitions.

2. For each of the three words, elicit game or sports examples from the participants. Some examples might be:
   - *Individualistic:* solitaire card game, mountain climbing, swimming, gymnastics
   - *Competitive:* chess, tug of war, basketball, drag racing
   - *Cooperative:* leap frog, see-saw, football team, relay team

3. Explain to the participants that they will be experiencing three quick but graphic examples of these interactions. Suggest that as the interactions take place, they are to focus on their *feelings* and *reactions.*

4. Distribute three sheets of paper to each participant. Instruct the participants to take one sheet of paper, and then introduce the *individualistic task* to the group by saying, "Each person is to tear his or her sheet to form a shape that meets all of the following criteria: two straight sides, two curved sides, and a hole. Any and all shapes that meet these criteria are acceptable." Repeat the criteria if necessary and/or write them on the flip chart.

5. Allow several minutes for individuals to complete the task. Do not provide any additional information for the task if participants ask questions. Once the participants complete the task, instruct them to hold up their shapes and to view what others have made. The shapes for this task might include figures that look like this:

6. Ask the participants to describe their feelings and reactions during the task. Using the prepared flip chart sheet headed "Individualistic Interaction," record the descriptive words that are generated from the discussion (for example, successful, non-threatened, satisfied, confused, alone). Post the newsprint sheet.

7. Direct participants to form groups of three to five persons each. When everyone is settled, instruct participants to use a different sheet of paper for the next task. Introduce the *competitive task* to the group by saying, "Each person is to tear his or her sheet to form a circle. The goal is to tear the *roundest* circle in your group. The winning circle will be judged by others for its *roundness*."

8. Allow several minutes for individuals to complete the task. Next, instruct each group to select its *roundest* circle. Provide each group with a pencil and ask each one to place an identifying mark on the chosen circle.

9. Collect the circles of the chosen finalists and place them on the overhead projector. Explain that the group as a whole will now select the best circle from among these. Using an "applause meter," judge the best circle and announce the winner. (For a large number of groups, three circles may be chosen as first-, second-, and third-place winners.)

10. Ask the participants to describe their feelings and reactions during the task. Using the prepared flip chart sheet for "Competitive Interaction," record the descriptive words that are generated from the discussion (for example, anxious, angry, threatened, motivated, energized). Use masking tape to post the newsprint sheet.

11. Instruct participants to use the last sheet of paper. Introduce the *cooperative task* to the group by saying, "The goal is for each group to decide on one shape that every person in the group will use to tear his or her sheet. The group will then form a collage symbolizing *cooperation*. The group members are to construct their collages by gluing them to the construction paper that will be provided."

12. Distribute one sheet of colored construction paper and a glue stick to each group. Allow several minutes for groups to

complete their collages. Instruct each group to display its final product. Some examples of the collage designs might include figures that look like this:

 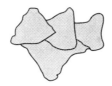 

13. Ask the participants to describe their feelings and reactions during the task. Using the prepared flip chart sheet for "Cooperative Interaction," record the descriptive words that are generated from the discussion (for example, supported, teamwork, pride, trust). Post the newsprint sheet.

14. Lead a concluding discussion by asking the following questions:
    • Overall, what were your feelings and reactions to these three types of interaction?
    • What were some reactions that you observed other participants exhibiting?
    • How can we relate these feelings and reactions to how we interact with others in the workplace?
    • We recognize that each of these three social interactions has advantages and disadvantages. In what workplace circumstances would an individualistic approach be beneficial? A competitive approach? A cooperative approach?
    • How can we use this information to improve workplace performance?

Variation   If time allows, participants within each group can close the activity by compiling a list of responses to the following lead-in: "Cooperation is like . . . because . . .." Each group then shares its responses with the large group.

➤ Three Blind Mice

Goals
1. To develop trust among group members.
2. To practice leadership skills.
3. To use effective communication in providing directions.

Group Size   Several triads.

Time Required   20 to 30 minutes.

Materials
1. A clock or timer.
2. A whistle.
3. A blindfold for each participant (optional).

Physical Setting   A large indoor or outdoor setting that allows for walking in various directions.

Process
1. Direct the participants to form triads.
2. Explain that each person will have the opportunity to close his or her eyes and be led around by the other two members of the group. The groups may choose where they will walk, but they should keep safety in mind at all times. Each person will be led for a 5-minute time period, which will end when you blow the whistle.
3. Ask the triads to select the first person to be led. Instruct these individuals to close their eyes or provide them with blindfolds. Signal for the groups to begin their walks.
4. Time the activity for 5 minutes, and then blow the whistle to stop the activity. Instruct the groups to choose the second person to be led. Instruct these individuals to close their eyes or provide them with blindfolds. Signal for the groups to begin their walks.
5. Time the activity for 5 minutes, and then blow the whistle. Instruct the last individuals to be led to close their eyes or

provide them with blindfolds. Signal for the groups to begin their walks.

6. Time the activity for 5 minutes, and then blow the whistle to stop the activity.

7. Lead a concluding discussion based on the following questions:

- Did you feel safe when you were being led by your guides? Why or why not?

- What behaviors helped to make you feel the safest? What behaviors made you feel uncomfortable?

- Was it easier being a guide or being led? Why?

- When you were a guide, did you ask the person how he or she wished to be led? Why or why not? Did you allow the person being led to set the pace?

- How important was clear communication when leading someone?

- When you were being led, did you feel like you were receiving conflicting directions from your guides? If so, how did this evidence itself to you?

- How are leadership and trust logically related to each other?

- How do we learn to trust others? What are some reasons why trust may break down?

Facilitator Note *Make sure to emphasize that safety is very important. The use of two guides helps ensure that risky behavior is not an issue. However, if anyone is acting in an unsafe manner, ask that individual to sit out the remainder of the activity.*

➤ Trust Bust

Goals

1. To discuss trust-building tips for group performance.
2. To assess a group's level of trust-building behavior.
3. To identify ways to improve the level of trust within a work group.

Group Size   Several groups of three or four persons, from an intact work group.

Time Required   Approximately 1 hour.

Materials

1. A copy of the Trust Bust Worksheet and a pencil for each participant.
2. A newsprint flip chart and felt-tipped markers for recording.
3. A newsprint sheet and a felt-tipped marker for each group.
4. Masking tape.

Physical Setting   A room large enough for groups to work without disturbing one another. Writing surfaces should be provided. Wall space is required for posting newsprint sheets.

Process

1. Begin the session with a general discussion of trust by asking the following questions:
   - How would you define trust?
   - What are some personal behaviors that exhibit trustworthy actions?
   - How does trust impact the performance of a group? What are some examples?
2. Explain that the group now will have an opportunity to assess its current level of trust-building actions.
3. Direct the participants to form groups of three or four persons each. Distribute a copy of the Trust Bust Worksheet and a pencil to each participant.

4. Instruct the groups to discuss the list of Trust-Building Tips and to add any other items they feel are important to include.

5. Allow approximately 10 minutes for discussion, and then ask groups to identify any additional items for the list of tips. Record any responses on the flip chart.

6. Distribute a newsprint sheet and a felt-tipped marker to each group. Ask the groups to continue their discussions and to identify the top five suggestions (those listed plus any additional ones) that are most important for the group to work well together. These are to be recorded on the sheets provided.

7. Allow approximately 15 minutes, giving a 2-minute warning before time expires. Direct the groups to post their sheets with the masking tape, and then ask each group in turn to report on its list.

8. Ask the groups to review the posted sheets and to identify those items that the group as a whole currently does very well. Use a felt-tipped marker to highlight these items with an asterisk.

9. Ask the groups to review the posted sheets and to identify those items that the group as a whole needs to work on to improve. Use a felt-tipped marker to circle these items.

10. Lead a concluding discussion by asking the following questions:
    • Referring to the items that the group does well, what are some reasons members have been successful at making these things happen?
    • Referring to the items that need improvement, what are some reasons members have been unable to succeed in these areas?
    • What are some things that the group can do to develop a better level of trust in general?

Variation   Ask the group to create a list of ground rules that would help increase its levels of trust.

Trust Bust Worksheet

Trust-Building Tips

1. *Be cooperative.* Use the Golden Rule and treat others as you would like to be treated. Remember, being trustworthy earns trust.
2. *Listen attentively.* Pay careful attention to what others say and give them good verbal and nonverbal feedback.
3. *Ask questions and verify understanding.* Discuss ideas and opinions to help solve problems and avoid conflicts resulting from misperceptions.
4. *Consider personal feelings.* Understand that the opinions of others are important. Deal with the emotions surrounding personal beliefs to gain better acceptance of one another.
5. *Communicate openly.* If something bothers you, talk about it candidly. Don't hint, play games, or expect others to read your mind.
6. *Be honest.* Say how you feel and be authentic in your actions.
7. *Be consistent.* Remember, actions do speak louder than words. Your behavior toward others should not change impulsively or randomly.
8. *Be neutral.* Keep an open mind and don't make hasty judgments.
9. *Be sincere.* Express your true feelings and really mean what you say.
10. *Be reliable.* Keep your word and stick to promises; do what you say you will. Most important, never break a confidence!
11. *Share authority.* Take turns leading and being in charge.
12. *Don't become defensive.* Be careful not to attack others or place blame in an effort to protect self-esteem.
13. *Move forward.* Don't bring up old issues or problems. People will feel that nothing is ever accomplished.
14. *Accept accountability.* Honestly admit when you are wrong and chalk up mistakes to experience. Learn from your mistakes so that you won't repeat them.
15. *Support teamwork.* Encourage one another as you work toward personal and professional growth.

➤ What You Herd

Goals
1. To practice negotiating with other groups for needed resources.
2. To investigate the role of interdependence across groups and its impact on task and relationship processes.
3. To identify how limited resources impact performance, goal setting, and strategic planning.

Group Size   Several groups of four to six persons each.

Time Required   30 to 40 minutes.

Materials
1. A small box of animal crackers (or approximately fifteen) for each group.
2. A newsprint flip chart and felt-tipped markers for recording.
3. Prizes for the winning group (optional).

Physical Setting   A room large enough for all participants to move about freely.

Process
1. Direct the participants to form groups of four to six persons each. Distribute the animal crackers to each group.
2. Explain that each group represents a ranch that will herd one particular type of animal. The group must decide which animal it will use, and then try to collect as many animal crackers of that type from the other groups as possible. The group with the largest herd will be declared the winning ranch. Signal for the task to begin.
3. Depending on the group size and the amount of interaction taking place, allow sufficient time (approximately 5 to 10 minutes) for group members to mingle and trade, and then stop the activity.

4. Ask each group to count the number of animals in its herd. On the flip chart, record the animal and the total number collected for each group. Announce the winning ranch (group) and give out prizes if you choose to do so.

5. Lead a concluding discussion based on the following questions:

   • What factors were considered in selecting your group's animal? Did the original selection change as the task progressed? Why or why not?

   • How well did the other groups work with your group during the trading process? What behaviors were evidence of this? What role did trust play in your interactions? How did this impact your group's performance?

   • How did limited resources (different number of animal types, groups using the same animal, broken crackers, and so on) impact your group's performance? Did the availability of resources (cookies) change your group's goals as the activity progressed? Why or why not? What are some examples of how workplace goals change as a reflection of the availability of resources? How does this impact a group's strategic planning process?

   • How did you personally react to changes in conditions? How did others in your group react? As conditions changed, what did your group do to adjust?

   • In preparing for negotiations or strategic planning, how important are your assumptions (or research of competition and market conditions)? What happens when your assumptions are wrong? How do you adjust?

   • What role does interdependence across groups play in accomplishing tasks? In establishing relationships?

➤ Section 4
Communication

Introduction to Communication

The Communication category includes activities that deal with various aspects of the communication process, including communication styles, nonverbal communication, listening, feedback, and coaching skills.

Effective communication is the cornerstone of all group interactions and human resource development efforts. In its absence, tasks fail; relationships wither; teams cannot function beyond anything more than collections of individuals; and organizations lose their best employees, and ultimately, their competitive edge. Because communication is essentially a perceptual process, it can be improved by increasing the probability that the receiver will accurately perceive a sender's communication attempt. Participating in communication activities can help people learn in a variety of ways. They can recognize their own as well as others' communication patterns; they can become aware of the factors that help or hinder communication; and they can develop an understanding of the effects of assumptions on communication. They can learn to express their feelings authentically, using both verbal and nonverbal means. They can learn to listen in ways that improve the flow of thoughts between people and that increase understanding within the group they belong to. They can see how communication patterns within a company affect the functioning of the entire organization, and they can explore ways to improve organizational communication.

Activities that explore *communication styles* explore ways in which individuals prefer to communicate with others in terms of encoding and decoding. They involve issues such as communication patterns, open communication, one-way and two-way communication, degrees of assertiveness and influence, language and word use, and so on.

Nonverbal communication activities specifically deal with the transmission of messages through any communication channel other than formal verbal language. It typically includes facial cues, hand or arm gestures, and body positioning, but also can include objects and symbols. Nonverbal communication channels often are used to supplement verbal communication by highlighting or reinforcing parts of the verbal message.

Listening activities underscore active listening and paraphrasing skills, which are key components of two-way communication. Listening is closely associated with feedback, which is the loop in the communication process that verifies that a message was received and that the message is understood. *Feedback* activities examine methods of providing the interpretation or evaluation of the information shared through the communication process. This includes the use of constructive feedback and coaching skills to guide changes in behavior or performance levels.

➤ Body Basics

Goals

1. To interpret para-verbal communication signals.
2. To examine the impact of nonverbal communication on personal interactions.
3. To improve the ability to receive and to send nonverbal communication.
4. To develop the ability to make clear and objective observations.

Group Size   Eight to twenty participants.

Time Required   45 minutes to 1 hour.

Materials

1. One copy each of the Body Basics—Role Card A and Role Card B.
2. Paper and a pencil for each participant.

Physical Setting   Any room in which the group regularly meets.

Process

1. Select two role players and instruct them separately and secretly from the rest of the group by providing one with Body Basics— Role Card A and the other with Body Basics—Role Card B. Be sure that "A" knows what experience he or she wants to relate and that "B" knows what engagement he or she is hurrying toward. They do not need to tell you, but they must be clear about these themselves before they start.
2. Explain to the rest of the group that they are to observe the two role players and look for "para-verbal clues." These are nonverbal signals that accompany words.
3. Begin the role play by telling the participants the situation: Two people meet and engage in a conversation. Allow the role play to run approximately 3 to 5 minutes, until some frustration or irritation becomes obvious.

4. Lead a general discussion of the experience by asking the following questions:
   - Role player A, were you aware of your partner's eagerness to leave? How did you feel about this? Did you believe "B" was really listening to you? What did you notice about your own physical behavior?
   - Role player B, how did you feel during the interaction? Were you aware of A's reactions to your eagerness to leave? What about "A" made you think this?
   - What did the observers notice about the gestures and facial expressions of the role players? How did you think the role players were feeling? What clues made you think this?
5. Direct the participants to form groups of four to six persons each. Distribute paper and a pencil to each participant.
6. Ask the groups to discuss ways in which we encourage or discourage others by nonverbal communication. They should look at the kinds of nonverbal communication that accompany words and the kinds we act out without words. Allow approximately 10 to 15 minutes for discussion, and then have the groups report.
7. Lead a concluding discussion by asking the following questions:
   - What are some things that can be better expressed verbally? What are some things that can be better expressed nonverbally? What things require both?
   - Is there really such a thing as verbal expression without nonverbal accompaniment? Does the nonverbal accompany the verbal, or does the verbal accompany the nonverbal? What is the basis for your answer?
   - How does this all relate to our interactions with others in general? How does it impact a work group?

Variation   Within subgroups of four to six persons each, have two members perform the role play with the others acting as observers.

Body Basics—Role Card A

Situation

Two people meet and engage in a conversation.

Role

You are feeling relaxed and comfortable, but you are also very eager to tell the other person about an exciting experience you have had recently.

Body Basics—Role Card B

Situation

Two people meet and engage in a conversation.

Role

You have another engagement and are eager to get away quickly. You try to be polite and to give the appearance of interested listening. You do not want to mention that you must leave now or you will be late for your appointment.

➤ Close Calls

Goals

1. To have many persons pass messages at the same time.
2. To examine factors that may influence the exchange of information.
3. To identify ways that groups can improve the overall communication process.

Group Size Eight to twenty participants.

Time Required 15 minutes.

Physical Setting Any room in which the group regularly meets.

Process

1. Direct the participants to sit or stand in a circle, square, or rectangular formation. Instruct the individuals to count off alternately, that is, as "one" or "two."
2. Explain that the purpose of the activity is to have many persons pass messages at the same time.
3. To begin, have each "one" think of a factual statement that will be passed along. Explain that each "one" will whisper the message to the "two" on the right. Next, the "two's" will pass the messages along so that many messages are being passed at once. The messages are to go around the entire circle until they return to the originators.
4. Signal for the messages to be relayed around the group.
5. When the messages complete their circuit, have the "one" participants tell their messages in both the original and altered versions.
6. Lead a concluding discussion based on the following questions:
   - How accurate were the final messages compared to the original ones?
   - What factors influenced the outcomes?
   - How does this activity relate to the exchange of information within a group? How does it relate to the acquisition of information in the general workplace?
   - What actions can groups take to improve the overall process of communication?

➤ Converse Proceedings

Goals
1. To practice clear and concise verbal communication.
2. To practice active listening skills.
3. To examine the dynamics of distorted communication.

Group Size   Seven to fifteen participants.

Time Required   20 to 30 minutes.

Materials
1. Paper and a pencil for the volunteer.
2. A stopwatch or a clock with a second hand.
3. A newsprint flip chart and felt-tipped markers for recording.

Physical Setting   A room with enough chairs for all participants. Chairs should be arranged in a circle.

Process
1. Direct the participants to be seated in the prearranged chairs.
2. Ask for a volunteer to initiate the exercise. Take the person aside, provide paper and pencil, and instruct the volunteer to write down ten features of the room in which the group is meeting. (The other members of the group are not to hear these instructions.)
3. When the volunteer has completed the task, take the list; then have the volunteer rejoin the group.
4. Explain to the group that the volunteer will pass along a description of the current surroundings. This will be accomplished by whispering information to the member on his or her right. The member listening may ask questions, but only 30 seconds is allowed for passing on the information to the next participant. This process will continue until all group members have participated.

5. Signal for the exercise to begin. Time each exchange for 30 seconds, indicating when time has expired if the exchange is not concluded beforehand.
6. When all the group members have received the information, ask the last member to report to the group what he or she heard. Once the report is completed, read aloud the list of features made by the volunteer and record them on the flip chart.
7. Lead a concluding discussion by asking the following questions:
   - Did the final description differ substantially from the initial one? What factors contributed to this?
   - Looking around the room, do you agree with the description given to you? What features would you have used to describe the surroundings?
   - What role did perception play in this exercise? How can we become more accurate in our perceptions? What is the difference between fact and inference?
   - In what ways do our distorted communications and perceptions influence our work together on the job?
   - How can we improve our ability to communicate effectively in a team environment?
   - What can a group do back on the job to encourage more effective communication?

➤ Count Down

Goals

1. To identify the advantages and disadvantages of delayed response time on the communication process.
2. To examine the influence of delayed response time on conflict situations.
3. To discuss delayed response time from a cultural perspective.

Group Size   Any number of triads.

Time Required   30 to 40 minutes.

Physical Setting   A room large enough for triads to work without disturbing one another.

Process

1. Direct the participants to form triads. Select one person from each group and ask these persons to step aside. Confidentially, tell these participants that they are to count silently and slowly backwards from 10 to 1 before responding to any comments or questions within their groups. Instruct them to return to their groups.
2. Explain to the groups that they should hold a discussion on the topic of gun control laws (or some other controversial topic you wish to assign).
3. Allow approximately 10 minutes for the discussion, and then stop the groups. Reveal the role of the person selected from each group to maintain a delayed response time.
4. Lead a concluding discussion based on the following questions:
   For those selected to use delayed responses:
   • Did you find it difficult to participate in the discussion? Why?
   • Were there any advantages to employing a delayed response time? If so, what were they?
   • In the United States, many people consider a quick response time a sign of high intelligence. This belief is not universally

held. How does this make you feel about a culture that values a slower response time? Based on your experience in this exercise, why do you think people in some cultures would think that a slow response time was favorable?

- How might a delayed response time create conflict, particularly in a tense or pressured situation?

For those not using delayed responses:

- Did you find it difficult to converse with the person employing the slow response time? Why? How did you react?

- What disadvantages did you observe about a person using a delayed response time? Did you see any advantages? If so, what?

- How might conflict result when a person from a country with a quick response time must interact with someone from a culture in which a delayed response time was customary in tense or pressured situations? What can individuals do to alleviate the potential causes of such conflict?

⊒ Dumblelop

Goals
1. To determine the meaning of words by using the context of the discussion.
2. To explore how negative personal feelings and reactions may lead to conflict situations.
3. To identify ways to clarify verbal and written communications.
4. To discuss the need for clarity in the problem-solving process.

Group Size   Even number of groups of four or five persons each.

Time Required   45 minutes to 1 hour.

Materials   Paper and a pencil for each participant.

Physical Setting   A room large enough for groups to work without disturbing one another.

Process
1. Direct the participants to form an even number of groups of four or five persons each. Distribute paper and a pencil to each participant.
2. Instruct each group to choose three nonsense words with which to replace three common expressions. For example, the nonsense word "dumblelop" might be used to replace the phrase "I know what you mean." Allow approximately 10 minutes to complete this task.
3. Ask each group to pair with another one. Provide a topic for discussion (for example, ways in which language can cause conflict in cross-cultural communication). Explain that during discussion, group members should include the use of the common expressions selected, replacing the actual expressions with the nonsense words they have chosen to represent them.

4. Allow the discussions to run at least 10 to 15 minutes so that adequate time has been provided for the expressions to be used several times. Stop the discussions and ask if members of the partner groups were able to identify the meanings of the nonsense phrases from the context alone. Poll the groups to see how many people were able to identify all three phrases from each group.

5. Lead a concluding discussion based on the following questions:
   - How did you feel about the use of the nonsense phrases? Was it disruptive to the general discussion? Why or why not?
   - In what way could the reactions and feelings of individuals toward the use of the nonsense phrases lead to conflict? How could negative reactions and feelings lead to conflict situations in the workplace?
   - What role did the context of the discussion play in determining the meaning of the nonsense phrases? How can we apply this to situations in the real world?
   - Why is a clear and understandable problem statement important to the group problem-solving process? How can this be achieved?
   - What are some things we can do to ensure that our verbal and written communications are clear to others?
   - What can a group do to make sure that its members are "speaking the same language"?

Variation   If the participants are from the same organization, have participants identify company acronyms or terms that outsiders might be puzzled by, using a newsprint flip chart to record the information. Lead a discussion on how individuals felt when they first joined the organization and had to learn this "language." Ask what problems this kind of "insider language" might cause.

➤ Feedback Forum

Goals

1. To review guidelines for constructive feedback.
2. To examine the impact of personal values and experiences on group decisions.
3. To practice consensus decision-making skills.

Group Size   Several groups of five or six persons each.

Time Required   Approximately 1 hour.

Materials

1. A copy of the Feedback Forum Worksheet and a pencil for each participant.
2. A newsprint flip chart and felt-tipped markers for recording.
3. A newsprint flip chart sheet with the following information: Purpose, Specific, Prompt, Time and Place, Feelings, Not Punishing, Suggestions, Summarize, Two-Way Communication, Support.

Physical Setting   A room large enough for groups to work without disturbing one another. Writing surfaces should be provided.

Process

1. Direct the participants to form groups of five or six persons each.
2. Distribute a copy of the Feedback Forum Worksheet and a pencil to each participant. Read aloud the instructions at the top of the sheet. Ask the participants to complete the INDIVIDUAL rankings, and then to wait for your signal.
3. Allow approximately 8 minutes for all the participants to complete the rankings, and then signal that the groups will have 30 minutes in which to complete their rankings. Time the activity, giving a 2-minute warning before time expires.

4. Ask each group in turn to reveal its group rankings, recording the numbers next to each item on the prepared flip chart. Lead a general discussion on the outcomes and general trends by comparing the rankings.

5. Lead a concluding discussion based on the following questions:
   • How closely did your personal ranking compare to the group's ranking? How did your own experiences and personal values influence your rankings? How do these factors logically relate to feedback?
   • What are some examples of personal experiences, good or bad, of how these guidelines can be used in a feedback situation?
   • How can these feedback guidelines improve the way in which a group functions in terms of task processes? In terms of relationship processes?
   • What are some examples where constructive feedback is critical?
   • What are some guidelines that can be established by a group to support constructive feedback? *(Record on flip chart sheet.)*

Feedback Forum Worksheet

Instructions: Below is a list of guidelines for giving constructive feedback. Review them and then rank each item in order of personal importance in the INDIVIDUAL column, with "1" being most important and "10" being least important. Then, at your facilitator's instruction, try to arrive at a consensus as a group (no voting and all must reasonably agree) on a second ranking of the items and place these in the GROUP column.

INDIVIDUAL	GUIDELINE	GROUP
	State the purpose and its importance.	
	Use specific observations to maintain objectivity.	
	Be prompt—let it occur close to the event.	
	Choose an appropriate time and place.	
	Acknowledge feelings and reactions.	
	Do not be punishing or angry.	
	Offer constructive suggestions.	
	Summarize points and key issues.	
	Use two-way communication.	
	Express support and offer assistance.	

➤ Fishing for Feedback

Goals
1. To practice objective group observation.
2. To provide constructive feedback.
3. To use persuasive communication in presenting a viewpoint.

Group Size   Two equal groups of five to ten persons each, preferably from an intact work group.

Time Required   Approximately 1 hour.

Materials
1. Two problem statements for discussion.
2. A copy of the Fishing for Feedback Observer's Guide and a pencil for each participant.
3. A newsprint flip chart and felt-tipped markers for recording.
4. Masking tape.

Physical Setting   A large room with one chair for each participant; the chairs should be arranged in two concentric (inner and outer) circles. Wall space is required for posting newsprint sheets.

Process
1. Prior to the session, determine the topics for group discussion. For intact work groups, select two issues or problems that the work group is currently facing. For a wide-ranging audience, select two topics of general interest that would elicit differing viewpoints (for example, gun control, the death penalty, working mothers, or home schooling). Write a specific problem statement for each topic.
2. At the session, direct the participants to form two equal-sized groups of five to ten persons each. Designate one group as A, to be seated in the chairs in the inner circle, and the other group as B, to be seated in the outer circle.

3. Explain that the groups will be using a fishbowl format in which the inner group discusses a topic and the outer group makes observations and provides feedback. Distribute a copy of the Fishing for Feedback Observer's Guide and a pencil to each member of Group B and tell them to read the instructions at the top of the page.

4. Read the first problem statement to Group A. Allow approximately 15 to 20 minutes for discussion and then call time. Ask Group B observers to provide comments and recommendations for improvement. Record significant issues on a flip chart sheet and then post with masking tape.

5. Instruct the groups to reverse positions, with Group B in the center and Group A on the outside. Distribute a copy of the Fishing for Feedback Observer's Guide and a pencil to each member of Group A and tell them to read the instructions at the top of the page.

6. Read the second problem statement to Group B. Allow approximately 15 to 20 minutes for discussion and then call time. Ask Group A observers to provide comments and recommendations for improvement. Record significant issues on a flip chart sheet and then post with masking tape.

7. Lead a concluding discussion based on the following questions:
   - How did you feel about voicing a personal viewpoint on a controversial issue? How effective were you in using persuasive communication? Why do you think that was?
   - How would you describe the climate in each of the two groups? What were the basic issues in each group that functioned as the current underlying agenda?
   - As an observer, was it difficult to make specific and objective observations? Why or why not? How difficult was it to give effective feedback? Why?
   - How helpful was the feedback you received? In what way was it helpful or not? How can you use the feedback you received to improve how the group works together? *(Refer to posted newsprint sheets.)*
   - What did the group do well that would help it act more effectively as a team in the future?

Fishing for Feedback Observer's Guide

Instructions: Use skills as a process observer to critically observe and record how the group is functioning and then write suggestions for improvement. Make note of specific examples of observed behaviors.

NORMS that developed for:

Openness

Politeness

Confrontation

GROUP CLIMATE

Participation Pattern *(circle one):*   Broadly shared   Paired   Individualized

Does group show dependence on a leader? How?

Do certain members dominate? How?

What basic underlying issue(s) exist in this group?

GENERAL COMMENTS:

RECOMMENDATIONS for improvement:

➤ Getting the Message Across

Goals

1. To explore the role of communication in the negotiation process.
2. To explore aspects of performance feedback.
3. To investigate the dynamics involved in consensus decision making.

Group Size   Several groups of five to eight persons each (a minimum of two groups is necessary).

Time Required   Approximately 1 hour.

Materials

1. A copy of the Getting-the-Message-Across Worksheet and a pencil for each participant.
2. A prepared flip chart sheet with the following information:
   Rules: You are not to use voting, trading, or polling.
   You must all agree with and accept the final decision.

Physical Setting   A room large enough for groups to work without disturbing one another. The room must be able to accommodate a final arrangement of all group members in a circle of chairs with one chair for each group representative, plus one additional, in the middle of the larger circle.

Process

1. Direct participants to form groups of five to eight persons each.
2. Distribute a copy of the Getting-the-Message-Across Worksheet and a pencil to each participant. Read the directions on the sheet aloud.
3. Referring to the prepared flip chart, review the rules. Instruct each group to select a recorder, who is to make sure that the rules are followed and to record the group's final decision. Remind the groups that they will have 15 minutes in which to make their decisions. Signal for the discussion to begin.

4. After 15 minutes stop the group discussions. Explain that the organization will be providing each group with the same recognition or reward, and each group will have the opportunity to present its idea. Instruct each group to select a representative to enter into negotiations with the other group(s) to attempt to reach a final decision.

5. Direct the representatives to be seated in the middle with the rest of the group seated in a circle around them. One additional chair in the middle circle is left open.

6. Tell the representatives:

   "You represent your group and are to enter into negotiations with the other representatives. You are to make a final decision as to how the groups will be recognized or rewarded. The rules are the same as before with the addition of one other: You cannot communicate with your original group members, who are now observers."

7. Tell the observers:

   "If you feel your agent is misrepresenting the discussion that your group had or you would like to assist in providing supporting information for your point of view, you may take the open chair and give your representative your input, and then leave the chair. You may not enter into a two-way conversation with your representative, nor may he or she ask you any questions, so make your feedback and input very clear."

8. Time the task for 15 minutes, giving the representatives a 2-minute warning. Stop the negotiations and ask the representatives for their final decision.

9. Lead a discussion with all the groups by asking the following questions:

   • What was your group's approach to coming to a decision on the proposed reward? How did individual group members articulate their ideas? Did you establish some criteria? If so, what were they and why did you establish them?

- How committed were individual group members to the initial group decision? How was this articulated (verbally or nonverbally)? How did this commitment impact the negotiations with other groups for a final decision?
- What role did communication play in the negotiation process? How important was active listening? Why? What could have been done to improve the overall process?

10. Ask the representatives:
- How did it feel to be your group's representative? Why did you feel that way? How effective was the one-way communication process for receiving feedback? How did you feel when you received feedback that you were misrepresenting the group? What did you do with the input you received? Ignore it, change tactics, or what?
- Did you feel that you were able to communicate your ideas clearly? Why or why not? Were the other negotiators willing to listen to your ideas? Why or why not? Were you willing to listen to theirs fully? Why or why not?

11. Lead a concluding discussion based on the following questions:
- Can all participants accept the final choice made by the negotiators? Why or why not? Could anything have been done differently to increase commitment to the final decision? If so, what?
- How important was open communication in the negotiation process? Why?
- How well did members of your group express themselves (verbally and nonverbally) throughout the exercise? Were you pleased with your group's behavior? Why or why not? What factors influenced behaviors and outcomes in the activity? How are these factors logically related to each other?
- How does your experience relate to what happens in similar situations in the workplace?
- What can group members do to support effective communication with other groups in order to achieve common organizational goals?

Getting-the-Message-Across Worksheet

Instructions: Your organization has determined that its employees have exceeded all performance expectations for the year. To get the message across that the employees are highly valued, management wants all employees to receive recognition for their efforts. All the groups will have an opportunity to present their ideas on what that recognition should be to management before a final decision is made. Following the rules for consensus, your group will have 15 minutes in which to decide on one specific way to recognize or reward *all* members of the group.

➤ Give and Take

Goals

1. To experience what happens when people do not communicate verbally.
2. To examine the impact of communication on group work.
3. To apply problem-solving skills.

Group Size   Several groups of four persons each.

Time Required   30 minutes.

Materials

1. A Give-and-Take Card Set of four envelopes for each group.
2. A prepared newsprint flip chart with the following information:
   "Dogs started running very fast."
   "The car is making noises."
   "The teacher has blue eyes."
   "We are not going home."
3. A clock or timer.

Physical Setting   A room with separate tables for each group.

Process

1. Prior to the session, prepare the card sets by duplicating the Give-and-Take Card sheets on card stock and cutting each sheet into individual pieces, keeping each set separate. Place each set of cards in an envelope, marking the outside with the appropriate card set number. Prepare a flip chart with the four sentences that comprise the solution and conceal it from the participants.
2. At the session, direct the participants to form groups of four persons each. Distribute one set of card envelopes (#1–4) to each group, handing one envelope to each group member.
3. Explain that groups will be given 5 minutes to solve a problem, which is for each group member to create one meaningful

sentence consisting of five words using the words found in
the envelopes provided to the group. That is, at the end of
5 minutes, all of the four members of the group will have a
meaningful five-word sentence in front of them. However, the
groups must observe certain rules while accomplishing the task.

4. Tell the groups:

"Players on a team may exchange cards, *but no member may
speak throughout the activity.* No team member may indicate in
any way that another player's card is wanted. Players must wait
until a card is presented to them before taking it. Team players
must accept a card from another player any time it is presented
to them. Players may offer their own cards to other members of
their team at any time. If your group finishes before the time
period ends, please remain silent."

5. Time the activity for 5 minutes and then stop the activity. Ask a
member from each group to read a formed sentence until all
solutions have been disclosed. Reveal the prepared flip chart,
presenting the four sentences that comprise the final
solution set.

6. Lead a concluding discussion by asking the following questions:

   • What were your personal reactions to this activity? How did
   others seem to react to it?

   • How difficult was this task? In what way? Since verbal
   communication was not permitted, how did your group
   approach the task?

   • During the activity, what kind of interactions took place? Did
   some people interact more than others? If so, why do you
   think this occurred?

   • What kind of nonverbal communication occurred? Was it
   effective? Why or why not? How does nonverbal communication lead to misunderstandings or conflict situations?

   • How does the overall communication process affect the way in
   which group members work together? What happens when
   there is poor communication or lack of information within a
   group?

Give-and-Take Card Set 1

THE	CAR
HOME	HAS
STARTED	

Give-and-Take Card Set 2

TEACHER	RUNNING
IS	NOISES
VERY	

Give-and-Take Card Set 3

EYES	NOT
GOING	ARE
FAST	

Give-and-Take Card Set 4

THE	BLUE
DOGS	WE
MAKING	

➤ Group Assembly

Goals
1. To accomplish a group task through nonverbal communication.
2. To enhance the expression and interpretation of nonverbal communication.
3. To observe what happens when conflicts arise that cannot be discussed verbally.
4. To discuss the influence of communication on task accomplishment and relationship development within a group process.

Group Size   Several groups of five to seven persons each.

Time Required   30 to 45 minutes.

Materials   A set of construction toys (for example, Legos® or Tinkertoys®) for each group.

Physical Setting   Each group should be located at a separate table.

Process
1. Direct the participants to form groups of five to seven persons each, with each group seated at a separate table.
2. For each group, dump a set of construction toys in the middle of the table. Tell the groups:

   "Without communicating verbally, you are to decide on something to build and then you are to build it. You must use every piece available. You will have 10 minutes to accomplish the task."
3. When the time is up, stop the groups and ask them to discuss the experience. Allow approximately 5 minutes, and then stop the discussion.

4. Lead a discussion by asking the following questions:
   - How did your group decide what to build? Did everyone agree on the decision? How did you know there was agreement or disagreement? Was everyone in the group aware of this? How was this evidenced? How does a shared goal influence group performance?
   - Were there any conflicts or disagreements during construction? How were these disagreements exhibited? How were disagreements handled? How does the communication process impact conflict management?
   - Did any member of the group not participate? Did others try to involve him or her? How? What was the result?
   - Was the group focus on the object being constructed or on the group members? Was this effective? In what way? Could anything have been done differently? If so, what?
   - How would the activity have changed if verbal communication had been allowed? What role does verbal communication play in task accomplishment for a group? In relationship development?
   - How does this activity relate to a group's overall ability to function in the workplace?

➤ Infomercial

Goals
1. To communicate ideas through a commercial advertisement.
2. To explore how verbal and nonverbal communication affect perception.
3. To apply creative thinking skills.

Group Size   Several groups of four to seven persons each.

Time Required   45 minutes to 1 hour.

Materials
1. Paper and a pencil for each participant.
2. A specific object that will be the subject of the advertisement (for example, a utensil, small appliance, toy, or game).

Physical Setting   A room large enough for groups to work without disturbing one another. A clock should be visible to all participants. Writing surfaces should be provided.

Process
1. Direct the participants to form groups of four to seven persons each. Distribute paper and a pencil to each participant.
2. Explain that the groups will be creating "infomercials." These commercial advertisements will involve a specific object (show the object) and should convincingly persuade someone to buy it. The commercial must meet the following specifications:
   • It should last approximately 2 minutes.
   • It must be convincing.
   • It must involve all group members.
3. Allow approximately 20 minutes for group work. Ask each group in turn to present its advertisement to the class.

4. Lead a concluding discussion based on the following questions:
   - Which group used the most creative approach in presenting its product? Did this grab your attention as a potential consumer? Why?
   - What parts of the commercial made the message believable? Which words had more appeal to you? Did any words "turn you off"? If so, which ones?
   - How did the body language of the actors impact their message?
   - How does the overall communication process affect the opinions or perceptions of others?

➤ Let Me Show the Way

Goals
1. To practice giving clear verbal instructions.
2. To develop strategies for improving the dissemination of information within groups.

Group Size   Several triads.

Time Required   Approximately 1 hour.

Materials
1. Paper for each participant.
2. A blindfold for each participant.
3. Two pencils or felt-tipped pens in different colors for each triad.

Physical Setting   A room large enough for triads to work without disturbing one another. Writing surfaces should be provided.

Process
1. Introduce the activity by explaining that groups will be exploring how communication affects task completion.
2. Direct participants to form triads. Distribute a sheet of paper and a blindfold to each participant. Provide each triad with two pencils or felt-tipped pens, in different colors.
3. Explain that each group member will perform a different role during each round of the activity: One member will be the *observer*, a second member will be blindfolded and act as the *receiver*, and the third will be the *guide*, who will draw a path on the paper and provide directions to the *receiver*. Group members should decide on these roles for the first round.
4. Start the first round by instructing the *receiver* to securely fasten the blindfold over his or her eyes. Next, have the *guide* draw a path on a sheet of paper with one of the colored pencils or

felt-tipped pens. Point out that the pencil/pen should not be lifted from the paper until the path is complete. The path may go in any direction and form any pattern, but the guide should place an arrow at the beginning of the path and an "X" at the end.

5. After the path has been drawn, the blindfolded person (*receiver*) should be given the remaining pencil or felt-tipped pen (different color), with the point positioned on the paper at the arrow (start). The *receiver* must trace over the path by following only the verbal instructions provided by the triad member who drew the diagram (*guide*). Any type of instructions may be given, but the guide cannot touch the pencil/pen or the receiver's hand. The *observer* should watch and make mental note of what occurs during the completion of the task.

6. When each group has completed the task, the blindfold should be removed and the participating pair should examine the drawing to see how closely the *receiver* was able to duplicate the original path made by the *guide*, discussing what helped and what hindered the process. Next, the *observer* should provide feedback on the process.

7. Instruct each triad to repeat the procedure for a second round, switching roles as *guide, receiver,* and *observer.*

8. Repeat the procedure for a third round, switching roles so that each member of the triad has had the opportunity to act in all the roles.

9. Lead a concluding discussion based on the following questions:
   - How difficult was this communication challenge? Why?
   - What could have been done to make the instructions clearer?
   - As each new round occurred, did the process improve from the previous round(s)? If so, what was improved?
   - What are some ways to improve the dissemination of information within groups?

➤ Listen to Me

Goals
1. To apply effective listening techniques during disagreements.
2. To examine the repercussions of continuing conflict within groups.
3. To develop strategies for supporting effective listening as a conflict management tool.

Group Size   Unlimited pairs.

Time Required   30 to 40 minutes.

Materials
1. A newsprint flip chart prepared with the following statements:
   - You must not interrupt the speaker at any time.
   - Paraphrasing must be accurate and accepted by the original speaker.
2. A copy of the Listen-to-Me Resource Sheet for each participant.

Physical Setting   Any room in which the group regularly meets.

Process
1. Direct the participants to form pairs, facing each other and fairly close but not touching.
   Tell the participants:
   "Try to come up with a topic on which the partners disagree (such as gun control, tax increase to support government services, or cloning) so that you can get the most out of this exercise. Begin by having one partner state how he or she feels about the chosen topic. If you cannot agree to disagree on a topic, you may talk about what you feel about this experience or about your partner. The first speaker should take enough time to develop his or her thoughts, and then the partner is to paraphrase what was said in his or her own words. The first speaker must accept the paraphrasing as accurate before the partner may begin to express his or her feelings as the second

speaker. When the second speaker has finished, the partner must paraphrase what was said. The second speaker must accept the paraphrased interpretation as accurate before the partner may speak again. The discussion should continue in this way until time is called."

2. Refer to the prepared flip chart and remind the participants to follow the rules. Signal for the discussions to begin.

3. Allow approximately 8 minutes for discussion, and then stop the participants. Ask them:
   - How effectively did you listen to your partner? What did you do to make you think this was true?
   - What specific behaviors contributed to effective listening?

4. Tell participants:
   "We often don't hear what another person is saying during a disagreement because we are too busy thinking up our own argument. If you learn to listen, you have made a major step in learning to handle arguments and settle conflicts. While you are listening, you may become aware of some good points in the other's argument that you may have overlooked. Even if this doesn't happen, you will have learned to control your emotions and deal effectively with differing opinions."

5. Distribute a copy of the Listen-to-Me Resource Sheet to each participant. Ask the participants to read over the guidelines for effective listening.

6. Instruct the partners to continue their original discussions using the statements on the resource sheet as guidelines. Allow approximately 5 minutes for discussion, and then stop the participants.

7. Lead a concluding discussion based on the following questions:
   - Did you feel you listened more effectively this time? What, if anything, did you do differently?
   - What are the repercussions of continuing disagreement or unresolved conflict situations within a group?
   - What specific strategies can group members use to support effective listening as a conflict management tool?

Variation Have the partners select a personal topic to discuss for 2 minutes. While one partner is speaking, the other is to display gradually more disinterested behavior. Reverse roles and repeat the procedure. Include the following discussion questions: How did you feel during the exchange? How did this impact your ability to get your message across? What behaviors would a good listener have exhibited?

Listen-to-Me Resource Sheet

Listening Effectively to Resolve Conflicts

1. Communication begins by listening and indicating that you have heard and understood what the person feels and means.
2. Effective listening involves eye contact and body posture that reveals a willingness to listen.
3. Avoid negative responses that use critical, threatening, or belligerent words. These tend to shut off communication.
4. Treat your respondents with respect and courtesy.
5. Respect involves accepting the other person's feelings and attitudes, even though you may disagree with them.
6. If you listen well, you can reflect on what the person has said and sum up the information.
7. Use responses that keep the communication door open. Don't slam it by giving the other person no face-saving way to respond.
8. Listen!

➤ Not Me!

Goals

1. To practice using persuasion in verbal communication.
2. To examine the effect of stereotyping on interpersonal relationships.
3. To identify unique personal characteristics, experiences, and interests.
4. To become better acquainted with other members of the group.

Group Size   Several groups of six to ten persons each.

Time Required   40 to 50 minutes.

Materials   Two 3-inch by 5-inch index cards and a pencil for each participant.

Physical Setting   A room large enough for groups to work without disturbing one another. Writing surfaces should be provided.

Process

1. Direct the participants to form groups of six to ten persons each. Instruct each group to select a leader.
2. Distribute two index cards and a pencil to each participant.
3. Explain that individuals are to write one statement on each card that describes something unique about themselves (qualities, experiences, accomplishments, interests, and so forth)— something that makes them unlike any other person. Emphasize that they should not write their names on the cards.
4. Allow approximately 5 minutes to complete the task, and then ask the group leaders to collect all of the cards from their groups and to shuffle them. Next, each group leader is to distribute two cards to each member of the group.
5. Explain that the group members, in turn, are to read one of the cards they are holding. After each reading, all the group

members should come to an agreement on who they think wrote the statement. During the discussion, the person described should gently try to persuade the other group members that it is someone else by making a logical argument to convince them. Emphasize that they should not draw attention to themselves by trying to persuade the others too strongly. Once the final guess is made, the person who wrote the statement should identify himself or herself. This process should continue until each person has had the opportunity to read at least one card or until all cards have been read, as you desire.

6. Ask the participants:

   - How were your predictions formulated? How accurate were your guesses?
   - How persuasive were the originators of the statements during the discussion period? What factors made the persuasive arguments believable or unbelievable?
   - What could have been done to improve the chances of making a correct match?
   - Were some statements harder to match than others? Why was that?

7. Explain that stereotypes are often applied to connect certain characteristics or abilities to people. These perceptions can influence our interactions with others, whether consciously or unconsciously. It is important to recognize the uniqueness of each person while still acknowledging that there are certain traits common to various groups of people. Ask:

   - What stereotypes do you or others have that get in the way of really knowing other people? What impact does this have on a group?
   - What types of questions can you ask that would allow you to get to know others better? Other than interpersonal communication, what else could you do to get to know others better?

➤ Otherwise

Goals

1. To use effective listening skills in accomplishing a task.
2. To explore the influence of listening skills on the task and relationship dimensions of a group.
3. To identify ways in which to improve listening skills.
4. To provide an icebreaker activity at the beginning of a session.

Group Size   Eight to thirty participants.

Time Required   15 to 20 minutes.

Materials

1. A copy of the Otherwise Puzzle Sheet and a pencil for each person.
2. A copy of the Otherwise Resource Sheet for the facilitator.
3. A newsprint flip chart and felt-tipped markers for recording.

Physical Setting   Any room in which the group regularly works. Writing surfaces should be provided.

Process

1. Distribute a copy of the Otherwise Puzzle Sheet and a pencil to each person. Tell the participants that you are going to test their concentration.
2. Use the Otherwise Resource Sheet to read all of the numbered instructions, allowing a few moments between each for the participants to complete the task. Do not repeat the instructions or make any type of clarification.
3. Ask the participants for the answer to the puzzle. Lead a discussion based on the following questions:
   • How did you feel about receiving instructions orally? Why did you feel that way?
   • Did this affect your motivation in completing the task? Why or why not?
   • What role did listening skills play in this activity?

4. Explain that the puzzle answer is the ending to a Turkish proverb, "If speaking is silver, then *listening is gold.*" Using the flip chart to record important issues, lead a concluding discussion by asking the following questions:

   • What impact does listening have on accomplishing tasks in general? What are some workplace examples where listening skills impacted the accomplishment of a task?

   • How does listening influence the relationship dimension of a group? What role does listening play in conflict management?

   • What are some ways in which a group member can improve his or her listening skills?

Variation   Make your own puzzle and clues based on some session content to use as a closing review activity.

Otherwise Puzzle Sheet

1	2	3	4	5	6	7	8	9	10	11	12	13	14	15	16	17

Otherwise Resource Sheet

1. If the letter X appears in the newspaper more than the letter E, put the letter X in space 5; otherwise, put an E there.
2. If the sky is sometimes gray, put an N in spaces, 2, 7, and 13, unless children sometimes laugh, in which case put an N in spaces 6 and 8.
3. If Carol and Karen are girls' names, put a K in space 10, unless Carroll is sometimes a boy's name, in which case do nothing.
4. If the River Seine is in Portugal, put a B in space 14, unless Perth is an Australian city, in which case put an I in space 11.
5. Put a G in space 1, unless an apple is a fruit, in which case put it in spaces 9 and 14.
6. If 7 and 8 are 16, put a T in space 12. If they do not equal 16, put a T in space 9, unless Tom Thumb is small, in which case put a T in space 4.
7. If a collie is a dog, put a D in space 17, unless lettuce is sold by the ear, in which case put an O in space 17.
8. If Jack Horner pulled a peach from his pie, put a P in spaces 1 and 16. If it was a prune, put an S there. If it was a plum, put an L in 1 and 16.
9. If spiders have 8 legs, put an O in space 15, unless fish can't swim, then darken space 15.
10. If a manatee is a mammal, put an O in spaces 3 and 12, unless a snake lays eggs, in which case put an S in those spaces.
11. If the moon is closer to us than the sun, darken spaces 10 and 13, unless zebras can sing, in which case put an O in those spaces.
12. If Charles Dickens wrote *A Christmas Carol*, place an I in space 2. If Herman Melville wrote *Moby Dick*, put another I in space 7. If George Bernard Shaw wrote *Hamlet*, destroy this puzzle.

➤ Perceptual Dimensions

Goals
1. To define words in terms of individual meanings and compare these against prescribed definitions.
2. To explore the interpretation of messages sent and received in the communication process.
3. To discuss individual perceptions and stereotyping.

Group Size   Several groups of five to seven persons each.

Time Required   Approximately 1 hour.

Materials
1. A copy of the Perceptual Dimensions Worksheet and a pencil for each participant.
2. A copy of the Perceptual Dimensions Definitions sheet for each group.

Physical Setting   A room large enough for groups to work without disturbing one another. Writing surfaces should be provided.

Process
1. Distribute a copy of the Perceptual Dimensions Worksheet and a pencil to each participant.
2. Ask individuals to write a personal definition of each of the six words listed on the sheet. Allow approximately 10 minutes to complete the task.
3. Direct the participants to form groups of five to seven persons each. Ask the groups to share their definitions of the words and to discuss the commonalities and differences. Allow approximately 15 minutes for discussion.
4. Distribute a copy of the Perceptual Dimensions Definitions sheet to each group. Explain that the dictionary is a public information system in which the common meanings of words

are recorded. Ask the groups to compare their meanings of the words with the dictionary meanings. Allow approximately 10 minutes for discussion.

5. Lead a discussion on perception and communication by asking the following questions:

   • What similarities and differences were there among the individual members' perceived meanings for each word?

   • What similarities and differences were there between personal meanings and the dictionary meanings? Since words generally have multiple definitions (the resource sheet provides two or three for each word), how do people determine the appropriate use of a word? How does perception affect usage and interpretation of certain words? How does this affect communication within the group? How can it affect communication with those outside the group?

   • In the communication process, how might perception affect the message that is sent and the one that is received? What can the sender do to help ensure the proper interpretation of the message? What can the receiver do to help improve the probability that the message is interpreted correctly?

6. Explain that a stereotype is defined as "a conventional, formulaic, and oversimplified conception, opinion, or image." Like a definition, a stereotype can also be viewed as a type of information system, but it is based on perceived meanings. Ask:

   • How do personal meanings and dictionary meanings play a role in creating stereotypes? How can they help break down stereotypes?

   • Do you use stereotypes in defining who you are? Is stereotyping a help or a hindrance in learning about yourself? Why do you think that?

   • How can diverse members of a group work together to gain a better understanding of one another?

PERCEPTUAL DIMENSIONS WORKSHEET

Write a personal definition for each of the following words:

Collaboration

Community

Culture

Ethic

Leader

Partner

Perceptual Dimensions Definitions

Collaboration: (1) working together, especially in a joint intellectual effort; (2) cooperating treasonably, as with an enemy occupation force in one's country.

Community: (1) a group of people living in the same locality and under the same government; (2) a group of people having common interests, similarity, or identity; (3) sharing, participation, and fellowship.

Culture: (1) the totality of socially transmitted behavior patterns, arts, beliefs, institutions, and all other products of human work and thought characteristic of a community or population; (2) intellectual and artistic activity and the works produced by it.

Ethic: (1) a principle of right or good conduct; (2) a system of moral principles or values; (3) a rule or standard governing the conduct of a person or the members of a profession.

Leader: (1) one who leads or guides; (2) one who is in charge or in command of others; (3) one who has influence or power.

Partner: (1) one who is united or associated with another or others in some activity or a sphere of common interest; (2) one who cooperates in a venture, occupation, or challenge; (3) one of a pair or team in a sport or game.

Source: *The American heritage dictionary* (4th college ed.). (2000). Boston: Houghton Mifflin.

➤ Picture That!

Goals
1. To practice writing a clear and concise description of an object.
2. To consider the role of perception in the communication process.
3. To identify ways to improve communication across groups.

Group Size   Two equal groups of no more than ten persons each.

Time Required   50 minutes.

Materials
1. An envelope with a picture of a person and a copy of the Picture That! Resource Sheet 1.
2. An envelope with a picture of a house and a copy of the Picture That! Resource Sheet 2.
3. Four pictures of individuals.
4. Four pictures of houses.
5. A pencil for each group.

Physical Setting   Two separate work areas so that each group can talk without being overheard. Writing surfaces should be provided.

Process
1. Prior to the session, use magazines to find five pictures of individuals, either all male or all female, that resemble one another in many respects, and then make a black-and-white copy of each picture. Place one of the picture copies in a large envelope along with a copy of the Picture That! Resource Sheet 1, setting the remaining four pictures to the side. Mark the envelope "PERSON." Repeat the same procedure for five pictures of houses that are similar in many ways and place one of the picture copies in a large envelope along with a copy of the

Picture That! Resource Sheet 2, setting the remaining four
pictures to the side. Mark this envelope "HOUSE."

2. At the session, direct the participants to divide into two equal
groups of no more than ten persons each.

3. Explain that each group will be compiling a written description
that will be used by the other group for identification purposes.
Distribute the PERSON envelope and a pencil to Group 1 and
the HOUSE envelope and a pencil to Group 2. Send the two
groups to separate work areas.

4. Allow approximately 10 minutes for group work, and then ask
each group to place its picture and the Resource Sheet back in
the envelope. Collect both envelopes, leaving the pencils with
the groups.

5. Instruct members of the groups to spend approximately 10 min-
utes discussing the overall process they used to perform the task
and its effectiveness. During the discussion time, place the four
additional PERSON pictures, set aside previously, into the
PERSON envelope along with the original picture and Resource
Sheet 1. Place the four additional HOUSE pictures into the
HOUSE envelope along with the original picture and Resource
Sheet 2. Stop the group discussions.

6. Distribute the HOUSE envelope to Group 1 and the PERSON
envelope to Group 2. Instruct each group to remove the pictures
and Resource Sheet from its envelope. Using the written
description, the group will try to locate the picture it feels is the
"real" one. Allow approximately 5 minutes for the task, and then
ask each group in turn to display its choice. Identify the correct
pictures.

7. Lead a concluding discussion based on the following questions:
   • What kinds of descriptions were most effective in enabling the
     group to select the "real" person? What kinds of descriptions
     were most effective in selecting the "real" house?
   • Are some things easier to describe than others? Why is that?
     What are some examples?
   • How did your group approach the task of compiling the
     description? Was the process effective? Why or why not?

- Why is the ability to describe something accurately an important skill to master?
- What role does perception play in descriptions? How can this affect the overall communication process?
- What are some suggestions for improving communication across groups?

Note to the Facilitator *You may wish to use the Picture This! activity, provided in this section, as a follow-up to this exercise.*

Picture That! Resource Sheet 1

Your pen pal, whom you have never met in person, is coming to visit you. At the last minute, you are unable to meet your pen pal at the airport so you are sending a friend in your place. You will need to provide your friend with an accurate description of your pen pal from the picture provided. Your group will have approximately 10 minutes to write the description in the space below.

Picture That! Resource Sheet 2

Your friend is being relocated to a new job in the state in which you live. Your friend wants to purchase a house and there is one in your neighborhood that you think is a good choice. You want your friend to have a good idea of what the house is like before coming to town. Write an accurate description of the house from the picture provided. Your group will have approximately 10 minutes to write the description in the space below.

➤ Picture This!

Goals

1. To consider the role of perception in creating and interpreting descriptions.
2. To develop guidelines for creating appropriate descriptions.
3. To assess the level of complexity needed for providing descriptions in various situations.

Group Size   Several groups of four to six persons each.

Time Required   1 hour.

Materials

1. A newsprint flip chart and felt-tipped markers for recording.
2. A copy of the Picture This! Questionnaire and a pencil for each participant.
3. Masking tape.

Physical Setting   A room large enough for groups to work without disturbing one another. Writing surfaces should be provided. Wall space is needed for posting newsprint sheets.

Process

1. Lead an opening discussion with the following questions:
   - What are some of the general qualities and purposes of descriptions?
   - Why is it important to use all of our senses when describing things? How does individual perception impact the outcome of this endeavor?
2. Ask the participants to suggest some guidelines to use when attempting to describe an object. Record responses on the newsprint flip chart, then post the sheet(s) for viewing.
3. Explain that the participants will take a look at how effectively the guidelines can be used in a variety of circumstances.

4. Distribute a copy of the Picture This! Questionnaire and a pencil to each participant. Read aloud the directions at the top of the sheet. Allow approximately 10 minutes for participants to complete the questionnaire, and then stop the activity.

5. Direct the participants to form groups of four to six persons each.

6. Instruct the group members to discuss the individual ratings for the various situations on the questionnaire and then to agree on the two that would require the most complex descriptions and the two that would require the least complex descriptions. In addition, group members should share their examples of unsuccessful and successful experiences. Allow approximately 15 to 20 minutes for discussion.

7. Ask the groups to report their choices for the two most complex, and then the two least complex. Record the results on the newsprint flip chart. Ask the following questions:

   • From these results, which require the most complex descriptions: objects, people, or events? Which require the least complex descriptions? Why?

   • What are some examples of your personal experiences with unsuccessful descriptions and the end results? What are some examples of personal experiences with successful descriptions and the end results?

8. Referring back to the posted description guidelines compiled earlier, ask the following questions:

   • How effective are these guidelines in terms of the various situations presented on the questionnaire? What made them effective or not?

   • What changes or additions, if any, would you make to these guidelines?

   Note to the Facilitator   *You may wish to use this exercise as a follow-up to the Picture That! activity, provided in this section.*

Picture This! Questionnaire

Instructions: Below are statements relating to objects, people, and events. Imagine that you have been asked to describe each of these. Rate each one on the complexity of the description that you would be required to give.

		Simple			Complex	
1.	You want your sister to bring you your shoes from another room.	1	2	3	4	5
2.	You are a restaurant critic reviewing a new pizza parlor in your town.	1	2	3	4	5
3.	You have been asked to identify a robber whom you saw crawling out of your neighbor's window.	1	2	3	4	5
4.	You are telling a colleague about your vacation trip to Australia and New Zealand.	1	2	3	4	5
5.	You are a real estate agent talking to a client on the phone about a house you would like to show him.	1	2	3	4	5
6.	You are fixing your best friend up for a blind date, and your friend wants to know something about the person.	1	2	3	4	5
7.	You are a journalist writing a story about a kidnapping that occurred in your town.	1	2	3	4	5
8.	Your roommates are going to the store, and you are telling them about the shirt that you want them to buy for you.	1	2	3	4	5
9.	You are the master of ceremonies for a fashion show describing the season's newest fashions.	1	2	3	4	5
10.	You are a sports commentator for the Olympic Games.	1	2	3	4	5

What were some times that you *unsuccessfully* described something? What were the results?

What were some times that you *successfully* described something? What were the results?

➤ Positive Charge

Goals
1. To experience the effects of positive versus negative statements.
2. To discuss elements of constructive feedback.
3. To identify effective coaching skills.

Group Size   Several triads.

Time Required   40 to 50 minutes.

Materials
1. A copy of each of the Positive Charge Assignment A, B, and C slips for each group.
2. Paper and a pencil for each group.
3. A clock or timer.
4. A newsprint flip chart and felt-tipped markers for recording.

Physical Setting   A room large enough for the triads to work without disturbing one another. Writing surfaces should be provided for one person in each triad.

Process
1. Direct the participants to form triads. Assign the letter designations of A, B, and C, one to each member of a triad.
2. For each group, distribute a copy of the Positive Charge Assignment C slip, paper, and a pencil to person C. Provide person A with the Positive Charge Assignment A slip.
3. Explain that persons A and B in each group will engage in a conversation for the next 3 minutes. Person C will act as observer for the interaction. Person B is to describe a past experience that was personally embarrassing or that turned out badly.
4. Signal for the conversation to begin, time for 3 minutes, and then stop the interaction.
5. Provide person B with the Positive Charge Assignment B slip. Explain that persons A and B will engage in another

conversation for 3 minutes as person A describes a past experience that was personally embarrassing or that turned out badly. Person C once again will act as observer.

6. Signal for the conversation to begin, time for 3 minutes, and then stop the interaction.

7. Instruct the triads to discuss the two interactions, focusing on the words and behaviors used and the reactions of persons A and B during the conversations. Allow approximately 10 minutes for discussion.

8. Lead a concluding discussion based on the following questions, recording responses on the flip chart:

   • What are some examples of the words and behaviors used during the "negative" interaction? How did person B feel during the exchange?

   • What are some examples of the words and behaviors used during the "positive" interaction? How did person A feel during the exchange?

   • What role does constructive criticism play in providing feedback? What are some guidelines to use when providing feedback to others? (*convey positive intent, be specific, state impact of action, use two-way communication and active listening, focus on solutions*)

   • How can we relate this activity to coaching situations in the workplace? What are some examples of supportive coaching skills? What can a group do to establish a supportive coaching climate for its members?

Positive Charge Assignment A

Follow these instructions as you engage in the conversation with person B for the next 3 minutes:

- You are to respond to everything that is said in a NEGATIVE way.
- React to the person in a CRITICAL manner.

Positive Charge Assignment B

Follow these instructions as you engage in the conversation with person A for the next 3 minutes:

- You are to respond to everything that is said in a POSITIVE way.
- React to the person in a SUPPORTIVE manner.

Positive Charge Assignment C

For each of the two conversations that occur between persons A and B, use the paper and pencil provided to make note of the words, behaviors, and reactions in terms of the following.

Conversation 1: Person A will be responding to everything that person B says in a NEGATIVE way. He or she is to react to the person in a CRITICAL manner.
Conversation 2: Person B will be responding to everything that person A says in a POSITIVE way. He or she is to react to the person in a SUPPORTIVE manner.

➤ Question Mark

Goals
1. To practice questioning skills.
2. To practice giving and receiving information.
3. To compare and contrast the use of open and closed questions.
4. To utilize problem-solving skills.

Group Size   Several triads.

Time Required   45 minutes to 1 hour.

Materials
1. Two identical sets of Lego® blocks in a bag for each triad.
2. A copy of the Question Mark Observer Sheet and a pencil for each triad.
3. A clipboard (or other portable work surface) for each participant.
4. A clock or timer.

Physical Setting   A room (with movable chairs) that is large enough for triads to work without disturbing one another. Each group should have two chairs placed back to back with the third chair to the side of these.

Process
1. Prior to the session, prepare two plastic bags containing Lego blocks for each triad. Each bag should contain an identical set (color and size) of approximately ten Lego blocks. (*Note:* The blocks do not need to be identical for *all* the groups, only *within* each triad.) Mark the bags in some way to indicate that they are a set.
2. At the session, direct the participants to form triads. For each group, one person will be designated as *A*, another *B*, and the

third C. Persons A and B should sit back to back, and person C should be in a position to see the partners.

Note to the Facilitator   If the number of participants in the total group is not divisible by three, form one or two groups of four, two of whom will be observers.

3. Distribute two identical sets of blocks to each group, giving one each to persons A and B. Distribute a copy of the Question Mark Observer Sheet and a pencil to person C. Provide each participant with a clipboard (or other portable work surface).
4. Instruct person A to construct a design using all of the blocks in the bag. Person B is not to see this design.
5. Explain that the goal of the activity is for person B to use his or her blocks to create an exact duplicate of person A's configuration. This is to be accomplished only by asking questions to obtain the necessary information to create the design. Any kind of question may be asked, but person A may respond only to the specific question being asked, without elaborating further. During the exchange, person C will use the Observer Sheet to indicate the types of questions asked and their purpose. The observers are not allowed to communicate in any way during the exercise.
6. Time the exercise for 8 to 10 minutes, and then stop the groups. Instruct the partners to compare the design made by person A with the one constructed by person B, listen to feedback from the observer, and discuss which questions were most effective in obtaining the necessary information. Allow approximately 10 minutes for the discussion.
7. Ask the following questions of the total group:
   • How did the "building" partners feel during the exercise? Why? How well did the questioner do in replicating the design? Why was this?
   • What were some general observations made during the activity regarding the communication process?

- How did different kinds of questions affect the information that was received? What are some examples of questions that were most effective in performing this task?

8. Explain that there are two types of questions: open and closed. Open questions result in an expanded explanation (bigger picture) and closed questions ask for specific details.
   - Which type of question was generally more effective for this task? Why?
   - What are some examples of work situations in which closed questions are best? What are some examples of work situations in which open questions are needed?

9. Lead a concluding discussion based on the following questions:
   - Which role was more difficult—asking the questions or responding? What made it difficult? How effective was the feedback from the observer? What did you learn from the feedback?
   - Is there anything that you could have done differently during the activity to improve your results? If so, what?
   - How important was it to change the position of various blocks as you proceeded in building the design? Why is flexibility important in diagnosing and solving problems?
   - How can we use the information gained in this exercise to improve our skills and behaviors in the workplace?

Variations

1. Repeat steps 4 through 6 two more times, rotating the roles of persons A, B, and C so that each has an opportunity to perform each role.

2. Use other building materials, such as Tinkertoys®, pipe cleaners, or Play-Doh®, in place of the Lego blocks.

Question Mark Observer Sheet

Instructions: Briefly make note of the questions used, the resulting information provided, and the effectiveness of each question.

Questions that ask for the *bigger picture*:

QUESTION	INFORMATION	EFFECTIVENESS

Questions that ask for *specific details*:

QUESTION	INFORMATION	EFFECTIVENESS

➤ Reading Between the Lines

Goals
1. To introduce the topic of open communication.
2. To investigate the influence of hidden meanings within communication.
3. To identify ways to improve communication within a group.

Group Size   Several groups of three to five persons each.

Time Required   30 to 45 minutes

Materials
1. A copy of the Reading Between the Lines Worksheet and a pencil for each participant.
2. A newsprint flip chart and felt-tipped markers for recording.

Physical Setting   A room large enough for groups to work without disturbing one another. Writing surfaces should be provided.

Process
1. Direct the participants to form groups of three to five persons each.
2. Distribute a copy of the Reading Between the Lines Worksheet and a pencil to each participant.
3. Referring to the worksheet, read aloud the directions at the top.
4. Allow approximately 15 minutes for completion of the task, and then stop the activity.
5. Determine how many groups were able to complete the entire exercise. Obtain feedback from the group as a whole, asking for each hidden word and its definition. Record on the flip chart as many of the five hidden words as groups were able to find.
6. If not all five hidden words were found, provide the following answers (definitions are in italic) and add the key words to the flip chart sheet:

A. OPEN: The thief stole money from the *unguarded* envel[ope n]ear the door.
B. CLEAR: It was *obvious* that the vehi[cle ar]riving at the station belonged to someone important.
C. MEANING: I got a *sense* that the ga[me, an ing]enious strategic contest, would be very competitive
D. VERBAL: We *spoke* to the tour guide about how to best disco[ver Bal]timore's historic locations.
E. LISTEN: I *heard* a loud crash after the cyc[list en]tered the cross-section.

7. Referring to the five words on the flip chart sheet, ask:
    • How do these words relate to the group communication process in general?
8. Lead a concluding discussion based on the following questions:
    • Why is it important for communication to be clear and concise?
    • In what way does communication sometimes hold hidden meanings? What are some examples? What influence does this have on the group process? How does this affect task accomplishment? How does it affect group member relationships? What can be done to prevent misunderstanding?
    • To what extent does communication affect your organization overall? How can organizations support open communication?
    • In general, what can a group do to facilitate an effective communication process within a group? *(Record responses on a flip chart.)*

Variation   If you are working with an intact work group, distribute a newsprint sheet to each subgroup and ask that the group members identify specific ways to improve communication within the group. After the subgroups have reported, ask all members to agree on a list of the top five suggestions.

Reading Between the Lines Worksheet

Instructions: Each sentence below has a hidden word that is defined somewhere in the line. For example, the sentence below conceals the word ERRAND, which is defined as "quick trip."

Yesterday, his moth[er ran d]owntown on a *quick trip* to the store.

Your group will have 15 minutes in which to underline the hidden word and circle its definition for each of the five sentences.

A. The thief stole money from the unguarded envelope near the door.
B. It was obvious that the vehicle arriving at the station belonged to someone important.
C. I got a sense that the game, an ingenious strategic contest, would be very competitive.
D. We spoke to the tour guide about how to best discover Baltimore's historic locations.
E. I heard a loud crash after the cyclist entered the crossing.

➤ Sounding Board

Goals

1. To practice coaching skills by giving constructive feedback.
2. To develop effective listening skills.
3. To encourage self-disclosure.

Group Size   Several triads.

Time Required   1 to 1½ hours.

Materials

1. A copy of the Sounding Board Resource Sheet and a pencil for each participant.
2. Prepared newsprint flip chart sheets, one for each of the following headings: Communication Process, Active Listening, Constructive Feedback, Coaching Skills.
3. Felt-tipped pens for recording.
4. Masking tape.

Physical Setting   A room large enough for triads to work without disturbing one another. Wall space is required for posting newsprint sheets.

Process

1. Direct the participants to form triads. Ask group members to count off so that each is assigned a number.
2. Distribute a copy of the Sounding Board Resource Sheet and a pencil to each participant.
3. Explain that the triads will have the opportunity to perform each of the roles listed on the sheet. Review each role, stating that the Observer is to use the bottom of the sheet for taking notes. For the first round, player #1 will be the Presenter, #2 will be the Consultant, and #3 the Observer. Signal for the consultations to begin. After approximately 8 minutes, stop the discussion

between the Presenter and the Consultant. Ask the Observer to provide feedback concerning the interaction (allow approximately 5 minutes).

4. Ask the members to switch roles for the second round: player #2 will be the Presenter, #3 will be the Consultant, and #1 the Observer. Signal for the consultations to begin. After approximately 8 minutes, stop the discussion between the Presenter and the Consultant. Ask the Observer to provide feedback concerning the interaction (allow approximately 5 minutes).

5. Ask the members to switch roles for the final round: player #3 will be the Presenter, #1 will be the Consultant, and #2 the Observer. Signal for the consultations to begin. After approximately 8 minutes, stop the discussion between the Presenter and the Consultant. Ask the Observer to provide feedback concerning the interaction (allow approximately 5 minutes).

6. Lead a discussion with the whole group by asking the following questions regarding each role performed. Record pertinent information regarding the communication process, active listening, constructive feedback, and general coaching skills on the appropriate flip chart sheets. Use masking tape to post the charts.

Presenters:

- Did you feel you were being listened to? Why or why not?
- How much did you actually disclose about yourself? Why was that?
- Were you surprised at the observer's comments? If so, why?
- Did you feel that you were given constructive feedback from your consultant? Why did you feel the way you did?

Consultants:

- Did you feel you were acting in a constructive capacity? Why or why not?
- Did the observer confirm this? If not, why do you feel there was a discrepancy? Did the observer provide you with constructive feedback on your role? What was constructive about the feedback?
- Did you feel distant or close to the presenter? Why? How might this influence the coaching relationship?

Observers:
- What types of feelings did you have about your role?
- What type of dynamics did you observe taking place? Do you feel the interactions could have been more constructive? If so, in what way?
- How effective was the communication process you observed? Give some examples of behaviors that supported the process. Give some examples of behaviors that hindered the process.

All:
- Why is constructive feedback important in a coaching situation? What role does active listening play?
- What guidelines should be followed during a coaching situation in the workplace? *(Record on Coaching Skills newsprint sheet.)*

Sounding Board Resource Sheet

The following roles will be assigned during each of three practice rounds.

PRESENTER: member who will discuss a personal change he or she is currently going through or would like to initiate.

CONSULTANT: member who will discuss the topic with the Presenter and provide constructive feedback on the change.

OBSERVER: member who will listen to the discussion and make comments to the Presenter and Consultant concerning the communication process and dynamics of the interaction following the discussion.

Observer Notes

Communication Process:

Active Listening:

Constructive Feedback:

Coaching Skills:

➤ Sum-Thing

Goals

1. To illustrate the difficulty of attentive listening.
2. To identify ways to increase attention and active listening.
3. To apply mathematical problem-solving skills.

Group Size　Unlimited number of participants.

Time Required　15 to 20 minutes.

Materials

1. A sheet of paper and a pencil for each participant.
2. Sum-Thing Directions Sheet for the facilitator.
3. A copy of the Sum-Thing Active Listening Guidelines for each participant.

Physical Setting　Any room in which the group regularly meets. Writing surfaces should be provided.

Process

1. Distribute a sheet of paper and a pencil to each participant. Instruct participants to write the numbers 1 through 10 on their sheets of paper.
2. Explain that you will be reading aloud a set of mathematical equations. The participants are to listen carefully to each question and do all calculations mentally, writing only the answers down on the paper.
3. Read the statements on the Sum-Thing Directions Sheet at a normal rate of speech. Pause *briefly* after each statement to allow the participants to write their answers.

4. Instruct the participants to score their papers as you provide the answers:
   - (1) 9
   - (2) 21
   - (3) 10
   - (4) 32
   - (5) 24
   - (6) 20
   - (7) 58
   - (8) 4
   - (9) 66
   - (10) 5

5. Lead a discussion based on the following questions:
   - How many equations did you solve correctly? Did you perform as well as you thought you would? Why or why not?
   - How many of you just stopped listening when you became confused or lost when a statement was read? Why did this happen?
   - Have you seen times when people seem to stop listening when you are providing verbal information or instructions? What are some signs that this is happening?

6. Explain that listening is not a passive activity, but a skill that requires concentration and practice. Ask the following question, recording the responses on a flip chart:
   - What are some specific things a person can do to prevent a loss of attention and to encourage active listening?

7. Distribute a copy of the Sum-Thing Active Listening Guidelines to each participant and use the information listed as a review for the session.

Sum-Thing Directions Sheet

1. Start with 4, triple it, add 6, then divide by 2.
2. Take half of 34, add 4, divide by 3, subtract 4, multiply by 7.
3. From a number that is 5 times larger than 3, subtract 3, add 8, and divide by 2.
4. In the series of numbers 8–4–11–9–6–18, add the first four numbers.
5. Subtract 18 from 26, divide by 4, multiply by 9, and add 6.
6. Multiply 7 by 8, divide by 4, subtract 6, add 12.
7. Add the series of numbers 5–7–9–18–6–13.
8. Take the square root of 36, add 5, add 14, divide by 5, add 7, divide by 4, add 1.
9. Double the sum of the numbers 4–1–6–8–5–9.
10. Take half of the sum of 4, 3, 8, and 5, multiply by 3, divide by 6.

Sum-Thing Active Listening Guidelines

1. Provide verbal and nonverbal awareness of the other (for example, eye contact, facial expressions, body language, tone of voice).
2. Respond to a person's basic verbal message by restating or paraphrasing what you have heard.
3. Put yourself in the speaker's place and try to understand the other's point of view.
4. Offer a tentative interpretation about the other's feelings or meanings.
5. Provide focus by summarizing or synthesizing information, feelings, and experiences.
6. Probe for more information or clear up confusions by questioning in a supportive way.
7. Give feedback by sharing perceptions of the other's ideas or feelings by disclosing relevant personal information.
8. Minimize distractions.
9. Be patient and refrain from showing frustration.
10. Put the speaker at ease by creating a "permissive environment."
11. Refrain from arguing or criticizing, which can make the speaker defensive.
12. Be quiet so that the other person has time to think as well as to talk.

➤ Unspoken Meanings

Goals

1. To identify nonverbal behaviors influencing the communication process.
2. To assess personal nonverbal behavior patterns.
3. To practice giving positive behavioral feedback.

Group Size   Several triads.

Time Required   20 to 30 minutes.

Materials

1. A prepared topic card for each participant.
2. A newsprint flip chart and felt-tipped markers for recording.
3. A stopwatch or a clock with a second hand.

Physical Setting   A room large enough for triads to work without disturbing one another.

Process

1. Prior to the session, prepare enough index cards (or slips of paper) with a variety of "inane" common topics to accommodate one card for each participant. The topics might include: toilet paper, paper clips, gum, lint, rain, fences, and so forth.
2. At the session, introduce the activity by asking the participants to think of all the behaviors to which people respond in addition to a person's words. Record answers on the flip chart. *(Possible answers might include: eye contact; smiles and facial expressions; body posture; hand gestures; vocal loudness, tone, and speed.)*
3. Explain that although the content of some social conversations is often insignificant, a lot is happening to contribute to developing impressions. The purpose of this activity is to help

participants recognize which behaviors people react to in others and to learn what others like about how they "come across."

4. Direct the participants to form triads and have each group decide who will be designated as A, B, and C. Explain that each person will have a turn to talk while the other two people listen. The primary learning will occur as a "listener" in this exercise.

5. Randomly distribute a prepared topic card to each person. Explain that each participant will talk conversationally about the topic on his or her card for 90 seconds. During this time, the two listeners are to be attentive, but should not talk. The listeners should be identifying the nonverbal behaviors that are effectively holding their attention.

6. Instruct participant A to begin the conversation when you give the signal to start. Time the discussions for 90 seconds, and then signal for participants to stop.

7. Repeat Step 6 for participant B, and then for participant C.

8. After all three persons have spoken, instruct the listeners to give positive behavioral feedback on what they liked about each speaker's nonverbal behaviors. Monitor the triads to check that the feedback focuses on how (nonverbal behavior) the speaker behaved rather than on what (content) the person said.

9. Lead a concluding discussion by asking the following questions:
   - How did you feel during your time as the speaker?
   - Was it difficult to give positive behavioral feedback to the speakers? Why or why not?
   - How do nonverbal behaviors influence our view of others and what they are saying?
   - What impact can these impressions have on our interactions in the workplace? How do these impressions influence feedback and/or coaching sessions specifically?

Variations

1. Following the nonverbal feedback activity, distribute paper and a pencil to each participant. Without placing direct focus on ineffectual behaviors, ask participants to reflect in general on their own nonverbal behaviors. Each person is to create a list

of specific behaviors that he or she would like to change and the reason why. Allowing approximately 5 minutes, instruct the participants to select at least one behavior and write a statement of commitment describing actions they will take to change the behavior.

2. Prepare index cards with a variety of poor listening or speaking behaviors (for example, refraining from eye contact, acting disinterested, diverting from the topic, using slang or jargon, talking down to listener). In step 5, provide each participant with a behavior card in addition to the topic card for use during the conversation. In leading the concluding discussion, ask whether the "listeners" observed the assigned behaviors or not, and then explore conditions of observation and the overall impact of the ineffective behaviors.

Note to the Facilitator   *It is important that the feedback be offered after all three group members have talked, rather than after each person talks. When each speaker in turn receives immediate feedback, the speakers are more likely to imitate the previous speaker and feel anxious about performing as well or better. When the speakers receive positive feedback after everyone has talked, they know that it is for their "uncoached" behavior. Participants usually expect critical reactions and relax when they do not occur.*

➤ Section 5

Personal Awareness

Introduction to Personal Awareness

The activities in the Personal Awareness category focus on the expansion of personal insight. They emphasize such topics as self-disclosure, values clarification, ethics, sensory and feelings awareness, perceptual set, motivation, and personal growth and development issues.

Personal Awareness activities can be useful in a variety of settings and with many different kinds of groups. Lack of self-understanding, inability to disclose one's thoughts and feelings, or lack of insight into sensory functioning and perceptual set can cause individuals to feel inadequate and can cause difficulties in interrelationships, such as those that exist in work and social groups. The activities in this category can be incorporated into interventions that the facilitator will find helpful in dealing with these situations. Because the individual is a key component in the group process, it is important to the effective functioning of the group for individual members to appraise their own strengths and weaknesses and examine their personal priorities and motivation in order to determine how they contribute to the group as a whole.

Self-disclosure activities provide the opportunity to reveal oneself to others. The ability or inability of an individual to reveal personal thoughts and feelings can have a tremendous effect on the dynamics of a group. In fact, most activities in all categories of this book contain discussion questions that invite participants to share their feelings and reactions to specific tasks or experiences. However, the facilitator is advised to consider the participants' willingness and readiness to disclose.

Values clarification activities help participants clarify the processes by which they make choices or take action. Values clarification is often a necessary step when individuals need to understand themselves and one another better in order to work toward common goals. Through values clarification, people can develop insight into how their values affect their decisions; they can identify the sources of their significant beliefs, pinpoint their reactions to those beliefs, and reconsider which ones they might want to modify; they can exchange points of view and learn the significance that others attach to their own points of view; they can examine their personal development and growth in the context of their values. Often relationships are improved when co-workers share and develop an understanding of one another's values. It is also an important part of goal setting, performing tasks, and strategic planning.

Perceptual set activities look at the process by which individuals receive and interpret sensations from the environment so they may act on them. Perception is the view that individuals have of things in the world around them. It is based on suggestions, beliefs, or previous experiences, and it has a significant effect on individual concept formation and personal behaviors.

➤ Cross-Circulation

Goals

1. To describe oneself through descriptive images.
2. To become acquainted with other members of the group.
3. To relate levels of interaction to personal motivation.
4. To explore the impact of group member similarities and differences on teamwork.
5. To use as an icebreaker activity at the beginning of a session.

Group Size Several groups of five or six persons each.

Time Required 20 to 30 minutes.

Materials

1. A 4-inch by 6-inch blank adhesive label and a felt-tipped pen for each participant.
2. A prepared newsprint flip chart with the following numbered statements:
   1. What best describes your <u>approach to life</u>?
      DOVE–OWL–EAGLE
   2. What best describes you when you <u>enter a room full of unfamiliar people</u>:
      HOT PIE–JELLO–ICE CREAM
   3. What best describes you in your <u>relationships with others</u>?
      BALL–PADDLE–NET
   4. What best describes how you <u>feel right now</u>?
      SNAP–CRACKLE–POP

Physical Setting A room large enough for all participants to move about freely. Writing surfaces should be provided.

Process

1. Distribute a blank adhesive label and a felt-tipped pen to each participant.

2. Instruct the participants to create their name tags by writing their first names in the center of the labels. Referring to the prepared flip chart, explain that individuals will complete the tags by answering the four forced-choice questions listed. These answers will be placed on their name tags according to the directions below, which can also be printed on newsprint:
   • Answer #1: across the top, left side
   • Answer #2: across the top, right side
   • Answer #3: across the bottom, left side
   • Answer #4: across the bottom, right side
3. Allow several minutes for all of the participants to complete their name tags, and then instruct them to wear the tags.
4. Explain that the participants will circulate around the room, trying to find others who have made the same four choices. Allow approximately 5 minutes, and then stop the activity.
5. Direct the participants to randomly form groups of five or six persons each. Group members should introduce themselves to the group by explaining their choices and reasoning. Allow approximately 10 minutes, and then stop the discussion.
6. Lead a concluding discussion based on the following questions:
   • How difficult was it for you to make your initial choices? Why was that? To what extent did your choices reflect your ability to interact with others? How do our interactions with others affect personal motivation?
   • How difficult was it to find individuals who had the same four choices as your own? Why was that? How does this relate to groups in general?
   • How do similarities and differences among group members impact teamwork?

➤ Eye of the Beholder

Goals
1. To discuss the impact of the individual on the performance of a group.
2. To examine distinctive and similar characteristics of individuals.
3. To explore perception through the senses of sight and touch.

Group Size   Several groups of five to eight persons each.

Time Required   20 to 30 minutes.

Materials   A potato for each participant.

Physical Setting   A room with a separate table for each group.

Process
1. Direct the participants to form groups of five to eight persons each. Distribute a potato to each participant.
2. Explain that each person is to study the various characteristics of the potato he or she received so that it can be identified by touch only. Allow a few minutes for observation and exploration.
3. Instruct the participants to close their eyes and then to pass their potatoes to the right until a signal is given to stop. When the potatoes have been passed several times around, signal for the groups to stop. Explain that, upon the next signal, each person is to pass a potato to the right while attempting to locate his or her original potato as it is passed along.
4. Signal for the group to pass the potatoes. Allow several minutes for the participants to locate their potatoes, and then stop the activity. Tell the participants to open their eyes.

5. Lead a concluding discussion based on the following questions:
   - Do you feel confident that you were able to locate the correct potato? Why or why not? How much of your success was due to your ability to observe? What other factors helped you identify your personal potato?
   - How can we relate this activity to the distinctive qualities of each individual in a group? How does it relate to how much people are alike?
   - What are some ways in which we "observe" or become aware of the individual characteristics of people?
   - Reflect on how you behave in your own group. What is the impact of your personal behaviors on the group?
   - How does the composition of group members impact the overall ability of a group to perform effectively? What can a group do to make the most effective use of individual characteristics as it establishes group roles and norms?

Variation   Use other objects that have slight physical differences (such as fruit, pinecones, stones, and so forth) for the identification process.

➤ Going Around in Circles

Goals
1. To demonstrate differences in perspective.
2. To discuss how individual perception influences outcomes.
3. To discuss how individual perception affects change initiatives.
4. To identify ways of helping individuals to see things from a common perspective.

Group Size   Unlimited participants.

Time Required   10 to 20 minutes.

Physical Setting   Any room in which the group regularly meets.

Process
1. Instruct each participant to hold one hand above his or her head and to point the index finger upward. In this position, ask the participants to look up at their fingers and to draw imaginary circles in the air in a clockwise direction. Instruct the participants to continue making the clockwise circles, *keeping their fingers pointing upward,* as they slowly lower their hands to waist level. Ask them to observe the direction of the circles from this view. *(The circles are now being made in a counterclockwise direction.)*
2. Use this demonstration to open up a general discussion on the topics of individual perspective and issues surrounding change.
3. Lead a concluding discussion based on the following questions:
   - What are some examples of an event in which two or more individuals may view things differently? *(a car accident or a business disagreement)* What are the possible outcomes of a difference in viewpoint?
   - How do varying individual viewpoints help a group formulate ideas? How do they hinder a group?
   - What guidelines can a group establish to help individual members work from a common perspective?
   - How does individual perspective affect change initiatives in the workplace? What can an organization do to positively influence change management strategies?

➤ High Impact

Goals
1. To reflect individually on the personal influence of another person.
2. To relate the extent of the person's influence on the individual.
3. To examine how the influence of others affects our actions and perceptions.

Group Size   Six to twenty participants.

Time Required   30 to 40 minutes.

Materials   Paper and a pencil for each participant.

Physical Setting   Any room in which the group regularly meets. Writing surfaces should be provided.

Process
1. Tell the participants the following:

   "As a human being, you are a learner. Other humans play a significant part in your learning because they are your models. When you get close to people, you begin to take on the behaviors that you like in them, and you also tend to avoid their behaviors that you dislike or find uncomfortable. Thus, the way you perceive yourself is influenced by the relationships you have with other people."

2. Distribute paper and a pencil to each participant. Have individuals identify one person who has influenced them in the past and whom they would be willing to talk about in a group setting. Next each person should list the ways this person has influenced what they are as well as what they feel, think, say, and do. The influence may be positive or negative. Allow approximately 10 minutes for this task.

3. After the lists are completed, instruct the participants to select the three ways they feel the person has influenced them the most. Allow several minutes for reflection.

4. Ask the participants to take turns sharing with the group the person they chose and the three most important ways this person influenced them.

5. Lead a concluding discussion by asking:
   - What do you find to be the most common ways people are influenced by one another?
   - How do role models influence our individual perceptions in general? What role do mentors and coaches play in influencing individuals in workplace situations? *(emulate successful behaviors, provide resources and information, facilitate networking)*
   - How can we use this type of reflective information for our own self-improvement efforts?

Variation   If the group is large and/or time is limited, rather than have each participant share his or her information with the entire group, have participants talk in groups of three to five persons each.

➣ In the Company of . . .

Goals

1. To compare behavioral responses to situations in which one interacts with friends versus when one interacts with strangers.
2. To examine the element of trust within a group.
3. To become acquainted with other members of a group.

Group Size   Several groups of three to five persons each.

Time Required   30 to 45 minutes.

Materials   A copy of the In the Company of . . . Worksheet and a pencil for each participant.

Physical Setting   Any room in which the group regularly meets. Writing surfaces should be provided.

Process

1. Distribute a copy of the In the Company of . . . Worksheet and a pencil to each participant. Read aloud the instructions at the top of the page. Allow approximately 5 to 8 minutes for completion of the worksheet.
2. Direct the participants to form groups of three to five persons each. Ask the group members to share their answers with one another. Allow approximately 15 minutes for discussion.
3. Lead a concluding discussion based on the following questions:
   • Is your "public self" similar to your "private self"? Why or why not?
   • Why do we sometimes wear "masks" as we perform certain roles in our lives? How does this influence the perception of an individual's trustworthiness?

- Were there any similarities among the feelings of individuals in your group? If so, what kind? How did you feel if your reactions were different from those of other members of your group?
- Why are people generally more comfortable in situations with people they know well? Is trust a factor? If so, in what way?
- What are some specific ways in which members of a group can become more comfortable with one another?

In The Company of . . . Worksheet

Instructions: For an interaction that occurs within each situation below (in the company of friends and in the company of strangers), write an analogous word for each category that generally describes how you feel and the reason why you feel that way.

WHAT I AM LIKE:	IN THE COMPANY OF FRIENDS	IN THE COMPANY OF STRANGERS
FOOD		
ANIMAL		
COLOR		
VEHICLE		
SHAPE		

➤ Keep On Role-ing

Goals
1. To recognize the variety of personal roles that individuals perform.
2. To identify the actions required in performing different roles.
3. To discover the interactions among the various roles an individual performs.
4. To assess the balance between work and personal life roles.

Group Size   Several groups of four to six persons each.

Time Required   45 minutes to 1 hour.

Materials   A copy of the Keep On Role-ing Worksheet and a pencil for each participant.

Physical Setting   A room large enough for groups to work without disturbing one another. Writing surfaces should be provided.

Process
1. Distribute a copy of the Keep On Role-ing Worksheet and a pencil to each participant.
2. Read aloud the instructions at the top of the sheet.
3. Allow sufficient time for the participants to complete the task, approximately 15 minutes, and then signal for the participants to stop.
4. Direct the participants to form groups of four to six persons each.
5. Instruct the members of each group to share their responses on the worksheet. Allow approximately 20 minutes for discussion, and then stop the activity.

6. Lead a concluding discussion based on the following questions:
   - In identifying the various actions for each role, did you see any similarities between those you use in your personal life and those you use in your work life? What are some examples? *("coach," "discipline," "have fun," "solve problems," and so forth)*
   - What analogies or parallels can you make between the roles you perform in your personal life and those you perform in your work life?
   - Do you feel that there is a sufficient balance between your work roles and your personal life roles? Why or why not? What factors currently contribute to this state? How does this impact your ability to perform the various roles?
   - What are some ways in which you can improve the balance of the demands of your work life and your personal life?

Keep On Role-ing Worksheet

Instructions

1. For each segment created by the spokes of the ship's wheel, identify the eight most important roles you play in your daily life, for example, spouse, parent, employee, supervisor, member of religious congregation, member of bowling team, and so forth.
2. For each role identified, list several action words (verbs) or phrases that describe the things you do in that role. For example, for "parent" you might write "coach," "drive places," "play," "discipline," or "mediate."
3. Underline the three words in each segment that you feel are the most important to functioning in that role.

➤ Making a Commitment

Goals
1. To reach a group definition of commitment.
2. To discuss aspects and examples of commitment.
3. To explore personal feelings relating to commitment as it relates to working within a group.

Group Size Several groups of three to five persons.

Time Required 1½ to 2 hours.

Materials
1. Paper and a pencil for each participant.
2. A newsprint flip chart and felt-tipped markers for recording.
3. Masking tape.
4. A copy of the Making-a-Commitment Questionnaire for each participant.

Physical Setting A room large enough for groups to work without disturbing one another. Writing surfaces should be provided. Wall space is required to post newsprint sheets.

Process
1. Introduce the session by explaining that commitment is an important factor in a group's ability to function effectively. However, commitment may have different meanings for different people.
2. Distribute paper and a pencil to each person. Ask the participants to complete the following statement in writing: "Commitment is . . . ." Instruct them that they are not to give examples but should try to *define* the word. Allow a few minutes for this task, and then ask them to write a one-sentence statement entitled "How I Feel About Commitment." Explain

that this should be an honest individual assessment and will not be shared with others. Allow several minutes for this task.

3. Ask the participants to give their definitions of "commitment" and record key ideas on a flip chart. Have the group as a whole come up with a working definition of commitment. Record this on a newsprint flip chart sheet and post it with masking tape so that it can be seen by all participants.

4. Lead a discussion by asking the following questions:
   - Did individuals share similar ideas on the definition of "commitment"? Why or why not?
   - How do personal values and interests influence an individual's view of commitment?

5. Direct the participants to form groups of three to five persons each. Distribute a copy of the Making-a-Commitment Questionnaire to each participant.

6. Have the groups review the questions and discuss them in any order they wish as each member records the group's opinions, viewpoints, and examples. Allow approximately 30 to 40 minutes for discussion.

7. Ask various group members to respond to the questions as you facilitate a general discussion of the various issues and answers that emerge. Record key ideas on the flip chart.

8. Instruct the participants to use the original sheet of paper to write a one-sentence statement entitled "How I Feel About Commitment Now." Remind them that this is an individual assessment and will not be shared with others. Allow several minutes for this task.

9. Lead a concluding discussion by asking the following questions:
   - Did your personal feelings about commitment change at all? Why or why not?
   - Are there various levels of commitment? Give some examples. How does this relate to risk taking, both as an individual and as a group?

- How does individual commitment affect the functioning of a group? How can personal commitments affect work commitments and vice versa?
- Commitment is a multifaceted concept. How does it relate to aspects of personal development? To areas of group development? Give some examples.

Variation   If you are working with an intact work group, have group members reach consensus on areas of commitment to the group and its goals. Create a list that can be posted back on the job.

Making-a-Commitment Questionnaire

The group definition of commitment is

1. Who or what are commitments made to in the work environment?

2. What purpose(s) do these commitments serve?

3. What examples of work commitments can you think of? (These can be ones that you made or ones that you have observed.)

4. How do you know when a commitment has been made?

5. What is the relationship between a promise and a commitment?

6. How long do commitments last?

7. In what ways can a commitment lead to conflict?

8. What benefits and problems can be connected to commitments in general?

➤ Me, Myself, and I

Goals
1. To describe oneself through words and a drawing.
2. To compare personal views of ourselves with how others view us.
3. To discuss the impact of individual group members on one another and on the group.

Group Size   Six to thirty participants.

Time Required   30 to 40 minutes.

Materials   Paper and a pencil for each participant.

Physical Setting   Any room in which the group regularly meets. Writing surfaces should be provided.

Process
1. Explain that one key to being an effective group member is the ability to value oneself. A good starting point is to look at how you view yourself as well as how others view you. That means looking honestly at your internal feelings and your external behaviors.
2. Distribute paper and a pencil to each participant.
3. Instruct participants to draw pictures of themselves. Tell them that the picture does not have to be perfect or accurate, but a representation of how they are as individuals. Allow approximately 5 minutes for the task.
4. When the pictures have been drawn, instruct the participants to turn the sheet over to the other side. Instruct them to draw a line down the center of the page to create two columns. They are to mark one column "Self" and one "Others." In the column marked SELF, they are to write five words or phrases that they feel describe them. In the column marked OTHERS, they are to

write five words or phrases that they think others would say describe them. Allow approximately 7 minutes to complete the task.

5. Ask the participants to pair with another person and to discuss their pictures and the words/phrases they chose as descriptions, for both columns. Allow approximately 8 minutes for discussion.

6. Lead a concluding discussion by asking the following questions:
   - How did you feel about drawing a picture of yourself?
   - When you made your drawing, how much of the paper was used for the figure? Was it a large or small drawing? Did you draw the whole body or just the face? How much detail did you use? How did you decide what to draw?
   - When you wrote the words describing how you see yourself, did you use positive or negative words? What factors influenced your view of yourself? Was there a match between how you view yourself and how you feel others view you? If not, why was that? What impact does this have on your feelings and behaviors?
   - What is the impact of individual group members on one another? How does the degree of congruence between how we view ourselves and how others view us impact the group as a whole?

➤ Music Box

Goals
1. To disclose personal information to others.
2. To become acquainted with other members of the group.
3. To examine the influence of rewards on motivation.

Group Size   Two equal-sized groups of ten to twenty persons each.

Time Required   15 to 20 minutes.

Materials
1. A source of music.
2. Paper and a pencil for each participant.
3. A prize or award.

Physical Setting   A large, open room with sufficient space for forming two concentric circles of participants. Writing surfaces should
be provided.

Process
1. Direct the participants to form two equal-sized groups of ten to
   twenty persons each. Instruct one group to form an inner circle
   and the other group an outer circle surrounding the first group.
2. Explain that when the music is played, the outer circle is to walk
   to the left and the inner circle is to walk to the right. Whenever
   the music stops, the two persons facing one another are to
   converse until the music starts again. Later give a prize to the
   person with the longest list of correct facts for each person met.
   Be sure to show the prize or award to the participants.
3. Play music, suddenly stop the music for approximately 30 to
   60 seconds, and then resume playing the music. Repeat this
   process for approximately 5 minutes.

4. Distribute paper and a pencil to each participant. Ask individuals to write the names of the people they met with as many facts as they remember about each one. Allow approximately 5 minutes for the task.

5. Determine who has the longest list and ask the person to read the names and facts. The participants who are listed are to confirm or deny the information as the list is revealed. Any incorrect facts are to be crossed off the list. If there are several incorrect facts on the list, you may need to determine whether someone else has a longer correct list. If so, repeat the process with the second person. Award the prize to the winner.

6. Lead a concluding discussion based on the following questions:
   - How much did you learn about other members of the group? Was it easy or difficult? Why?
   - How willing were your partners to share information about themselves? What are some other ways in which you can become acquainted with other members of your group?
   - How does knowledge of individual member interests and background help a group become more effective overall? How does this information help in establishing group norms?
   - Did the prize or award influence your individual behavior? Why or why not?
   - In general, how do rewards and recognition influence behaviors in the workplace? What impact might they have on a group?
   - What can group members do to move from an individual focus to a more team-related focus?

➤ Pipe Dreams

Goals

1. To creatively express one's persona.
2. To allow participants to become better acquainted.
3. To build cohesion within a group.
4. To provide an icebreaker activity at the beginning of a session.

Group Size   Ten to thirty participants.

Time Required   30 to 45 minutes.

Materials   Six pipe cleaners in a variety of colors for each participant.

Physical Setting   A room large enough that the participants can move about in an unrestricted fashion. A centrally located table to hold the pipe cleaners is desirable.

Process

1. Prior to the session, set the pipe cleaners out so that all the participants are able to access them.
2. Begin the session by asking the participants to come and select a pipe cleaner whose color in some way reflects their personality or current mood.
3. After everyone has chosen a pipe cleaner, ask the participants to mill about looking for others with the same color, stopping to compare ideas on why each chose that color. After several minutes of milling and sharing, stop the activity.
4. Instruct the participants to come and select five additional pipe cleaners in any color combination from those remaining. Ask the participants to create a structure with the pipe cleaners that in some way represents them. Allow approximately 5 minutes for building.

5. Ask the participants to find another person who has built a structure that is similar in some way to the one they built and to share some ideas about their designs. Allow 2 or 3 minutes for sharing.

6. Ask the pairs to join one or two other pairs of participants to form groups of four or six persons. Each is to take 1 minute to introduce the original partner, using the pipe cleaner structure as the basis for the introduction.

7. Lead a concluding discussion by asking the following questions:
   - How difficult was it to use the pipe cleaners to represent yourself? Why was that?
   - As a member of a group, why is it important for an individual to be self-aware? Why is it important to gain insight into others in the group? How can this information build a more cohesive group?
   - What are some specific ways in which group members can get to know one another better?

Variations

1. Instead of forming pairs initially, the group can be divided into groups of five or six and individuals can introduce themselves to the group, using their structure as part of the introduction.

2. If the participants are members of an intact work group, as a final step they can connect all the individual structures in some way to represent the team.

➤ Point of View

Goals

1. To identify personal influential events or situations.
2. To discuss how personal experience shapes individual perceptions.
3. To explore the impact of individual perceptions on group functions.

Group Size   Several groups of four or five persons each.

Time Required   30 to 45 minutes.

Materials   A copy of the Point-of-View Worksheet and a pencil for each participant.

Physical Setting   A room large enough for the groups to work without disturbing one another. Writing surfaces should be provided.

Process

1. Distribute a copy of the Point-of-View Worksheet and a pencil to each participant.
2. Ask the participants to recall some of the events or situations that helped shape their personal points of view (for example, position in the family, important life event, influential institution). Using the worksheet, each person is to quickly sketch two pictures, one in each lens of the glasses, to represent two events or situations that influenced him or her significantly. Allow approximately 10 minutes for the task.
3. Direct the participants to form groups of four or five persons each. Ask the group members to share how their personal "glasses" affect their perceptions of situations. Allow approximately 10 to 15 minutes for discussion.

4. Lead a concluding discussion by asking the following questions:
   - What personal impressions and insights did you gain from this activity?
   - How do individuals' past experiences influence how they perceive things? What are some examples of other events or situations that have influenced your perceptions?
   - How does the past experience of individual group members impact the functioning of a group?
   - What can a group do to draw on these experiences as a way to improve its overall performance? How can this information be used to establish group norms and roles?

Point-of-View Worksheet

Instructions: Quickly sketch a picture in each of the lenses in the glasses below to represent two significant events or situations that have influenced you.

➤ Powers of Observation

Goals
1. To make general observations about a work group or organization.
2. To examine factors that influence personal observations.
3. To identify ways to promote shared expectations.

Group Size   One or more groups of four to six persons each, with members of an intact work group or from the same organization.

Time Required   45 minutes.

Materials
1. A sheet of paper and a pencil for each participant.
2. A newsprint sheet and a felt-tipped marker for each group.
3. Masking tape.

Physical Setting   A room large enough for groups to work without disturbing one another. Writing surfaces should be provided. Wall space is required for posting newsprint sheets.

Process
1. Direct the participants to form one or more groups of four to six persons each.
2. Distribute a sheet of paper and a pencil to each participant.
3. Ask participants to think about various aspects of their work group (or *organization*) that they have observed. Allow a few minutes for reflection, and then instruct them to write one observation (or feeling) about the work group (or *organization*) on their individual sheets of paper.
4. Next, instruct participants to pass each sheet to the next person to their immediate right. Each individual is to write another observation (or feeling) about the work group (or *organization*) that is different from the one already written on the current

paper or that the person wrote previously. Repeat the process two more times, reminding participants to write new observations (or feelings) that have not been written on the paper or made previously by them. At the end of the final pass, there should be four different observations (or feelings) recorded on each sheet of paper.

5. Direct the participants to locate their original sheets of paper. Explain that each group will have 15 minutes to discuss the entries made on the sheets and to select the four most significant observations. These are to be recorded for posting. Distribute a newsprint sheet and a felt-tipped marker to each group.

6. Allow approximately 15 minutes, giving a 2-minute warning before time expires. Provide masking tape, and direct the groups to post their newsprint sheets. Ask each group in turn to present its most significant observations.

7. Lead a concluding discussion based on the following questions:
   • Were your own observations (or feelings) shared by others in your group?
   • What are some similarities in the observations made by all groups? What are some differences?
   • What factors influence our personal observations? How does this influence our perceived expectations?
   • Since people often perceive things in different ways, how can we promote shared expectations?
   • What are the implications of the observations made here for the future condition of the group (or *organization*)?

Variation   For general-population audiences, use an object or a specific concept (for example, conflict or communication) as the focus of observation.

Note to the Facilitator   This activity is best suited for groups that have had some experience working together. You should be familiar with both the culture of the organization and of the group. Since this activity may result in discussion of controversial issues (compensation, work direction, us versus them, and so forth), it requires that you be experienced in knowing how to open up or close down discussions of these issues.

➤ Pride and Prejudice

Goals
1. To identify situations demonstrating prejudice.
2. To analyze the relationships among invalid generalizations, emotions, and prejudice.
3. To suggest actions that can diminish or prevent prejudiced acts.

Group Size   Eight to twenty participants.

Time Required   2 hours.

Materials
1. A newsprint flip chart and felt-tipped markers for recording.
2. Masking tape.
3. A copy of the story "All Summer in a Day" by Ray Bradbury.

Physical Setting   Any room in which the group regularly meets. Wall space is required for posting newsprint sheets.

Process
1. Ask the participants to think of an event that demonstrates prejudice. After a few minutes of reflection, have them share the event they identified with two or three partners. Allow sufficient time for sharing.
2. Have the participants present several examples of events that showed prejudice, record these on a newsprint flip chart, and use masking tape to post the sheets. Identify any generalizations used in the incidents described. Lead a discussion on the extent to which each generalization is valid.
3. Develop and record lists of the causes, events, and effects of prejudice in each case. Use these lists to have the group develop a tentative definition for prejudice. List the definition on a newsprint sheet and post it.
4. Read aloud to the group the story "All Summer in a Day" by Ray Bradbury. (The story is set on a rainy planet where the sun shines for only a few minutes once every 9 years. Margot, who was born

on Earth, remembers sunny days, and she is persecuted for this. She is locked in a closet and forgotten, only to be released after the rain resumes.)

5. Lead a discussion on why the others prevented Margot from seeing the sun. Ask:
    • What are your reactions to this story?
    • How is prejudice displayed in this story?
    • How is generalization related to the events in the story?
    • How are feelings involved in the events of the story?
    • Should Margot have been allowed to see the sun? Why or why not?
    • What examples can you give of prejudice against people who know more than others or who have had experiences others have not had?

6. Have participants work with two or three other partners to suggest what any character in the story might have done to make it possible for Margot to see the sun. Allow approximately 10 minutes for discussion, and then ask for some suggestions.

7. Lead a concluding discussion by asking the following questions:
    • How might individuals have acted to change the situations we described at the beginning of the session?
    • Is it easy to take a stand against prejudice? Why or why not?
    • Is there a difference between preventing prejudice and preventing the effects of prejudice? If so, what is the difference?
    • If you can't prevent prejudiced feelings, how can you act to prevent acts of prejudice? What are some examples?

Note to the Facilitator   *This activity can surface a variety of reactions from individuals. It is important that participants understand that prejudice is not only the result of faulty thinking through generalizations, but that human feelings (emotions) are also involved in displays of prejudice.*

Resource

Bradbury, R. (1998). All summer in a day. In *A medicine for melancholy.* New York: Avon Books. (*Note:* A version of the story can be found at www.intermed.it/bradbury/Allsummer.htm.)

➤ Proverbially Speaking

Goals
1. To evaluate the legitimacy of accepted beliefs represented by proverbial sayings.
2. To consider personal preconceptions.
3. To investigate how previously established information influences current actions.
4. To help participants identify the underlying organizational culture of their own organizations.

Group Size   Several groups of four or five persons each.

Time Required   1 to 1½ hours.

Materials
1. A prepared Proverb Card for each group.
2. A copy of the Proverbially Speaking Proverbs Sheet for each participant.

Physical Setting   A room large enough for the groups to work without disturbing one another.

Process
1. Prior to the session, prepare the Proverbs Cards by duplicating the Proverbially Speaking Proverbs Sheet on card stock, then cutting it into individual cards. Alternatively, print each proverb on a 3-inch by 5-inch index card.
2. Direct the participants to form groups of four or five persons each.
3. Introduce the session with the following:
   "Proverbs are like heirlooms, passed on from generation to generation. These pithy, familiar sayings seem to sum up timeless wisdom about human nature. But are these truisms really true?"

4. Randomly distribute one proverb card to each group.

5. Explain that each group is to discuss the proverb that is printed on its card. Members are to examine whether or not the saying is "true," citing examples from the workplace to support or dispute the saying. Groups will have approximately 15 minutes to complete the discussion.

6. Allow sufficient time for the group discussions to occur, and then stop the task.

7. Ask each group in turn to make a report by reading the proverb and recounting highlights of its discussion and supporting workplace examples.

8. Lead a discussion based on the following questions:
   - Did group members share similar views on the "truth" of the proverbs? Why or why not?
   - What are some of your organization's proverbs?
   - How do preconceived ideas influence our individual values, beliefs, and actions?
   - How does the history of an organization impact the way in which current activities are conducted?
   - What can be done to help ensure that this history has a positive influence on current decisions and actions?

9. After the discussion, provide the following information: "What occurs in an organization is influenced by its unique organizational culture, which consists of such characteristics as rules, interpersonal relationships, supervision, trust, communication, decision making, conflict management, reward systems, risk taking, innovation, and change."

10. Distribute a copy of the Proverbs Sheet to each participant.

11. Ask each group member to select one of the sayings that represents the best description of the culture for the organization in which he or she works. Next, group members should share their selections and reasoning with other members of the group.

12. Allow sufficient time, and then stop the group discussions. Lead a closing discussion with the entire group by asking: How does organizational climate affect characteristics of the group process?

Proverbially Speaking Proverbs Sheet

The squeaky wheel gets the grease.	Actions speak louder than words.
Out of sight, out of mind.	Birds of a feather flock together.
You can't teach an old dog new tricks.	You're never too old to learn.
Look before you leap.	Haste makes waste.
A stitch in time saves nine.	Many hands make light work.
Variety is the spice of life.	He who hesitates is lost.

➤ Search for Tomorrow

Goals
1. To identify individual habitual responses to group situations.
2. To identify feelings and attitudes for elimination and expansion.
3. To generate planned actions for personal development.

Group Size   Unlimited number of participants.

Time Required   45 minutes to 1 hour.

Materials   A copy of the Search for Tomorrow Survey and a pencil for each participant.

Physical Setting   A room large enough for groups to work without disturbing one another. Writing surfaces should be provided.

Process
1. Explain that this activity is designed as an inward search to identify areas for personal development. Distribute a copy of the Search for Tomorrow Survey and a pencil for each participant.
2. Referring to the instructions on the survey, tell the participants to complete Section 1 by first placing a check mark in front of any words that describe a habitual response to group situations. Next they should place an X in front of those words that describe personal feelings and attitudes that they would like to eliminate. Finally, they are to place a plus sign in front of those words that describe responses they would like to expand. Allow approximately 8 minutes for individual work.
3. Explain that most people have feelings that contradict one another. Tell the participants:
   "You can feel discouraged and optimistic at the same time. Even when change takes place, old habits pop up when least expected. First think about how you would like to change your behavior. Then begin where you feel comfortable by picking

one developmental area that would help you perform more effectively in group situations. Describe some specific, practical steps you can take to carry it out. Then take the key word from the list and write it in a prominent place as a reminder."

4. Allow approximately 10 minutes for individuals to complete the task.

5. Ask the participants to pair up and to discuss briefly their plans for personal development. Allow approximately 10 minutes.

6. Lead a concluding discussion based on the following questions:
   - How do you habitually respond to a group situation?
   - Do feelings get in your way and block your effectiveness? Why does that happen? How does this impact the overall group process?
   - What can individuals do to *commit* to actively following a personal development plan? How can other members of the group support the process?

Search for Tomorrow Survey

Section I. From the 30 adjectives below: (1) place a check mark in front of any words that describe your habitual response; (2) place an X in front of those words that describe feelings and attitudes you would like to eliminate; and (3) place a plus sign in front of those words that describe responses you would like to expand.

_____ Agitated	_____ Happy
_____ Angry	_____ Hostile
_____ Apathetic	_____ Hurt
_____ Bored	_____ Involved
_____ Calm	_____ Not Sure
_____ Compassionate	_____ Optimistic
_____ Confident	_____ Pessimistic
_____ Confused	_____ Resentful
_____ Cynical	_____ Satisfied
_____ Discouraged	_____ Serious
_____ Disgusted	_____ Skeptical
_____ Enthusiastic	_____ Stimulated
_____ Fearful	_____ Weary
_____ Frantic	_____ Withdrawn
_____ Frustrated	_____ Worried

Section II. Write your changes here:

1. I would like to stop being so _____ and _____ .
2. I would like to become more _____ and _____ .
3. Specific things I can do to make this happen:

➤ Seeing Things My Way

Goals

1. To examine perception in terms of personal mindset.
2. To explore how perceptual mindset impacts change management and conflict resolution.
3. To discuss ways to change mindsets.

Group Size   Unlimited number of participants.

Time Required   15 to 20 minutes.

Materials   A ball or other small object.

Physical Setting   Any room in which the group regularly meets.

Process

1. Explain that individuals have unique perceptual mindsets that affect the ways in which they view the world. Individuals also have certain inherent physical traits; for example, a physical dominance in the way that they view objects—they are either left-eyed or right-eyed. The participants now will have an opportunity to determine their own eye dominance.
2. Hold up a ball or other small object. Instruct the participants to extend one arm and to point their index finger at the ball so that the finger appears to touch it when they look with both eyes open. Next, instruct the participants to close the right eye, open it, and then close the left eye. Whatever eye is in use when the finger remains fixed on the ball is the dominant one.
3. Poll the participants to determine how many are right-eye dominant and how many are left-eye dominant. (In most cases, the number of each type is approximately half the group.)

4. Explain that a "set" is a person's tendency to see and do things in a certain way; it causes us to stick to what's familiar because it is more comfortable than changing. Ask:

- How does perceptual mindset affect a person's ability to be a high-performing group member? *(expectations, communication, conflict management, problem solving, goal setting, creativity, and so forth)* How does it affect a person's ability to accept change?

- How does perceptual mindset impact our ability to resolve conflicts?

- How can we adapt our particular mindsets? *(see things from another person's point of view)* What can be done to persuade another person to change a particular mindset? *(understand the other person's mindset, don't argue or be confrontational, stick to facts, build trust, show benefits of new ideas, and so forth)*

➤ Take Flight

Goals

1. To identify one's most important personal value or belief.
2. To practice making decisions under time pressure.
3. To examine the role of personal values in decision making.

Group Size   Six to twenty participants.

Time Required   20 to 30 minutes.

Materials

1. A large balloon for each participant.
2. Ten Post-it® Notes and a pencil for each participant.

Physical Setting   Any room in which the group regularly meets. Writing surfaces should be provided.

Process

1. Distribute a balloon to each participant. Instruct everyone to inflate their balloons and tie them off.
2. Distribute ten Post-it Notes and a pencil to each participant. Ask participants to write on each one a value or belief that they have regarding their work or personal life. Allow several minutes for this task to be completed. When finished, ask the participants to stick the notes onto their balloons.
3. Read the following narrative to the participants, pausing only a few moments each time you instruct them to remove a note:
   "You are on a hot air balloon ride. Each value or belief is like a weight on the balloon. As you start on your trip, you are advised that high winds are ahead of you and you must rise up to fly over them by releasing one weight from your balloon. *(Instruct participants to quickly remove one note.)* The view from the higher altitude is breathtaking, but short-lived. You release your hot air slowly to lower to a better height and you release one weight in error. *(Instruct participants to quickly remove one*

note.) You now see black clouds coming toward you. Quickly release two weights! *(Instruct participants to quickly remove two notes.)* You realize that you are in the middle of a storm and severe rains are in view. You decide that you must release three weights to be able to hover above the troubled atmosphere. *(Instruct participants to quickly remove three notes.)* You are running out of hot air, but you must maintain your height. You need to drop two more weights in order to reach the coast from the water below. *(Instruct participants to quickly remove two notes.)* You have now survived the journey and you still have one weight left. This one will allow you to descend in safety."

4. Conduct a general discussion on how difficult it is to make decisions that require quick responses rather than having time for thoughtful consideration.
5. Lead a concluding discussion based on the following questions:
   - How well did you survive the journey? What was your most "troubled" time and why?
   - Was your final "weight" chosen or did it remain by accident? Is it the most important value or belief to you? If so, how did you manage to keep it under pressured conditions?
   - Would anyone like to comment on how they chose what to release and when?
   - Would anyone like to share what his or her final weight is? How important is this last value or belief to you?
   - What did you learn about your ability to make important choices quickly? How does this relate to decision making under time pressure in the work environment?
   - What role do values play in our everyday lives? How do our choices of values impact the workplace?

Variation   Rather than focusing on quick decision making, explore matters relating to decisions made through thoughtful consideration of issues. Allow sufficient time for reflection during the reading of the narrative as participants are asked to choose which notes to remove.

➤ Taste of Success

Goals
1. To reflect on the meaning of success and ways in which it is measured.
2. To identify types of success.
3. To recall personal successes.

Group Size   Several groups of four or five persons each.

Time Required   Approximately 1 hour.

Materials
1. A copy of the Taste of Success Worksheet and a pencil for each participant.
2. Two newsprint sheets and a felt-tipped marker for each group.
3. Masking tape.
4. A newsprint flip chart and felt-tipped markers for recording.

Physical Setting   A room large enough for groups to work without disturbing one another. Writing surfaces should be provided. Wall space is needed for posting newsprint sheets.

Process
1. Distribute a copy of the Taste of Success Worksheet and a pencil to each participant. Have the participants reflect on the word "SUCCESS," recording all the thoughts that come to mind.
2. After allowing several minutes for individuals to complete the task, direct them to form groups of four or five persons each.
3. Distribute a newsprint sheet and a felt-tipped marker to each group. Have group members discuss and then list their combined thoughts on the term SUCCESS. Allow approximately 10 minutes for groups to complete the task. Distribute masking tape, and ask groups to post their lists and share their ideas with the total group.

4. Using the flip chart to record responses, ask the following questions:
   - What are some types of success?
   - What are some things that people succeed in doing?
   - Who are some successful people and why do you think of them as successful?
5. Instruct the participants to use the back of the Taste of Success Worksheet to list some successes they have personally had in their own lives. Allow approximately 5 minutes to complete the task.
6. Distribute another newsprint sheet to each group. Ask group members to discuss and list the qualities or characteristics shared by successful people. Allow approximately 15 minutes to complete the task. Ask groups to post their lists and share their ideas with the total group.
7. Lead a concluding discussion based on the following questions:
   - What are some ways that success can be measured?
   - Is success the same thing as winning? Why or why not?
   - How did you view success when you were a child? Did these images change as you grew older? If so, how did they change? What do you think about it now?
   - Why do most individuals perceive success in different ways?

Variation   Locate magazine or newspaper articles on successful people and have the participants discuss these individuals in terms of the various definitions of success and the qualities or characteristics they listed.

Taste of Success Worksheet

Record all the thoughts that come to mind when you hear the following word:

SUCCESS

➤ Think About It

Goals
1. To describe the thinking process.
2. To explore individual preferences for learning and problem solving.
3. To relate the thinking process to learning and problem-solving styles.

Group Size   Ten to thirty participants.

Time Required   45 minutes to 1 hour.

Materials
1. A copy of the Think About It Worksheet and a pencil for each participant.
2. A newsprint flip chart and felt-tipped markers for recording.
3. Masking tape.

Physical Setting   Any room in which the group regularly meets. Writing surfaces should be provided. Wall space is needed for posting newsprint sheets.

Process
1. Explain that this exercise will help participants think about thinking. Distribute a copy of the Think About It Worksheet and a pencil to each participant. Allow approximately 10 minutes for individual work.
2. Ask the participants to form groups of three or four persons each to discuss their answers to the questions. Allow approximately 15 minutes for discussion.
3. Using a separate flip chart sheet to record responses to each question, ask:
   • What are some examples of ways in which people like to learn something new?
   • What are some examples of ways in which people like to solve a problem?

4. Use masking tape to post the newsprint sheets and lead a concluding discussion based on the following questions:
   - What is different about thinking about the past and thinking about the future? How does this impact learning? How does it impact problem solving?
   - How are learning and problem solving logically related to one another?
   - What can a group do to better meet the needs and preferences of its individual members?
   - What are some specific things a group can do to use individual learning and problem-solving styles to help it perform more effectively?

Think About It Worksheet

1. When, if ever, do you stop thinking? Why?

2. Are your thoughts in color? Why or why not?

3. Do thoughts have shape? If so, what kind?

4. What is the earliest event in your life that you can remember?

5. What is different about thinking of the past and thinking about the future?

6. How do you prefer to learn something new?

7. How do you prefer to solve a problem?

➤ To a "T"

Goals

1. To describe oneself through descriptive images.
2. To become acquainted with other members of the group.
3. To discuss the influence of similarities and differences among group members.

Group Size   Eight to twenty participants.

Time Required   Approximately 1 hour.

Materials

1. Paper and a pencil for each participant.
2. A plain white T-shirt for each participant.
3. A prepared newsprint flip chart with the following information:
   - Write two adjectives to describe yourself.
   - Draw a picture showing you doing something you enjoy.
   - List two things that are of great value to you.
   - Draw a symbol to represent something else about yourself.
4. A piece of stiff cardboard for each participant to put inside T-shirts when marking.
5. A variety of colored felt-tipped markers for each participant.

Physical Setting   A flat work surface for each participant.

Process

1. Distribute paper and a pencil to each participant. Explain that individuals will be decorating T-shirts to describe themselves to others; however, they will be planning the design on paper first. Referring to the prepared flip chart, tell the participants that they are to include the listed information on various parts of the fronts of their T-shirts. Allow approximately 15 minutes to complete the task.

2. Distribute a T-shirt, a piece of cardboard, and a variety of colored felt-tipped markers to each participant. Instruct the group to place the cardboard piece inside the shirt to prevent "bleeding" from the markers. They are to draw on the shirts, using the paper template as a guide. Allow approximately 15 minutes to complete the task.

3. Instruct the participants to put on their T-shirts. Ask the participants to work in pairs to discuss the markings on their shirts. Allow approximately 5 to 7 minutes for this task, and then have the participants introduce one another to the group, referring to the T-shirts as necessary.

4. Lead a concluding discussion based on the following questions:
   - How difficult was it to decide on the descriptive images of yourself? Why? How did you feel about revealing this information to others? Why?
   - Why is it important to know this kind of information about other members of a group? How does this information help establish roles and behavioral norms within a group?
   - How do similarities among group members help the group process? In what ways do the similarities hinder the group process? How do differences among group members help the group process? How do they hinder it?

Variations

1. Instead of T-shirts, the participants can decorate other articles of clothing, such as plain white painters' caps, aprons, visors, and so forth.

2. As a final step, have the participants form groups of three or four based on similarities and then on differences, spending about 5 to 7 minutes on discussion after each formation.

➤ Top Ten

Goals
1. To determine the basic values underlying one's actions.
2. To examine the extent to which one pursues valued activities.
3. To explore conditions influencing one's ability to do valued activities.

Group Size   Unlimited number of participants.

Time Required   30 to 40 minutes.

Materials   A copy of the Top Ten Worksheet and a pencil for each participant.

Physical Setting   Any room in which the group regularly meets. Writing surfaces should be provided.

Process
1. Distribute a copy of the Top Ten Worksheet and a pencil to each participant.
2. Instruct the participants to use the worksheet to list *ten* activities that they like to do and that they think are of value to them. Allow approximately 10 minutes to complete the task.
3. After the participants have completed the list, tell them to go back and write down how long it has been since they have done the various activities. Allow approximately 5 minutes to complete the task.
4. Lead a general discussion on what impacts our ability to do the things that we say we value.
5. Instruct the participants to go back to the worksheet list and to place an "X" in the left margin for those activities that require MONEY to do them.

6. Next, instruct the participants to again refer to the list and place an "A" in the right margin for those activities that are done ALONE and an "O" for those that are done with OTHERS.

7. Instruct the participants to consider the tasks they have just completed. Ask the following questions:
   - In general, what kinds of activities do you value most: Those that are free or that require money? Those done alone or with others?
   - How well does your current work situation support your ability to do these activities?

8. Lead a concluding discussion based on the following questions:
   - What role do values play in our everyday lives?
   - How are personal values formed?
   - How do differences in values affect our ability to interact with others?
   - What happens when our actions contradict our value system?
   - What can we do to help maintain a good work/life balance in regard to what we value?

Note to the Facilitator   *Be sure that participants understand the concept of values. Values are not behavioral traits that can be observed outwardly, but they are expressed in a person's thinking, speech, and behavior. Values are acquired early in childhood, through contact with surroundings and experiences in it. They are absorbed through relationships with family, friends, neighbors, institutions, and all parts of the community and society in which you live.*

Top Ten Worksheet

ACTIVITY	HOW LONG?
1.	
2.	
3.	
4.	
5.	
6.	
7.	
8.	
9.	
10.	

➤ Toss Away

Goals
1. To experience the release of negative thinking.
2. To examine the relationship of negative experience to risk taking.

Group Size   Unlimited number of participants.

Time Required   10 to 15 minutes.

Materials   Paper and a pencil for each participant.

Physical Setting   Any room in which the group regularly meets. Writing surfaces should be provided.

Process
1. Distribute paper and a pencil to each participant.
2. Ask each individual to use one side of the paper to write the biggest mistake made in his or her life. On the other side of the sheet, each person is to write three adjectives to describe how he or she felt at the time of making this mistake.
3. Ask the participants to put the paper in their hands and to raise their hands high above their heads. Tell them to crumple the paper into a ball and to toss the papers toward the front of the room.
4. Lead a discussion on how the individuals' moods changed from concentration on the most negative thing in their lives to concentration on throwing the stigma away.
5. Lead a concluding discussion based on the following questions:
   • How did you feel when you released the paper with the "mistake" you had made on it?
   • How do we have an individual choice to concentrate on those things that are positive rather those things that are negative? How can we change how we feel at any time by changing what we focus our attention on?

- What are some other things an individual can do to concentrate on positive feelings in the face of "mistakes"?
- How can we relate negative feelings to our ability to take risks? How does fear hold us back? What circumstances in the workplace contribute to this?

➤ Turning 21

Goals
1. To prioritize a set of values in terms of importance to the individual.
2. To reach a group consensus on prioritizing a set of values.
3. To examine the impact of personal values on group work.

Group Size   Several groups of four or five persons each from intact work teams.

Time Required   45 minutes.

Materials
1. A set of Turning 21 Cards for each group.
2. A copy of the Turning 21 Worksheet and a pencil for each participant.
3. A newsprint sheet and a felt-tipped marker for each group.
4. Masking tape.

Physical Setting   A room with a separate table provided for each group. Wall space is needed for posting newsprint sheets.

Process
1. Prior to the session, prepare the Turning 21 Cards by duplicating the sheet on card stock and cutting into individual cards. One set is needed for each group.
2. At the session, begin by explaining:
   "Each person has certain personal values that are very important to him or her. These values are acquired through contact with your surroundings and your experiences in it, as well as through your relationships with your family, friends, teachers, neighbors, institutions, the community, and society in general. Your personal values have a significant impact on your thinking and behavior, especially in terms of interacting with

others. We are going to explore how each of you, as an individual, views a certain set of values, and then we will work as a team to reach a consensus on rank ordering the same set of values with the purpose being to work better as a group in the future."

3. Distribute a copy of the Turning 21 Worksheet and a pencil to each participant. Read aloud the directions at the top of the sheet. Allow approximately 10 minutes for completion of the task.

4. Direct participants to form groups of four or five persons each. Distribute a set of the Turning 21 Cards to each group.

5. Explain that the groups will have 20 minutes to work together in arranging the Turning 21 cards in order of priority to the group as a whole. Groups are to refer to the Turning 21 Worksheet for definitions of the values.

6. After approximately 20 minutes, tell the participants to stop. Distribute a newsprint sheet and a felt-tipped marker to each group. Instruct groups to record their lists on the sheets in order of importance. Provide masking tape and ask groups to post the newsprint sheets.

7. Lead a concluding discussion with the following questions:
   - How difficult was it for you to prioritize your own set of values?
   - How closely do the values of your current work group reflect your personal values? In what ways does this influence your ability to work with others?
   - How difficult was it for your group to reach consensus on prioritizing the values of everyone in it? Why? What impact might this have on a work group?

Reference

Allport, G.W., Vernon, P.E., and Lindzey, G. (1960). *Study of values manual.* Boston: Houghton Mifflin.

Turning 21 Worksheet

Instructions: Rank order these twenty-one values according to their importance to you, with "1" being the most important and "21" being the least important.

	Achievement: accomplishment; result brought about by resolve, persistence, or endeavor
	Aesthetics: appreciation and enjoyment of beauty for its own sake
	Altruism: regard for or devotion to the interests of others
	Autonomy: ability to be a self-determining individual
	Creativity: creating new and innovative ideas and designs
	Emotional well-being: freedom from overwhelming anxieties; peace of mind; inner security
	Health: freedom from physical disease or pain; the general condition of the body
	Honesty: fairness or straightforwardness; integrity; uprightness of character or action
	Justice: being impartial or fair; conformity to truth, fact, or reason; righteousness
	Knowledge: seeking of truth, information, or principles for the satisfaction of curiosity, for use, or for the power of knowing
	Love: affection based on admiration or benevolence; warm attachment or devotion
	Loyalty: maintaining allegiance to a person, group, institution, or political unit
	Morality: the belief in and keeping of ethical standards
	Physical appearance: concern for the beauty of one's own body
	Pleasure: the agreeable emotion accompanying the possession or expectation of what is greatly desired; gratification
	Power: possession of control, authority, or influence over others
	Recognition: being made to feel significant and important; being given special notice or attention
	Religious faith: communion with, obedience to, and activity in behalf of a supreme being
	Skill: ability to use one's knowledge effectively and readily in performance; technical expertise
	Wealth: abundance of valuable material possession; affluence
	Wisdom: ability to discern inner qualities and relationships; insight; judgment

Turning 21 Cards

ACHIEVEMENT	HONESTY	PLEASURE
AESTHETICS	JUSTICE	POWER
ALTRUISM	KNOWLEDGE	RECOGNITION
AUTONOMY	LOVE	RELIGIOUS FAITH
CREATIVITY	LOYALTY	SKILL
EMOTIONAL WELL-BEING	MORALITY	WEALTH
HEALTH	PHYSICAL APPEARANCE	WISDOM

➢ Value of Work

Goals
1. To assess personal work values.
2. To review characteristics of the current job environment in relation to work values.
3. To gain insight into personal levels of job satisfaction.

Group Size Five to thirty participants.

Time Required 30 to 40 minutes.

Materials
1. A copy of the Value-of-Work Survey and a pencil for each participant.
2. A copy of the Value-of-Work Score Sheet for each participant.

Physical Setting Any room in which the group regularly meets. Writing surfaces should be provided.

Process
1. Explain that a value is anything to which a person ascribes worth, merit, or usefulness. Work values are important because they give meaning and purpose to your job. An individual's level of job satisfaction can impact the performance of the group as a whole. Say that individuals will have an opportunity to explore their own personal preferences through a short questionnaire.
2. Distribute a copy of the Value-of-Work Survey and a pencil to each participant. Referring to the sheet, read aloud the instructions at the top. Allow approximately 10 minutes for individuals to complete the questionnaire.
3. Distribute a copy of the Value-of-Work Score Sheet to each participant. Referring to the sheet, read aloud the instructions at the top of the form. Allow approximately 8 to 10 minutes for individuals to complete the scoring.

4. Explain that the ten work values listed on the Value-of-Work Score Sheet are just a few of the many different categories that describe desired qualities of a job. Say that these were chosen because they reflect many of the characteristics of today's work teams. Instruct the participants to review their Score Sheets and circle their top five scores.

5. Lead a concluding discussion based on the following questions:
   - What are some of the work values on which you scored high?
   - Is your current work group providing an appropriate environment to sustain the values you desire? In what way does it do so or fail to do so? How does this impact individual motivation?
   - How do members' work values impact the performance of a work group? What are some specific examples in your own groups?
   - What can individuals do to increase the amount of job satisfaction they experience working in a group?

Variations

1. Ask participants to think about the various tasks they perform in their current jobs. Instruct them to write a few action items that each can do to help increase his or her own level of job satisfaction.

2. As a replacement for step 4, instruct the participants to use the Work Value Descriptions table at the bottom of the Score Sheet to prioritize the ten work values in order of importance to them. This should be a reflection of the individual's assessment of his or her own preferences and should be done without considering the total scores obtained for the work value statements. After the rankings have been completed, instruct individuals to compare this ranking with the order of work values obtained as a result of the total scores for the survey statements. Participants can form groups of four or five persons each to discuss the similarities/ differences among individual rankings and the comparisons of preference rankings to the order of the survey statements scores.

Note to the Facilitator   *Be sure to delineate the difference between values and interests. Even though someone may not have liked some work activities he or she has performed, the tasks may have contained something of value to that person in terms of their context or results.*

Value-of-Work Survey

Instructions: The statements below reflect values that have various degrees of importance to people and can bring them satisfaction in their work. Read each sentence and respond to it according to your first impression. Indicate its IMPORTANCE TO YOU by ranking it according to the following key:

4 = VERY IMPORTANT
3 = IMPORTANT
2 = OF AVERAGE IMPORTANCE
1 = OF LITTLE IMPORTANCE
0 = NOT IMPORTANT

I need work in which I . . .

_____ 1. feel I have accomplished something with excellence.
_____ 2. compete with others either by myself or on a team.
_____ 3. use my imagination to create something new.
_____ 4. know that the policies of my workplace are reasonable.
_____ 5. make new friends among my work associates.
_____ 6. can do my job in the way I want.
_____ 7. perform tasks in my main field of interest.
_____ 8. manage and direct the work of other people.
_____ 9. know other people are aware that I have done a good job.
_____ 10. have many changes of duties and assignments.
_____ 11. know I have achieved the goals I have set for myself.
_____ 12. must come out ahead of others in order to move forward.
_____ 13. design new or different things, products, or ideas.
_____ 14. have a boss who is impartial and treats everyone alike.
_____ 15. meet people I like and enjoy.
_____ 16. have freedom to make my own decisions.
_____ 17. am challenged by new problems to solve.
_____ 18. have the power to make decisions that affect other people.
_____ 19. am praised and esteemed by others.
_____ 20. have a variety of functions within the same job.
_____ 21. see the results of a job well done.

_____22. compete with other people for honors, prizes, or bonuses.

_____23. bring into being a new product or way of doing something.

_____24. know my supervisors and co-workers are honest and truthful.

_____25. cooperate closely with fellow employees.

_____26. control my own area of responsibility.

_____27. become so involved that I don't notice the passing of time.

_____28. am responsible for the work that other people do.

_____29. am rewarded with extra pay and promotion.

_____30. face new problems, people, and situations frequently.

Value-of-Work Score Sheet

Instructions: Transfer the ratings for each of the thirty survey statements to this summary score sheet. Next, add the three responses across each row to obtain a total score for each of the designated work values, which are described at the bottom of this sheet.

Total Scores

1. _____	11. _____	21. _____	_____ Achievement
2. _____	12. _____	22. _____	_____ Competition
3. _____	13. _____	23. _____	_____ Creativity
4. _____	14. _____	24. _____	_____ Fairness
5. _____	15. _____	25. _____	_____ Friendship
6. _____	16. _____	26. _____	_____ Independence
7. _____	17. _____	27. _____	_____ Interesting Work
8. _____	18. _____	28. _____	_____ Leadership
9. _____	19. _____	29. _____	_____ Recognition
10. _____	20. _____	30. _____	_____ Variety

	WORK VALUE DESCRIPTIONS
Achievement	Feel a sense of accomplishment in reaching a goal, attaining excellence, or exercising resolve and persistence
Competition	Experience the challenge of competing for honors, awards, or recognition
Creativity	Originate new ideas and new ways of doing things
Fairness	Work where people are treated fairly and honorably
Friendship	Be in work that allows me to make friends and have a social life with work associates
Independence	Do the work in my own way and structure my own time
Interesting Work	Do work that is challenging, absorbing, and in a field of personal interest
Leadership	Have an opportunity to be in charge of and responsible for others
Recognition	Receive acknowledgment, attention, and approval for work
Variety	Do work that involves diverse activities and functions

➤ Value Judgment

Goals
1. To discuss the ethical considerations of various situations.
2. To explore the impact of ethical challenges on decision making.
3. To examine personal values.

Group Size   Several groups of four or five persons each.

Time Required   Approximately 1 hour.

Materials
1. A copy of the Value Judgment Worksheet and a pencil for each participant.
2. A clock or timer.

Physical Setting   A room large enough for the groups to work without disturbing one another. Writing surfaces should be provided.

Process
1. Direct the participants to form groups of four or five persons each.
2. Distribute a copy of the Value Judgment Worksheet and a pencil to each participant. Read aloud the instructions at the top of the sheet. Tell the groups that they will have approximately 30 minutes for group discussion.
3. Time the activity for approximately 30 minutes, giving the groups a 5-minute warning before time expires. Reading each situation in turn, ask a representative from each group to report on the issues that were discussed and the group's decision on acceptability of the action.
4. Lead a concluding discussion based on the following questions:
   - What general insights and impressions did you gain from this activity?
   - Is there a difference between an action that is acceptable and one that is ethical? Why or why not?

- What have you learned about differing ethical viewpoints? How difficult was it for group members to agree on the acceptability of the actions? Were some situations more difficult to agree on than others? Why is that?
- How is decision making affected when ethical challenges are involved?
- What are some examples of other situations in the workplace that involve ethical challenges? *(for example, doing personal business on company time, long-distance calls abuse, bribery, conflicts of interest, accepting gifts, special favors, drug use, unscrupulous business practices, not reporting product flaws)*
- What factors make the issue of ethical behavior difficult for organizations to handle? *(for example, people have individual values and respond differently to moral questions, cultures interpret morality differently, abuse isn't reported, employees feel the company can afford the loss, "everyone else does it")*

Variation   Assign one situation to each group and allow approximately 10 minutes for group discussion. Have the groups identify specific issues regarding the situation; for example, stakeholders, possible consequences, cost, and long-term implications.

Value Judgment Worksheet

Instructions: Discuss the following situations in your group. Each person should reflect on the actions taken, and then the group should decide whether or not the actions are acceptable.

1. Evan accidentally erases a very important file from a co-worker's computer. He is certain that no one will ever know who deleted it, so he says nothing about it to the co-worker. Evaluate Evan's actions.

2. Sue makes a mistake that will cost the company thousands of dollars, but a co-worker is blamed for it. Sue doesn't admit that she was the one responsible for the mistake. Evaluate Sue's actions.

3. Sam comes across a private memo in his boss's office regarding cutbacks. It includes the names of those who will be affected in his department, and he sees that he is not on the list. He secretly tells his co-workers in advance that they are about to be laid off. Evaluate Sam's actions.

4. Chris works for a small company that gives each department a limited budget for supplies. Last year, the Sales Department ran out of pens and paper pads, so people had to go buy their own. Now Chris sees a good friend who works in Sales taking home a box of office supplies. Chris doesn't say anything about it to anyone. Evaluate Chris's actions.

5. Linda has a job that allows her vacation time and an additional ten days a year for illness. She wakes up one morning and isn't ill, but she just doesn't feel like going to work. She calls in and tells them that she is sick, and she takes the day off. Evaluate Linda's actions.

➤ Valuing Yourself

Goals
1. To list personal qualities and career values.
2. To identify personal areas for growth and development.
3. To relate the concepts of personal qualities and career values to group effectiveness.

Group Size   Unlimited number of participants.

Time Required   30 minutes.

Materials   A copy of the Valuing Yourself Worksheet and a pencil for each participant.

Physical Setting   Any room in which the group regularly meets. Writing surfaces should be provided.

Process
1. Distribute a copy of the Valuing Yourself Worksheet and a pencil to each participant.
2. Explain that the participants will be doing a self-evaluation exercise to examine their personal qualities and career values in terms of both strengths and areas for improvement. Tell them that they will be sharing the results with others in a small group situation. Referring to the top of the worksheet, read the instructions aloud. Allow approximately 10 minutes for completion of the worksheet, and then stop the participants.
3. Instruct the participants to place an asterisk (*) next to the top three items in each section. Allow a few minutes, and then ask the participants to partner with two or three others. Individuals are to describe themselves by using the words they picked, explaining any perceived value contradictions that others point out. Allow approximately 5 to 10 minutes for discussion.

4. Lead a concluding discussion based on the following questions:
   - What insights did you gain about yourself from doing this exercise? What insights did you gain about others in your group?
   - How do personal qualities and career values logically relate to one another?
   - How closely aligned were your current and desired career values? Why is that?
   - What can you do to achieve growth in your desired areas?
   - How can a group use the information gained from its members to perform more effectively?

Variations

1. If working with intact work groups, use the composite information to review current roles and responsibilities to determine whether individual strengths and interests are being used effectively.
2. Instruct the participants to use the information to develop a personal development plan with actions, timelines, and resources.

Valuing Yourself Worksheet

Instructions: In the lists that follow each statement, place a check mark in front of EVERY word that finishes the statement correctly for you, as you are NOW. Put a plus sign in front of every word that describes things you would like to *develop more.*

Personal Qualities

I am (✓); I'd like to be more (+):

____ Accepting	____ Disciplined	____ Poised
____ Ambitious	____ Efficient	____ Prompt
____ Balanced	____ Enthusiastic	____ Self-accepting
____ Brave	____ Friendly	____ Sensitive
____ Caring	____ Honest	____ Strong
____ Competitive	____ Intelligent	____ Successful
____ Confident	____ Joyful	____ Trusting
____ Conscientious	____ Kind	____ Understanding
____ Cooperative	____ Loyal	____ Verbal
____ Courteous	____ Mature	____ Warm
____ Creative	____ Needed	____ Wise
____ Decisive	____ Peaceful	

Career Values

In my career, I do (✓); I would like to (+):

____ Create ideas	____ Create beauty
____ Make things	____ Explore ideas
____ Design systems	____ Follow directions
____ Help people	____ Take responsibility
____ Perform physical tasks	____ Experience variety
____ Organize things	____ Improve society

➤ Wishing Well

Goals
1. To clarify personal values and desires.
2. To choose from among many desirable alternatives.
3. To examine differences in group member values and goals.

Group Size   Several groups of four to six persons each.

Time Required   Approximately 1 hour.

Materials   A copy of the Wishing Well Worksheet and a pencil for each participant.

Physical Setting   A room large enough for groups to work without disturbing one another. Writing surfaces should be provided.

Process
1. Begin the session by telling the participants:
   "Ten experts have agreed to provide their services to members of the group. Their extraordinary skills are guaranteed to be 100 percent effective. It is up to you to decide which of these people can best provide you with what you personally want."
2. Distribute a copy of the Wishing Well Worksheet and a pencil to each participant.
3. Explain that individuals are to choose the *four* experts whose services they would MOST want to receive by placing an X in front of those names. Allow several minutes for selection. Now ask the participants to select another *three* experts whose services they would NEXT prefer to receive by placing a check mark in front of those names. Allow several minutes for selection. Point out to the participants that this process has left three experts who constitute a "least desirable" group.
4. Direct the participants to form groups of four to six persons each. Ask the group members to discuss their individual choices

and to see whether or not they can discover any patterns in the various groupings. Allow approximately 20 minutes for group discussion.

5. Ask individual volunteers to share responses to the following questions:
   - How did you feel about having to make your choices?
   - What seemed to link together the four most desirable people for you? Were your choices reflective of your personal goals?
   - What linked the three least desirable people for you?
   - What values were you upholding in your choices?
   - What are you now doing yourself to achieve what the top experts could do for you?

6. Lead a concluding discussion based on the following questions:
   - What patterns were you able to identify within groupings? Were there any choices that may have seemed out of place with others in either of the two groupings? Which ones?
   - How closely did members of the group share similar choices? In what areas? How does having a diverse collection of personal values and desires help a group? How can it hinder a group?
   - How do personal values influence individual behaviors and the choices we make? How does this impact a group? What effect does it have on setting and accomplishing group goals?
   - What did your group members seek in common? How might your group best use these shared values to perform more effectively back on the job?

Variations

1. Have members of a group work together to reach a consensus in ranking the ten experts in order of importance.
2. Have the participants do role plays of the various experts, with individuals arguing why they are more needed or more useful than the others.

Wishing Well Worksheet

Instructions: (1) Choose the *four* experts whose services you would MOST want to receive and place an X in front of those names. (2) Select another *three* experts whose services you would NEXT prefer to receive and place a check mark in front of those names.

_____ *Carey Ahn*—This world-famous leadership expert will train you to be listened to, looked up to, and respected by those around you.

_____ *Crystal Ball*—All of your questions about the future will be answered, continually, through her powerful insights.

_____ *Ann Ecksbert*—This job-placement guru can find you the job of your choice in whatever location you desire.

_____ *Bill Moore*—As a financial wizard, he will assure that wealth will be yours, with guaranteed schemes for earning millions within weeks.

_____ *Rob Pauer*—An expert on power and influence, he will make sure that you are never again bothered by those in authority. His services will make you immune from all control that you consider unfair by your work, the police, and the government.

_____ *"Pop" O'Larrity*—He guarantees that you will have the friends you want, now and in the future. You will find it easy to approach those you like and they will find you easily approachable.

_____ *Prof. May Noe*—She guarantees that you will have self-knowledge, self-liking, self-respect, and self-confidence. True self-assurance will be yours.

_____ *Dr. Sue Smart*—She will develop your common sense and intelligence to a genius level. It will remain this way throughout your entire lifetime.

_____ *Prof. Claire Voyant*—With her help, you will always know what you want, and you will be completely clear on all the issues.

_____ *Candy Zyre*—A top-notch interpersonal consultant, she guarantees that you will be well-liked and admired by everyone you meet.

➤ About the Author

Lorraine Ukens, owner of Team-ing With Success (www.team-ing.com), is a performance-improvement consultant who specializes in team building and experiential learning. Her business experience has been applied in designing, facilitating, and evaluating programs in a variety of areas. She has teamed with private companies, nonprofit organizations, and government agencies to help them achieve higher levels of success.

Lorraine is the author of several training activity resources that make learning interactive and fun. These include books (*Getting Together, Working Together, All Together Now, Energize Your Audience, Pump Them Up, SkillBuilders: 50 Customer Service Activities*), consensus activities (*Adventure in the Amazon, Arctic Expedition, Stranded in the Himalayas*), and games (*Common Currency: The Cooperative-Competition Game, Lexi-Connection*). Lorraine was the editor of *What Smart Trainers Know: The Secrets of Success from the World's Foremost Experts,* for which she wrote a chapter on team training. She also has contributed training activities to a variety of edited books, including the *Pfeiffer Annuals.*

Lorraine earned her B.S. degree in psychology and M.S. degree in human resource development from Towson University in Baltimore, Maryland. She has been an adjunct faculty member at Towson since 1997, where she teaches a core graduate course in training and development. Lorraine is an active member of ASTD and served as president of the Maryland Chapter from 1999–2000.

Lorraine lives in the Baltimore area with her husband. Whenever they have time, they like to travel, and they have visited six continents so far. They hope to make it to the seventh one in the near future!

➤ How to Use the CD

System Requirements

PC with Microsoft Windows 2003 or later
Mac with Apple OS version 10.1 or later

Using the CD With Windows

To view the items located on the CD, follow these steps:

1. Insert the CD into your computer's CD-ROM drive.

2. A window appears with the following options:

   Contents: Allows you to view the files included on the CD.
   Software: Allows you to install useful software from the CD.
   Links: Displays a hyperlinked page of websites.
   Author: Displays a page with information about the author(s).
   Contact Us: Displays a page with information on contacting the publisher or author.
   Help: Displays a page with information on using the CD.
   Exit: Closes the interface window.

If you do not have autorun enabled, or if the autorun window does not appear, follow these steps to access the CD:

1. Click Start → Run.

2. In the dialog box that appears, type d:\start.exe, where d is the letter of your CD-ROM drive. This brings up the autorun window described in the preceding set of steps.

3. Choose the desired option from the menu. (See Step 2 in the preceding list for a description of these options.)

In Case of Trouble

If you experience difficulty using the CD, please follow these steps:

1. Make sure your hardware and systems configurations conform to the systems requirements noted under "System Requirements" above.

2. Review the installation procedure for your type of hardware and operating system. It is possible to reinstall the software if necessary.

To speak with someone in Product Technical Support, call 800-762-2974 or 317-572-3994 Monday through Friday from 8:30 A.M. to 5:00 P.M. EST. You can also contact Product Technical Support and get support information through our website at www.wiley.com/techsupport.

Before calling or writing, please have the following information available:

- Type of computer and operating system.

- Any error messages displayed.

- Complete description of the problem.

It is best if you are sitting at your computer when making the call.

Pfeiffer Publications Guide

This guide is designed to familiarize you with the various types of Pfeiffer publications. The formats section describes the various types of products that we publish; the methodologies section describes the many different ways that content might be provided within a product. We also provide a list of the topic areas in which we publish.

FORMATS

In addition to its extensive book-publishing program, Pfeiffer offers content in an array of formats, from fieldbooks for the practitioner to complete, ready-to-use training packages that support group learning.

FIELDBOOK Designed to provide information and guidance to practitioners in the midst of action. Most fieldbooks are companions to another, sometimes earlier, work, from which its ideas are derived; the fieldbook makes practical what was theoretical in the original text. Fieldbooks can certainly be read from cover to cover. More likely, though, you'll find yourself bouncing around following a particular theme, or dipping in as the mood, and the situation, dictate.

HANDBOOK A contributed volume of work on a single topic, comprising an eclectic mix of ideas, case studies, and best practices sourced by practitioners and experts in the field.

An editor or team of editors usually is appointed to seek out contributors and to evaluate content for relevance to the topic. Think of a handbook not as a ready-to-eat meal, but as a cookbook of ingredients that enables you to create the most fitting experience for the occasion.

RESOURCE Materials designed to support group learning. They come in many forms: a complete, ready-to-use exercise (such as a game); a comprehensive resource on one topic (such as conflict management) containing a variety of methods and approaches; or a collection of like-minded activities (such as icebreakers) on multiple subjects and situations.

TRAINING PACKAGE An entire, ready-to-use learning program that focuses on a particular topic or skill. All packages comprise a guide for the facilitator/trainer and a workbook for the participants. Some packages are supported with additional media—such as video—or learning aids, instruments, or other devices to help participants understand concepts or practice and develop skills.

- *Facilitator/trainer's guide* Contains an introduction to the program, advice on how to organize and facilitate the learning event, and step-by-step instructor notes. The guide also contains copies of presentation materials—handouts, presentations, and overhead designs, for example—used in the program.

- *Participant's workbook* Contains exercises and reading materials that support the learning goal and serves as a valuable reference and support guide for participants in the weeks and months that follow the learning event. Typically, each participant will require his or her own workbook.

ELECTRONIC CD-ROMs and web-based products transform static Pfeiffer content into dynamic, interactive experiences. Designed to take advantage of the searchability, automation, and ease-of-use that technology provides, our e-products bring convenience and immediate accessibility to your workspace.

METHODOLOGIES

CASE STUDY A presentation, in narrative form, of an actual event that has occurred inside an organization. Case studies are not prescriptive, nor are they used to prove a point; they are designed to develop critical analysis and decision-making skills. A case study has a specific time frame, specifies a sequence of events, is narrative in structure, and contains a plot structure—an issue (what should be/have been done?). Use case studies when the goal is to enable participants to apply previously learned theories to the circumstances in the case, decide what is pertinent, identify the real issues, decide what should have been done, and develop a plan of action.

ENERGIZER A short activity that develops readiness for the next session or learning event. Energizers are most commonly used after a break or lunch to stimulate or refocus the group. Many involve some form of physical activity, so they are a useful way to counter post-lunch lethargy. Other uses include transitioning from one topic to another, where "mental" distancing is important.

EXPERIENTIAL LEARNING ACTIVITY (ELA) A facilitator-led intervention that moves participants through the learning cycle from experience to application (also known as a Structured Experience). ELAs are carefully thought-out designs in which there is a definite learning purpose and intended outcome. Each step—everything that participants do during the activity—facilitates the accomplishment of the stated goal. Each ELA includes complete instructions for facilitating the intervention and a clear statement of goals, suggested group size and timing, materials required, an explanation of the process, and, where appropriate, possible variations to the activity. (For more detail on Experiential Learning Activities, see the Introduction to the *Reference Guide to Handbooks and Annuals*, 1999 edition, Pfeiffer, San Francisco.)

GAME A group activity that has the purpose of fostering team spirit and togetherness in addition to the achievement of a pre-stated goal. Usually contrived—undertaking a desert expedition, for example—this type of learning method offers an engaging means for participants to demonstrate and practice business and interpersonal skills. Games are effective for team building and personal development mainly because the goal is subordinate to the process—the means through which participants reach decisions, collaborate, communicate, and generate trust and understanding. Games often engage teams in "friendly" competition.

ICEBREAKER A (usually) short activity designed to help participants overcome initial anxiety in a training session and/or to acquaint the participants with one another. An icebreaker can be a fun activity or can be tied to specific topics or training goals. While a useful tool in itself, the icebreaker comes into its own in situations where tension or resistance exists within a group.

INSTRUMENT A device used to assess, appraise, evaluate, describe, classify, and summarize various aspects of human behavior. The term used to describe an instrument depends primarily on its format and purpose. These terms include survey, questionnaire, inventory, diagnostic, survey, and poll. Some uses of instruments include providing instrumental feedback to group members, studying here-and-now processes or functioning within a group, manipulating group composition, and evaluating outcomes of training and other interventions.

Instruments are popular in the training and HR field because, in general, more growth can occur if an individual is provided with a method for focusing specifically on his or her own behavior. Instruments also are used to obtain information that will serve as a basis for change and to assist in workforce planning efforts.

Paper-and-pencil tests still dominate the instrument landscape with a typical package comprising a facilitator's guide, which offers advice on administering the instrument and interpreting the collected data, and an initial set of instruments. Additional instruments are available separately. Pfeiffer, though, is investing heavily in e-instruments. Electronic instrumentation provides effortless distribution and, for larger groups particularly, offers advantages over paper-and-pencil tests in the time it takes to analyze data and provide feedback.

LECTURETTE A short talk that provides an explanation of a principle, model, or process that is pertinent to the participants' current learning needs. A lecturette is intended to establish a common-language bond between the trainer and the participants by providing a mutual frame of reference. Use a lecturette as an introduction to a group activity or event, as an interjection during an event, or as a handout.

MODEL A graphic depiction of a system or process and the relationship among its elements. Models provide a frame of reference and something more tangible, and more easily remembered, than a verbal explanation. They also give participants something to "go on," enabling them to track their own progress as they experience the dynamics, processes, and relationships being depicted in the model.

ROLE PLAY A technique in which people assume a role in a situation/ scenario: a customer service rep in an angry-customer exchange, for example. The way in which the role is approached is then discussed and feedback is offered. The role play is often repeated using a different approach and/or incorporating changes made based on feedback received. In other words, role playing is a spontaneous interaction involving realistic behavior under artificial (and safe) conditions.

SIMULATION A methodology for understanding the interrelationships among components of a system or process. Simulations differ from games in that they test or use a model that depicts or mirrors some aspect of reality in form, if not necessarily in content. Learning occurs by studying the effects of change on one or more factors of the model. Simulations are commonly used to test hypotheses about what happens in a system—often referred to as "what if?" analysis—or to examine best-case/worst-case scenarios.

THEORY A presentation of an idea from a conjectural perspective. Theories are useful because they encourage us to examine behavior and phenomena through a different lens.

TOPICS

The twin goals of providing effective and practical solutions for workforce training and organization development and meeting the educational needs of training and human resource professionals shape Pfeiffer's publishing program. Core topics include the following:

    Leadership & Management

    Communication & Presentation

    Coaching & Mentoring

    Training & Development

    E-Learning

    Teams & Collaboration

    OD & Strategic Planning

    Human Resources

    Consulting

Discover more at Pfeiffer.com

- The best in workplace performance solutions for training and HR professionals
- Online assessments
- Custom training solutions
- Downloadable training tools, exercises, and content
- Training tips, articles, and news
- Author guidelines, information on becoming a Pfeiffer Partner, and much more

Discover more at www.pfeiffer.com